Mic It!

Bound to Create

You are a creator.

Whatever your form of expression — photography, filmmaking, animation, games, audio, media communication, web design, or theatre — you simply want to create without limitation. Bound by nothing except your own creativity and determination.

Focal Press can help.

For over 75 years Focal has published books that support your creative goals. Our founder, Andor Kraszna-Krausz, established Focal in 1938 so you could have access to leading-edge expert knowledge, techniques, and tools that allow you to create without constraint. We strive to create exceptional, engaging, and practical content that helps you master your passion.

Focal Press and you.

Bound to create.

We'd love to hear how we've helped you create. Share your experience:

www.focalpress.com/boundtocreate

Focal Press
Taylor & Francis Group

Mic It!

Microphones, Microphone Techniques, and Their Impact on the Final Mix

Ian Corbett

Focal Press
Taylor & Francis Group

NEW YORK AND LONDON

First published 2015
by Focal Press
70 Blanchard Road, Suite 402, Burlington, MA 01803

and by Focal Press
2 Park Square, Milton Park, Abingdon, Oxon OX14 4RN

Focal Press is an imprint of the Taylor & Francis Group, an informa business

Notices
Knowledge and best practice in this field are constantly changing. As new research and experience broaden our understanding, changes in research methods, professional practices, or medical treatment may become necessary.

Practitioners and researchers must always rely on their own experience and knowledge in evaluating and using any information, methods, compounds, or experiments described herein. In using such information or methods they should be mindful of their own safety and the safety of others, including parties for whom they have a professional responsibility.

Product or corporate names may be trademarks or registered trademarks, and are used only for identification and explanation without intent to infringe.

Library of Congress Cataloging in Publication Data
Corbett, Ian, 1972-
Mic it! : microphones, microphone techniques, and their impact on the final mix / Ian Corbett.
pages cm
ISBN 978-0-415-82377-7 (paperback)
1. Microphone. 2. Sound–Recording and reproducing. I. Title.
TK6478.C67 2015
621.389'30284–dc23
2014022955

ISBN: 978-0-415-82377-7 (pbk)
ISBN: 978-0-203-54978-0 (ebk)

Typeset in Times New Roman PS MT by
Servis Filmsetting Ltd, Stockport, Cheshire

Printed and bound in the United States of America by Sheridan Books, Inc. (a Sheridan Group Company).

In memory of Dionne Jeroue.

On stage and off stage, you were loved.

Table of Contents

About the Author

Ian Corbett is the Coordinator of the Audio Engineering Program, and Professor of Audio Engineering at Kansas City Kansas Community College. He also owns and operates "off-beat-open-hats – recording and sound reinforcement" which specializes in servicing the needs of classical and jazz ensembles in the Kansas City area. Since 2004 he has been a member of the Audio Engineering Society's Education Committee, and has mentored, presented, and served on panels at local, regional, national, and international AES events, and been an invited presenter at many other audio events in the USA and Europe. He has also authored articles on audio recording related subjects for *Sound On Sound* ("The World's Best Recording Technology Magazine"). Ian holds a Doctor of Musical Arts degree in music composition from the University of Missouri-Kansas City, and can frequently be found playing saxophone in various jazz clubs and restaurants around Kansas City. For more information, please see:

www.offbeatopenhats.com

www.focalpress.com/cw/corbett

Acknowledgments

Thank you to everybody who helped throughout the various stages of production of this project, from proposal to final copy edit, including: Bob Beck, Mark Drews, Dave Greenspan, Dr. Eric Honour, Kerry-Anne Kubisa, Dave Maclaughlin, Wes Maebe, Megan Turner, Anaïs Wheeler, and Meagan White. Additionally, Eric Honour and Dave Maclaughlin, thank you for your invaluable assistance as Technical Editors.

Thank you for letting me take and use photographs of you, your musical instruments, or your studio facilities: Bob Beck, Patrick Conway, Ian Dobyns, Chris Hazelton, Levi Holgerson, Dionne Jeroue, Kansas City Kansas Community College, Jennifer Kim, Margaret Kocher, Ken Lovern, Jim Mair, Armond McDonald, Erin McGrane, Chandler Meierarend, B. Scott Nelson, Jim Schrader, Sky Recording (Kansas City), Andrew Tremain, and Elizabeth Vallé. Thank you too, Larry Kopitnik, for letting me use your photograph on the dedication page.

Thank you to the professionals who graciously let me interview them so their valuable insights could fill the last chapter: Lenise Bent, David V. R. Bowles, Kerry-Anne Kubisa, Wes Maebe, Matt Ross-Spang, and Mark Rubel.

Thank you to the musicians and engineers who generously provided their talents for the accompanying web site audio examples:

- Carswell & Hope (carswellandhope.com): Nick Carswell (guitar and vocals), Dan Hines (bass), Austin Quick (keys), Jason Slote (drums). *Hunger* from the album *Carswell & Hope*. Written, recorded and produced by Carswell and Hope. Audio Example 2.21 mixed by Jason Slote and Nick Carswell. Audio Examples 1.5, 1.6, 1.7, 1.8, 2.20, 5.12, 5.13, 5,15, and 5.16, remixed by Ian Corbett.

- Bryan Corbett (trumpets, flugelhorn, flute, recording and mixing) and Chris Dodd (bass, drums, piano, keyboards, recording and mixing): *Funk 75*, written by Chris Dodd and Bryan Corbett, from the album *Green*. Audio Examples 2.7, 2.8, and 2.9.

- Ian Corbett (saxophones), Audio Examples 2.10, 5.9– 5.11.

- Ian Corbett (all instruments and drum programming), David Garibaldi (Tower of Funk drum samples) and Sarah Williams (vocals): *Smile!*, Audio Examples 1.1–1.4, 5.14, and *The Closer I Get To You,* Audio Examples 2.17–2.19, written by Ian Corbett, from the album *If That's You*.

- Aaron Crawford (drums). Audio Examples 2.15, 2.16, 3.5, 3.6, 3.12–3.15, 6.1–6.10, 7.6–7.9, 8.1, 8.2, 10.1–10.13, 13.4–13.7, 13.18–13.21.

- Ian Dobyns (acoustic and electric guitars). Audio Examples 2.11, 2.12, 3.16, 3.17, 7.1–7.5, 11.1–11.4, 11.11–11.14, 13.8–13.15.
- Eboni Fondren (vocals and narrations). Audio Examples 1.1–1.8, 1.13, 2.10, 2.13, 2.14, 2.22–2.26, 3.1–3.4, 8.3, 8.4, 13.1–13.3.
- Kelley Gant (vocals). Audio Examples 3.18–3.20, 9.1–9.4, 13.16, 13.17.
- Levi Holgerson (acoustic and electric bass). Audio Examples 11.5–11.10.
- Dr. Nahyun Kim (piano). Audio Examples 5.1–5.8, 11.15–11.21.
- Now Now Sleepyhead (www.facebook.com/nownowsleepyhead): Aaron Crawford (drums, percussion, programming, additional vocals), Phil Park (vocals, guitar, bass, and additional programming), Megan Zander (additional vocals). *Influenza* from the album *The Violator*. Written by Phil Park and Aaron Crawford. Produced, engineered, mixed, and mastered by Aaron Crawford. Audio Examples 2.1–2.6.
- Steven Sterner (vocals and narration). Audio Examples 1.13, 3.7–3.11.
- "The Standard" Vocal Jazz Ensemble: Natalie Bennett, Stormy Borsella, Deandre Clark, Laquita English, Allison Her, Lauren Irving, Andrew Roberson, Andrea Rodriguez, Shelby Stephenson, Morgan J. Tinsley. John Stafford, Director, Kansas City Kansas Community College. Audio Examples 9.5 and 9.6.

Last but not least, lots of love to my family in the UK, and friends and "family" in the USA and Europe.

To anybody I've omitted, I apologise!

C H A P T E R   1

Audio Basics

An engineer who knows how to use a mic is more important than the mic.
-Wes Maebe, Engineer/Producer, Sonic Cuisine, London, UK

1.1   IT'S NOT ALWAYS ABOUT THE GEAR!

Gear, gear, gear! We all want to get our hands on new toys, plug that gear in and make sound… And there's nothing wrong with that! But even the best audio equipment available won't produce great sound unless you understand how to use it properly. Lower quality equipment used well, will always sound better than great quality equipment used poorly. You'll be much better prepared to produce great recordings, and to get the most from the concepts discussed later in this book if you have a good understanding of fundamental audio theory and studio basics.

Sound is our artistic medium. As sound engineers, we create sonic artwork from it. The more we understand sound, the more we can predict its behavior, and more easily produce better recordings. Even if you think you know the basics, there might be something in this chapter that will dramatically change the way you think about sound, use your equipment, or hear what you're listening to – improving the audio you record and mix. *So please take the time to read this chapter, and don't skip ahead!*

1.2   WHAT IS SOUND?

What is it that we are trying to capture and craft into a hit record?

Examples of objects that produce sound include the strings on a guitar or violin, the reed in a wind instrument mouthpiece, a trumpet player's lips, and the head on a drum. All of these sources have one thing in common – they *vibrate*, creating variations in air pressure, called *sound waves*. Sound does also travel through other mediums, such as water and solid objects – but seeing as air is the medium that usually surrounds us, we'll concentrate on that!

Figure 1.1 shows a simplified, illustrative picture of a vibrating guitar string. The string is anchored at both ends, and stretched so it is taut. When it is plucked, bowed, or struck, it is set in motion and vibrates. During this motion it moves from its point of rest (the position it naturally returns to when not in motion), labeled **A**, and out to an extreme, labeled **B**. As it approaches **B**, the tension in the string increases until it is not able to move any further, and it rebounds back in the opposite direction, through **A** to the opposite extreme, **C**. Tension builds as it moves towards **C**, and causes the string to reverse its direction again, so it moves back through **A** towards **B**. A little energy is lost with each consecutive change in direction, so the string gradually moves less and less (getting quieter and quieter) until it is stationary and silent back at its point of rest, **A**.

As the string moves from **A** to **B**, it squashes the air molecules to the left of the string closer together. This increases the air pressure in that spot, causing a *compression*. This compression

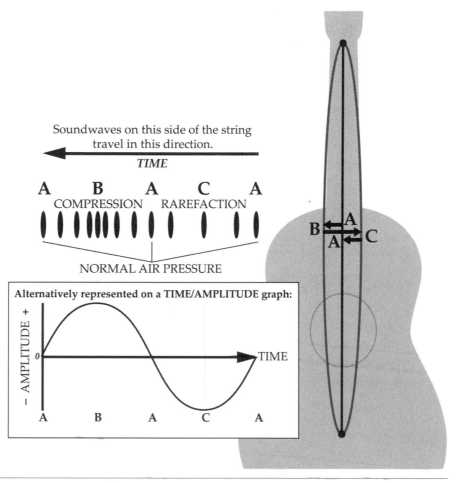

Figure 1.1   The motion of a vibrating string, and a resulting sound wave.

then travels outwards from this source at the speed of sound. The air molecules themselves do not move far – the compressed group of molecules bump into the adjacent molecules, which bump into the next set, passing the compression on.

THE SPEED OF SOUND

The speed of sound is commonly quoted as being around 344 meters (1130 ft) *per second* – for dry air, at 20°C (68°F), at sea level. As general principles, the speed of sound:

• Increases as air temperature rises, and decreases as air temperature falls.

- Decreases slightly as altitude increases (though this has more to do with the altitude-associated temperature decrease than the change in air pressure).
- Increases a little as humidity rises.

As the compression travels outwards, the string moves back through **A**, where normal atmospheric air pressure is restored. During the subsequent motion from **A** to **C**, the air molecules to the left of the string are drawn further apart, to fill the space where the string used to be. This causes a decrease in air pressure adjacent to the left of the string, called a *rarefaction*. This rarefaction travels outwards, following the previous compression. As the string returns to **A**, normal air pressure is once again restored behind the rarefaction. This continuing motion propagates the alternating compressions and rarefactions of *sound waves* behind each other. Greater motion and displacements from the point of rest create greater variations in air pressure and louder sounds.

If we analyzed the resulting sound wave from the right of the string in the diagram, the compressions and rarefactions would be reversed.

Figure 1.1 also shows two ways of graphically representing these sound waves. The first is a series of blobs representing the relative spacing of the air molecules – the air pressure. The second is a time/amplitude graph. This graph may look familiar. It is the shape of a sine wave – a pure tone made up of one single frequency. An actual vibrating string produces a much more complex harmonic waveform than a sine wave, shown in **Figure 1.2**.

A loudspeaker functions in a similar way. A *speaker cone*, or *driver*, is set in motion – it pushes outwards and sucks inwards, propagating compressions and rarefactions in front of it, which then travel towards the listener.

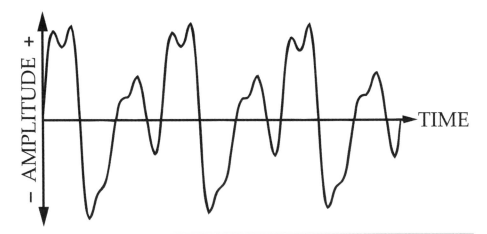

Figure 1.2 The waveform produced by an actual guitar string, showing the overall motion of the string produced by the interaction of all the frequencies present.

Time/amplitude graphs are based on measurements taken at a single point in space, over a duration of time. This is similar in principle to what a microphone does – a mic is positioned at a single point in space and takes measurements of air pressure over time, capturing frequency and amplitude information.

1.3   THE DECIBEL (DB)

The *amplitude*, or "amount of" a sound's energy is measured in Decibels. Meters, faders, and the scales on many equipment knobs are in dBs, so it is vitally important to understand the concept in order to use microphones and recording equipment correctly. The dB is a unit of convenience. By itself it *only* implies that we have reduced a much larger range of numbers into a smaller, more manageable range of numbers in the form of a dB scale of some sort.

For example, a unit familiar to more people might be the *watt* – used for measuring *power*. Power is a measure of the energy consumption or energy transfer of a device. The human ear is capable of detecting sounds with a power of 0.000000000001 W to almost 100 W. *Do not confuse these figures with amplifier power!* These numbers represent the energy of the sound waves in the air (that you're actually listening to) and *not* the electrical amplifier power required to propagate that sound from a loudspeaker. Clearly, this huge range of numbers is unusable and impractical!

The dB is a logarithmic unit that folds this large power range down into a smaller range of numbers that represent power ratios. The dB unit always requires clarifying with a second unit – in the form "dB *something*."

1.4   POWER RELATIONSHIPS

Don't be fooled when buying amplifiers. A 200 W amp is not twice as loud as a 100 W amp! Exactly how loud it will be depends upon the loudspeaker, and how many loudspeakers are attached to it.

Sound Pressure Level, or *SPL*, is a measure of how loud a sound actually is, as and where you're listening to or measuring it.

- Doubling the power of a sound causes a 3 dB increase in SPL, which we perceive as "slightly louder."
- Conversely, halving the power of a sound causes a 3 dB decrease in SPL, which we perceive as "slightly quieter."

So in a hypothetical sound system, doubling the amplifier power from 100 W to 200 W results in a "slightly louder" sound system (if your loudspeakers are rated to handle the increased power).

Doubling the electrical voltage representing a sound causes a 6 dB increase – however, this does not double the perceived loudness of the sound.

- In order to perceive something as being "twice as loud," a 9 or 10 dB increase is necessary.

In order to create a 9 or 10 dB increase, the power has to be doubled (= +3 dB), doubled again (+3 dB = 6 dB total increase), and then doubled again (+3 dB = 9 dB total increase). So to double the perceived SPL of a 100 W sound system, an 800 W amplifier is required – along with loudspeakers that will handle that extra power!

These same calculations and observations apply to *any control scaled in dB* on *any piece of audio equipment*.

KNOW YOUR POWER RELATIONSHIPS!

- Turning something up by 3 dB means that you have made it "slightly louder."
- Turning something down by 3 dB means that you made it "slightly quieter."
- Turning something up by 9 dB means that you have made it "twice as loud."
- Turning something down by 9 dB means that you have made it "half as loud."

Knowing just these simple facts, you're already a more informed, educated, and better audio engineer! If you're mixing and thinking "the vocal is *slightly* too quiet," you should now *know* what you need to do in order to achieve the right correction, and anticipate the results of that correction, before moving any controls:

- If the vocal is "slightly" too quiet, increasing the vocal fader level by +3 dB will make it "slightly louder" – and should come close to correcting the problem.
- If you're thinking, "the sax needs to be *half* as loud," then you should be able to make an informed judgment, reduce the sax fader level by about –9 dB, and come close to correcting the problem.

This process is much more professional than grabbing the fader and randomly moving it until you stumble across the correct level!

Amplitude Changes

Example 1.1: A music excerpt, and then the same excerpt +3 dB (slightly louder).

Example 1.2: A music excerpt, and then the same excerpt –3 dB (slightly quieter).

Example 1.3: A music excerpt, and then the same excerpt +9 dB (twice as loud).

Amplitude Changes (continued)

Contextual Mix Changes

Example 1.4: A music excerpt, and then the same excerpt −9 dB (half as loud).

Example 1.5: A mix example with the lead vocal +3 dB (slightly louder) in the second excerpt.

Example 1.6: A mix example with the lead vocal −3 dB (slightly quieter) in the second excerpt.

Example 1.7: A mix example with the bass +9 dB (twice as loud) in the second excerpt.

Example 1.8: A mix example with the bass −9 dB (half as loud) in the second excerpt.

1.5   DECIBEL SCALES

dB SPL

dB SPL is a measure of how loud a sound actually is in an environment, at a specific point in space. It is measured with an SPL meter. The most commonly encountered SPL scale is 0 to 140 dB SPL – which is based on the human ear's threshold of hearing (0 dB SPL) and threshold of pain (130 dB SPL). The SPL scale does in fact go up to about 194 dB SPL – which is the point at which the air cannot handle the amount of sonic energy, and distorts the sound.

dBV

dBV (*decibel volt*) scales are used on analog audio equipment, or digital devices and software trying to emulate an analog experience. They are a measure of the electrical voltage representing the sound wave. Bargraph meters commonly use dBV scales. Their range is usually −∞ dB (or some negative value) through 0 dB, to approximately +15 or +18 dB. **Figure 1.3** shows some typical dBV meters.

On a dBV meter, "0" is considered *nominal* – the optimum level at which the equipment is designed to operate most linearly. However, analog equipment can be pushed and operated above this quite happily, hence the typical +15 dB or +18 dB range. dBV meters are *peak meters* – they show the actual maximum voltage peaks of the electricity representing the sound waves. It is normal and desirable to have peak levels in the "+" ranges – but *do not* light any "overload" lights.

Some meters can be switched between peak and RMS (root mean squared) and other non-peak averaging modes.

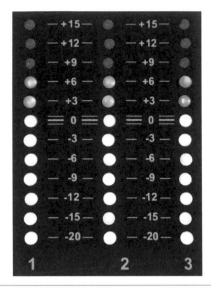

Figure 1.3   Some dBV meters, as found on many analog devices.

Figure 1.4   A VU meter with a dBu scale, as found on many analog devices.

dBu

Volume Unit meters, as shown in **Figure 1.4**, use the dBu scale. Their mechanical needles (or software simulations) cannot react to instantaneous peak levels. Instead, they show an averaged amplitude measurement – more of an indication of the perceived loudness of the sound. Many VU meters have a peak LED that lights when finite peak levels are exceeded. A VU meter's usual range is from −30 or −20 dBu or so, through 0 dBu, and up to approximately +6 dBu. VU meters are appropriate on analog devices (analog mixing consoles, tape machines, etc.), where "0" can be happily exceeded, and are useful because of their indication of the sound's average intensity. VU meters are not found on digital devices because it is imperative to know the actual peak level in order to avoid digital distortion.

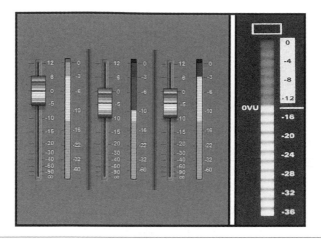

Figure 1.5 Left: A software dBFS meter. Right: A modern hybrid meter with a dBFS scale on the right, and 0 dBu on the left, correlating to −14 dBFS.

When using a VU meter it is imperative to leave enough headroom for instantaneous peak levels without lighting the peak LED. Desirable levels on a VU meter are generally lower than on a peak dBV meter, particularly for percussive or high frequency sounds.

dBFS

Most digital audio devices feature *dBFS* meters – *decibels* (relative to) *full scale* – which are instantaneous peak meters. A typical meter is shown in the left of **Figure 1.5**. "Full scale" is the maximum amplitude a digital device can handle without horrible distortion, and is labeled 0 dB. A dBFS meter's range is from −∞ dB (or some detectable negative value) up to 0 dB. The only thing above 0 dB is the "clip" or "over" indicator.

Digital devices cannot be overloaded in the same way as analog devices. There are no potentially desirable distortions or non-linearities above zero, as there might be on analog equipment – only ugly, and potentially equipment damaging, square wave digital nastiness! When using digital devices it is essential to leave enough *headroom* ("spare" level) so the "clip" or "over" indicators do not light if the signal's amplitude increases unexpectedly.

0 dBV on an analog device with a maximum dBV level of +15 correlates to −15 dBFS on a digital device. The right of **Figure 1.5** shows a hybrid meter found on a modern analog mixer that would, today, typically be connected to a digital recording system.

1.6   DYNAMIC RANGE

Measured in dB, audio dynamic range is the difference between the lowest and highest signal levels an audio device (or system) can record, store, or reproduce. Larger (or wider) dynamic ranges are better. The lowest extreme of this range, considered 0 dB, is the level below which the system is unable to resolve details. This limit is usually set by the naturally occurring hiss and noise in a system (its *noise floor*) overpowering and masking low level details, or in a microphone it could be a lack of low-level sensitivity and inability to respond to low levels. The high level limit of a system's dynamic range is the maximum level, relative to 0 dB, that the system can handle before a certain amount of distortion of the audio signal occurs.

Analog devices (mixers, tape and tape machines, outboard gear, etc.) all exhibit hiss and noise that dictate their lower performance limit. As the electronic components in an analog device are gently overloaded with voltage, or the magnetic particles on tape are over-saturated with magnetism, slight, often "pleasing" distortions occur. Dynamic range is usually quoted as being "*for x% THD*" (*Total Harmonic Distortion*). This is a measure of the amount of waveform *distortion*, changing it from what it should really be.

Digital devices do not exhibit gentle and "pleasing" distortions if their maximum limit is exceeded. Digital distortion is a square wave type of distortion, which adds sharp corners to the waveform, and is neither pleasing to the ear nor good for loudspeakers! **Figure 1.6** shows an input waveform, and how analog and digital systems would change it if it exceeded their maximums slightly.

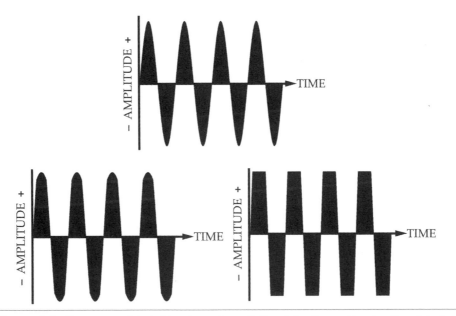

Figure 1.6   Top – an undistorted input waveform. Bottom left – the gentle saturation distortion characteristics of an analog device. Bottom right – harsh, undesirable, and potentially damaging digital distortion (clipping).

1.7   SIGNAL-TO-NOISE RATIO

SNR, or *S/N*, and dynamic range are quite similar. Whereas dynamic range is a measure of the difference between the loudest and quietest perceivable signals in a sound (or that a system can resolve), *signal-to-noise ratio* is a measure of the difference between a specific reference level (not the maximum level) and the noise floor. As with dynamic range, the higher the quoted SNR specification, the technically better it is.

1.8   FREQUENCY

In addition to amplitude, another way we categorize or identify musical sound is by its pitch. Pitch is our perception of how low or high a musical note is. So what is frequency?

Earlier in this chapter the motion of a vibrating string was analyzed. A vibrating sound source's motion from a starting point, through both extremes, and back to the same starting point and direction, is known as one *cycle*. The typical analysis of one cycle is shown in **Figure 1.7** – this is the motion **A-B-A-C-A** of the vibrating string in **Figure 1.1**. Additionally, **Figure 1.7** also shows that we can identify cycles that start from other points in the waveform.

Frequency is measured in *Hertz*. The abbreviation is *Hz*. The definition of 1 Hz is one cycle per second – so imagine the string pictured earlier taking one second to move **A-B-A-C-A**.

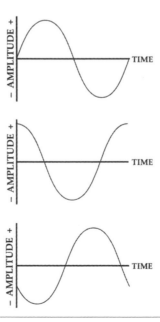

Figure 1.7   Top: A single cycle identified starting from the vibrating source's point of rest. Middle: A single cycle analyzed starting at one extreme. Bottom: A single cycle analyzed starting mid-cycle.

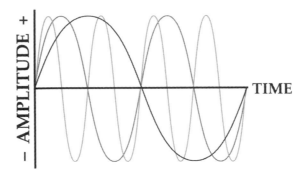

Figure 1.8 Three octave frequencies superimposed on each other show how zero crossing points regularly line up at the beginning, middle, and end of the lowest frequency's cycle, making the combined sound pleasingly powerful and solid.

In music, the interval of an octave is very special – octaves are "the same note," but in a higher or lower register. Octaves are created by doubling or halving the frequency. Given that the standard Western tuning note A is 440 Hz, the octave above that is 880 Hz, and the octave below that is 220 Hz. **Figure 1.8** shows the integer relationships between these octave frequencies that cause their waveforms to interact with each other in a way we find complementary and pleasing.

Frequency is an *exponential* scale – it is non-linear. The difference between tuning note A and the octave below it is 220 Hz. The difference between tuning note A and the octave above it is 440 Hz. The difference between, and the frequency of each higher octave, increases exponentially – continuously doubling. The frequency, and difference between each lower octave is continuously halving – or decreasing exponentially, never reaching zero.

1.9   FREQUENCY RESPONSE

The frequency response of an audio device or system is the range of frequencies it can efficiently capture, store, or reproduce. The standard range of audio frequencies, based on the limitations of human hearing, is from 20 Hz to 20 KHz (kilohertz, 20,000 Hz) – but many audio devices have frequency responses that extend beyond that range.

1.10 WAVEFORMS, FUNDAMENTALS, AND HARMONICS

The amplitude of the compressions and rarefactions of a sound wave plotted along a time axis produce a graphical *waveform*. **Figure 1.9** shows several waveforms:

• The upper graph shows a loud, low frequency sine wave.

- The middle graph shows a quieter, higher frequency sine wave. The positive and negative deflections are smaller, representing lower amplitudes, and there are more cycles in the same amount of time, representing a higher frequency.
- The bottom graph shows the waveform of a musical instrument playing a note. The larger overall cyclic shape represents the *fundamental* frequency, which gives the note its pitch. The multiple faster cycling, higher frequencies superimposed on the fundamental are the *harmonics*, which give the sound its *timbre* or *tone color*. Harmonics are usually found at multiples of the fundamental frequency, and are usually lower in amplitude than the fundamental frequency.

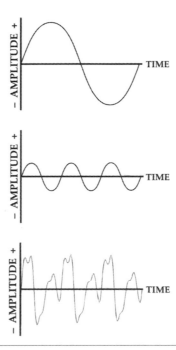

Figure 1.9   Top: A louder, lower frequency sine wave. Middle: A quiet, higher frequency sine wave. Bottom: A complex real world sound is a combination of a louder fundamental frequency, and multiple higher, quieter harmonic frequencies.

Simple Waveforms

Example 1.9: A pure (single frequency) sine wave.

Example 1.10: A square wave, produced by the addition of odd harmonics.

Example 1.11: A triangle wave, produced by the addition of odd and even harmonics.

1.11 WAVELENGTH, VELOCITY, PHASE

As previously discussed, sound waves travel at a finite speed, which for transmission through air is quoted as being 344 m/s or 1130 ft/s. A high frequency cycle takes a shorter time to be propagated than a low frequency cycle, so it doesn't travel as far from the sound source before the next cycle is propagated behind it – a low frequency cycle takes up more physical space in the air than a high frequency cycle.

Figure 1.10 shows a loudspeaker cone generating two frequencies. The top one is a lower frequency; the middle one is a higher frequency. The wavelengths of one cycle of each can be calculated by using the following equations:

$$\lambda = \frac{v}{f}$$

$$Wavelength\ in\ meters = \frac{speed\ of\ sound\ in\ meters\ per\ second}{frequency\ in\ Hertz}$$

$$Wavelength\ in\ feet = \frac{speed\ of\ sound\ in\ feet\ per\ second}{frequency\ in\ Hertz}$$

If the low frequency is 100 Hz its wavelength is 344 ÷ 100 = 3.44 meters (3 m, 44 cm). In feet, 1130 ÷ 100 = 11.3 ft (11 ft 3.6 in).

If the high frequency is 500 Hz, its wavelength is 344 ÷ 500 = 0.688 meters (68.8 cm). In feet, 1130 ÷ 500 = 2.23 ft (2 ft 3.1in)

The bottom waveform in **Figure 1.10** is the result of the loudspeaker generating both frequencies simultaneously – the shorter wavelengths of the higher harmonic frequency are superimposed on the longer wavelength of the lower fundamental frequency.

When looking at a waveform, the sine wave in **Figure 1.11** for example, it is impossible to describe any non-peak or non-zero-crossing position along the waveform accurately using non-technical language. Imagine trying to describe the position of the dot on the waveform – "It's almost at the first peak, but not quite…" Anything other than an approximation of its position is impossible to describe. An understanding of phase is necessary to be able to overcome this issue.

Waveform cycles can be divided into 360 degrees of phase:
- 0° and 360° are the same – the beginning or end of the cycle and at the zero-crossing point.
- 90° and 270° are the positive and negative peaks respectively.
- 180° is the mid-cycle zero-crossing point.

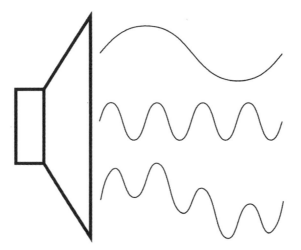

Figure 1.10   A loudspeaker cone generating different frequencies. Top: The low frequency. Middle: The high frequency. Bottom: The actual waveform produced by summing the two frequencies together.

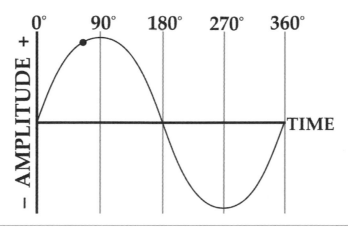

Figure 1.11   A sine wave, with degree "phase" markings.

Using degrees, it is possible to accurately describe the phase difference between two identical waveforms that differ in time. The difference between the waveforms **A** and **B** in **Figure 1.12** is 90° – they are 90° out of phase. **A** and **C** are 180° out of phase, and **A** and **D** are 270° out of phase.

Phase is frequency dependent. If the waveforms in the figure were replaced with higher or lower frequencies, displaced by the same amount of time, the relative phase relationships would not be the same.

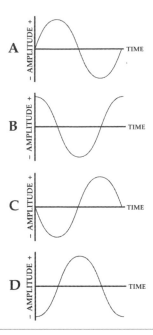

Figure 1.12   The relative phases of two identical waveforms which are displaced in time. **A** is 0°, "in phase." **B** is 90° out of phase compared to **A. C** is 180° out of phase compared to **A. D** is 270° out of phase compared to **A**.

1.12 AMPLITUDE SUMMATION

Summing together two waveforms can cause:

- Constructive interference – increasing the amplitude of the positive and negative peaks.
- Destructive interference – decreasing the level of the positive and negative peaks.

If two identical and "in phase" waveforms (or the in phase frequency components of a more complex waveform) are acoustically summed together in the air, they will constructively interfere, and become 3 dB louder because the power is doubled.

If two identical and "in phase" waveforms (or the in phase frequency components of a more complex waveform) are electrically summed together in a mixer or DAW (digital audio workstation), they will constructively interfere, and become 6 dB louder because the voltage is doubled.

This type of constructive amplitude summation is shown in **Figure 1.13**.

If two summed waveforms (or frequency components of a more complex waveform) are 180° out of phase, the positives and negatives happening simultaneously cancel, causing those frequencies to disappear, as in **Figure 1.14**.

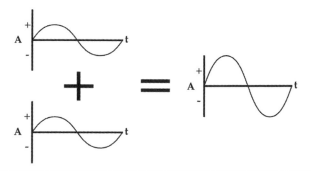

Figure 1.13 Two "in phase" sine waves acoustically sum together constructively, and become 3 dB louder. Two loudspeakers playing the same material would be 3 dB louder than a single loudspeaker.

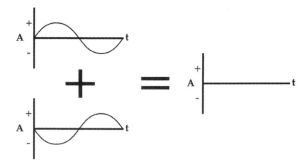

Figure 1.14 Two 180° out of phase sine waves destructively cancel completely.

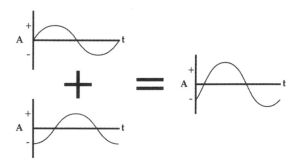

Figure 1.15 Two slightly out of phase waveforms interact partially constructively.

If two frequency components have a more "in-between" phase relationship, their behavior is more complex – there will be amplitude increases and decreases alternating throughout the summed waveform, as shown in **Figure 1.15**.

COMB FILTERING AND MICROPHONES

Phase relationships and summation characteristics are important to consider and understand when using microphones.

If two microphones are positioned different distances from a sound source, the wave front is picked up slightly later in the more distant mic – sound takes approximately 2.9 ms to travel 1 meter (0.9 ms to travel 1 ft). This causes different frequencies to arrive at each mic at different points in their relative phase cycles. When these time displaced signals are electrically summed in a mixer or DAW, both constructive and destructive summation occurs at different frequencies, creating *comb filtering* – a strange, funky, usually undesirable sound caused by narrow frequency band cancellation:

- The peaks of some of the frequencies in both signals will be one or more complete cycles out of phase (360° out of phase, or in-phase but delayed by an integer multiple number of cycles), and will combine constructively to become louder.
- The peaks of any frequencies in both signals that arrive at each mic a half cycle out of phase (180° out of phase, or 0.5, 1.5, 2.5, etc. cycles out of phase) will combine destructively to cancel.
- Frequencies that arrive at the mics with phase relationships in-between these two extremes partially sum or cancel.

Similar problems can occur if sound travels two different distances to reach a single microphone – for example directly from a sound source to the mic, and additionally via reflecting off the floor or a wall. Summation of these two wave fronts (that have each traveled different distances and therefore arrive at the mic time displaced and out of phase with each other) occurs acoustically at the single microphone, as described in **Chapter 13**.

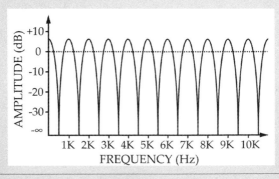

Figure 1.16   Alternating bands of cancellation and summation – comb filtering.

In the two mic examples described above, changing the distance between the two mics will change the frequencies at which comb filtering occurs. In the single mic, direct plus reflected sound example, changing the mic distance will change the frequencies affected. It is impossible to completely remove the effects of comb filtering in these situations, but unless used as a deliberate effect, it should be reduced as much as possible by adjusting the mic positions to put its effects in less noticeable frequency ranges, before exploring other solutions such as electronic time alignment and acoustical absorption – which are discussed in later chapters.

Phase Relationships

Example 1.12: The phase relationship of two slightly detuned sine waves cycles in and out of phase as they interact, at times constructively, and other times destructively.

Example 1.13: A vocal excerpt. In the second part of the example, two slightly time delayed versions of the same material produce the frequency dependent constructive and destructive interference of comb filtering.

1.13 HUMAN HEARING

Figure 1.17 shows a sound wave's compressions and rarefactions travelling through the air to a listener's ear. They are reflected by the pinna of the ear into the ear canal and to the eardrum, a thin membrane of skin-like material.

- If a compression travels towards the eardrum, the pressure in the ear canal becomes greater than normal, causing the eardrum to stretch inwards to equalize the air pressure difference on both sides of the eardrum.
- A rarefaction lowers the air pressure in the ear canal, causing the eardrum to flex outwards to equalize the air pressure difference on both sides of the eardrum.

The eardrum's motion is an analog of the sound wave's air pressure differences, which are an analog of the motion of the vibrating sound source.

The eardrum is connected to the auditory ossicles – an "acoustical gearbox" made up of three tiny bones. The eardrum and auditory ossicles change acoustical sound waves into mechanical motion, and then into pressure waves in the fluid of the cochlea. The cochlea is a very small helix-shaped organ lined with hair-like cells that transmit signals to the auditory cochlear nerve when stimulated. Different regions of hair-like cells in the cochlea are stimulated by different frequencies. The brain then processes these signals, and the listener perceives sound.

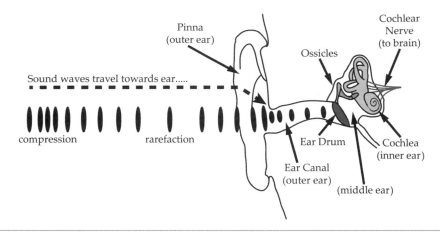

Figure 1.17   Sound waves and the human ear.

The commonly quoted 20 Hz to 20 KHz frequency range of human hearing is a best case scenario, and different from person to person. Factors such as age and exposure to loud sound reduce this range.

- High frequency sensitivity deteriorates as we get older. By the age of thirty, 20 Hz to 16 KHz would be a more typical audible frequency range.
- Extended exposure to loud sounds can impair upper mid-range (and high frequency) sensitivity.

Our ears are not equally sensitive to all frequencies. They are most sensitive to the middle of the frequency spectrum (where essential speech intelligibility frequencies are), and less sensitive to extreme high and low frequencies. The linearity (or non-linearity) of our hearing's frequency response also changes with amplitude:

- At quiet levels, our ears are very insensitive to extreme low and high frequencies.
- At higher SPLs we perceive frequencies more equally across the spectrum.

THE PHON

The *phon* is a measurement used to describe the relative sound pressure levels of frequencies above and below a 1 KHz reference tone, required in order for our ears to perceive *all* frequencies at the same loudness as that 1 KHz range. The phon equates to the actual SPL we are listening to at 1 KHz, so 85 phons = 85 dB SPL at 1 KHz.

At low SPLs, 40 phons for example, extreme low and high frequencies need to be at significantly higher SPLs than the 1 KHz range, and around 4 KHz the SPL must be a little less than the 1 KHz range for our ears to perceive the entire frequency spectrum as being the same loudness as 1KHz at 40 dB SPL. To perceive frequencies around 20 Hz at the same level as 1 KHz at 40 phons, an actual SPL of almost 80 dB is required at 20 Hz. To perceive frequencies around 10 KHz at equal loudness to 1 KHz, an actual SPL of almost 60 dB is necessary at 10 KHz. To perceive frequencies around 4 KHz at equal loudness to 1 KHz, an actual SPL of approximately 35 dB SPL is necessary at 4 KHz. The phon scale, and a level of "40 phons" implies these differences.

At high SPLs, 100 phons for example, (meaning that 1 Khz is perceived at 100 dB SPL) our ears are more linear, requiring almost no increase in the low frequencies, an actual SPL of approximately 95 dB at 4 KHz, and the extreme high frequencies to be slightly louder than the 1 KHz range. Quoting "100 phons" implies these compensations have been made.

Because of our ear's non-linear perception, it is important to monitor and mix at an average (and safe) overall level – not too quiet, and not too loud. 80 to 85 dB SPL is recommended. You should briefly check how your mix sounds at lower and higher levels though, so that you know it will sound good at a variety of playback levels.

Frequencies

All these tones are presented at identical amplitudes – **try not to adjust your volume knob between examples!** *The mid frequencies (around 1 KHz to 2 KHz) should appear much louder than the lower and higher extremes.*

Example 1.14: A 32 Hz tone.

Example 1.15: A 63 Hz tone.

Example 1.16: A 125 Hz tone.

Example 1.17: A 250 Hz tone.

Example 1.18: A 500 Hz tone.

Example 1.19: A 1 KHz tone.

Example 1.20: A 2 KHz tone.

Example 1.21: A 4 KHz tone.

Example 1.22: An 8 KHz tone.

Example 1.23: A 16 KHz tone.

Example 1.24: A 20 KHz tone.

Example 1.25: A smooth sweep from 20 Hz to 20 KHz, and back down.

Humans hear amplitudes between the *threshold of hearing* and *threshold of pain*:

• The threshold of hearing is quoted as 0 dB SPL – any sounds below this level are theoretically inaudible, and any sounds at or above this level are theoretically audible.
• The threshold of pain is around 130 dB SPL. This is the level at which the sensation of sound changes from being a sonic one, to one of physical pain.

These levels are theoretical "best case" scenarios, and vary not only from person to person, but also depending upon frequency. Hearing damage and age affect each person's threshold of hearing, and individual tolerance and age change the threshold of pain for each individual.

A leading cause of hearing damage is exposure to loud sound. Various governments around the world require hearing protection and regular hearing screenings to be made available to employees if noise in a general industry workplace exceeds 85 dBA SPL. Needless to say, sitting behind a drum set, in front of a guitar amp, going to a rock concert, or working in a recording studio or audio production environment often exceeds these levels – but these industries are not covered by the same government legislation in most countries. A drummer's ears can be exposed to over 115 dB SPL while playing!

SAFE SOUND!

If you wish to have a long career as an audio professional or musician it is important to practice safe sound:

• Monitor loudly for brief periods only.
• If you are in a situation where you are exposed to loud sounds, wear earplugs.

Protect your hearing. Loud noise exposure eventually destroys the sensitive hair cells in the cochlea – modern medicine cannot yet make them grow back!

WEIGHTING

SPL measurements are usually *weighted*, meaning that they are biased, to better reflect how our ears perceive amplitude at different frequencies:

• *dBA* weighting severely reduces the measurement tool's sensitivity to the low and high frequency extremes (much like we hear at lower SPLs), and is related to the 40 phon scale described earlier.
• *dBC* weighting is flatter, only slightly reducing the measurement tool's sensitivity to lows and highs (much like we hear at high SPLs), and is related to the 100 phon scale described earlier.

So, some essential theory out of the way, let's discuss some gear-related topics!

1.14 SIGNAL FLOW AND AUDIO LEVEL STANDARDS

Signal flow refers to how an audio signal flows through a chain of devices while it is being recorded or played back. If you plug a mic in and there's no sound, or the sound is distorted, a thorough understanding of signal flow makes it possible to quickly troubleshoot and fix the problem – and makes you a better and more employable audio professional.

Signal flow is case-specific, and differs depending upon the type of facility and specific gear in use – so it's impossible to describe every scenario in this book. However, typical hardware mixing console and computer/digital audio workstation recording chains are shown in **Figure 1.18**.

MICROPHONES AND MIC LEVELS

Microphones change acoustical sound waves into electricity – specifically, variations in voltage. This voltage is very small, measured in millivolts. This type of signal level is known as *mic level*.

A mic level signal needs amplifying before it can go through the main mixing console circuits, or the analog to digital converters in a DAW system. A *pre-amplifier*, *pre-amp*, or *mic pre* is the first circuit in the signal flow of a mixer that the mic is plugged into. A pre-amp can also be a separate device, external to the mixer or audio interface. The pre-amp is a critical circuit – it needs to amplify the tiny voltage coming from a microphone, without increasing noise, undesirable distortions, or negatively affecting the frequency response or sound of the microphone.

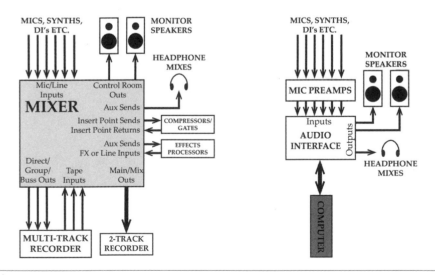

Figure 1.18 Left: The signal flow of a typical hardware recording chain, including a mixing console. Right: An example computer/DAW recording chain.

LINE LEVELS

A pre-amp applies *gain* (amplification) to the mic level signal to raise it to *line level*, which is the level the rest of the mixing console (or audio interface) operates at. There are two standards for line level signals:

- *"+4 dBu"* or *professional level* represents the audio waveform as voltages of up to about ±1.7 V.
- *"−10 dBV"* or *consumer level* represents the audio waveform as voltages of up to about ±0.4 V.

Consumer level "−10" interconnects are commonly found on domestic devices such as CD, DVD, Blu-ray players, and gaming systems.

- If you connect a −10 dBV device to a +4 dBu input you will see low levels (about 12 dB lower than they should be) and have to apply a lot of gain.
- If you connect at +4 dBu output to a −10 dBV input you will probably overload that input unless there is an input gain stage you can turn down on the receiving device.

Connections between studio hardware are usually "+4" professional line level.

- For a "direct to stereo" recording, the main outputs of the mixing console are connected to a stereo recording device – a CD recorder, portable recording device, or an audio interface attached to a computer-based recording system.
- For multi-track recording, the subgroups, multi-track busses, or direct outs from the console can be used to send individual microphones to individual tracks in a DAW, hardware multi-track recorder, or an analog tape machine – yes, analog tape is still used!

The playback outputs from a multi-track recording device will return into individual inputs on a mixing console. If mixing is taking place "in the box" (inside the DAW system), only a stereo left/right (or a set of surround outputs if mixing in surround) may come out of the DAW and be routed to the monitor speakers.

LOUDSPEAKER LEVEL

If passive monitor speakers are being used, the line level output of the mixer or DAW will need amplifying to *loudspeaker level* – which is the *many* volts required to move a loudspeaker cone (± several volts to ±50 V or more). The line outputs are connected to a power amplifier, which will handle that task. This amplification is built into *powered* or *active* monitors – hence the input is line level, and the speaker requires an AC electrical power connection for its amplifiers and crossover circuitry.

INSTRUMENT LEVEL

Electric guitars and basses feature *instrument level* connections. In terms of signal level, they are not dissimilar to mic level – so plugging a guitar or bass directly into a mic input will usually result in decent levels. However the impedances (the electrical load each device presents to the other) of the two devices are not designed to work together – and the sound will be muddy and dull. Some audio interfaces and pre-amps have an instrument input or two on them. If yours does not, you will need to use a *direct box* or *DI* to convert the instrument level signal to a balanced mic level signal (fixing the impedance problem) if you wish to plug a guitar or bass directly into your recording chain.

1.15 GAIN STRUCTURE

Levels, levels, levels! A beautifully clean recording (as opposed to one that is full of hiss, noise, or distortion) is created in part by setting appropriate levels as signals leave one device and enter the next:

- If too low a signal enters a device, that device will add a greater relative percentage of its own hiss and noise to the signal. That extra noise will end up being turned up to compensate for the low input level somewhere later in the signal flow.
- If too high a level enters a device, then subtle or not so subtle distortion will result.

Both these types of noise and distortion are undesirable.

With the exception of a *pad* control (which attenuates a microphone's output by a fixed amount) mics do not feature a gain control on their output. They are connected to a pre-amp, and the gain control on the pre-amp is used to set the amount of amplification that the mic signal receives in order to bring it up to an appropriate line level.

On a digital dBFS scale, the golden rule is "*do not clip.*" To avoid potentially nasty distortion the "clip" or "over" indicators must not light. There are two schools of thought on digital recording levels:

- The older approach was to record with the levels as high as possible, without going "over," while making sure enough headroom was left to avoid clipping unexpected louder moments.
- Given the huge dynamic range offered by modern 24 and 32 bit recording systems, it is much less necessary to "max the meters." Peaking a little lower, maybe around −12 dB or so, leaving plenty of headroom means that that the digital convertors are not constantly running at or close to their upper limit. Many engineers claim they sound better that way.

CLIP INDICATORS

In addition to the generally preferred sound of analog to digital converters running 6 to 12 dB below maximum levels, other reasons to keep levels below maximum are:

- Often, clip indicators don't indicate clipping unless several consecutive samples are "over" – by which time the problem is more serious than a single sample being over.

- This also means that if a single sample is clipped, but multiple samples in a row do not, the clip will not be indicated. Just because it doesn't show up, doesn't mean it hasn't happened and distorted the sound.

A big difference between competing digital recording devices and systems is how they distort when overloaded. Some are more sonically forgiving than others. You can expect a cheap device to produce ugly clicks and chirps immediately on clipping, while you might be able to get away with the occasional and light clip on a more expensive, better quality device.

On an analog device, with a dBV peak meter, the level can happily be pushed past "0," and into the "+" values. On many analog devices, more of the unit's real character will be picked up by doing just that. Care must be taken not to light any "over" light though!

A VU needle type meter cannot show you peak level, so good levels peaking at, or just above "0" are appropriate for less percussive sounds, and lower for more percussive sounds. Again – the "peak" light should not come on.

With good input levels established, it should be easy to get good levels to the recording device.

FROM THE MIXER TO THE RECORDING DEVICE

Mixer outputs to the recording system may be pre-fader or post-fader, and pre-panner or post-panner. If they are post-fader and/or post-panner, faders in-between the pre-amps and outputs to the recorder should be set at unity (which is marked "0" near the top of the fader's travel), and pan controls should be set correctly if odd/even panning rules apply to the outputs in use.

- In its unity position, a fader does not boost or cut the level of the signal on that channel. What leaves the channel is the same level as was set at the input gain/pre-amp stage – possibly minus a few dB depending upon the output being used, because of the stereo panning laws used to maintain perceived equal amplitudes when a sound is panned to different positions. (When a sound is panned centrally for example, two loudspeakers reproduce it – that's twice as much power than if it was hard panned and only reproduced by one loudspeaker. Panning laws attenuate the sound's amplitude slightly as it is panned towards center so that it is perceived at equal amplitude regardless of where it is panned.)
- Turning a fader above unity also turns up mixer channel noise. If a channel needs turning up above unity, it usually implies that the input gain is too low, so the input level to the channel should be checked.
- Turning a fader down below unity is fine during mixing, but if post-fader sends to the recording device are used during tracking, low levels will be sent to the recorder.

When mixing, good main/master output levels can be achieved by setting the faders for the most important, loudest channels of the mix at around unity, and other faders below unity. If too

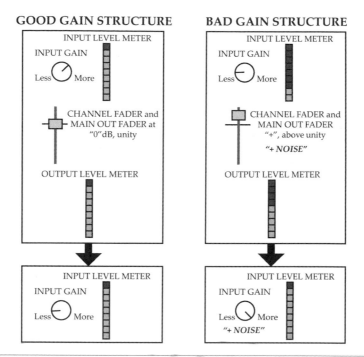

Figure 1.19 Left: Good input levels and good unity gain output levels on the top device produce good input levels on the bottom device. Right: Low input levels and undesirable fader gain on the top device, and increased input gain on the bottom device results in a more noisy signal, due to the two additional stages of amplification after the top device's input gain.

many faders are set above unity, the main output levels can be too high, clipped, or overloaded; or noisy, due to the additional amplification applied by faders that are above unity. Conversely, running too many faders too low will result in low main/master output levels and an increased relative percentage of noise. A compensating gain increase will be required in the next recording device that, while turning up the desired signal, will also turn up the undesired extra noise.

1.16 ANALOG AUDIO CONNECTORS

Microphones and all of the equipment in the recording chain diagram (**Figure 1.18**) need to be plugged in and connected together correctly. You need specific cables to do this, so you need to know the names of the connectors used, and what each type of connector is commonly used for.

XLR CONNECTORS

XLR connectors are the preferred connectors for single channel analog connections. They are robust and lock into place – a little release button needs to be pushed to disconnect them. They can be found with varying numbers of pins in the connector. Three-pin connectors are usually used for standard audio connections. XLR connectors can be male or female – the male plug is the one with the pins, the female (jack) the one with little holes. Signal always flows out of the male and into the female, so if you're ever wondering "which end do I need," think about signal flow – if you're connecting to the output of a device (outputs always have a male connector) you need the female end of the cable, and if you're connecting to an input (inputs are always female) you need the end of a cable with a male plug. XLR connectors are most commonly used for mic connections, and many line level connections on a lot of professional equipment.

QUARTER-INCH PHONE CONNECTORS

Quarter-inch phone connectors are also used on a lot of audio equipment. They come in two types:

- *quarter-inch TRS* connectors have three segments to the connector – the tip, ring, and sleeve.
- *quarter-inch TS* connectors have just two segments to the connector – the tip and sleeve.

Quarter-inch connectors come in male and female sexes – the male plugs and the female jacks. The genders of quarter-inch connectors are not dedicated to inputs or outputs like XLR connectors – sound can go in or out of a male plug or female jack.

Line level connections commonly use quarter-inch TRS connectors. Instrument level, standard "instrument cables," and some speaker level connections use quarter-inch TS connectors. From the outside, all female quarter-inch jack sockets – instrument, line or speaker level, TRS or TS – look identical, so it's really important to know what you're hooking up and use a cable with the correct connectors and wire for the job! *You don't want to fry a mixer channel by connecting a speaker level output to a line level input!*

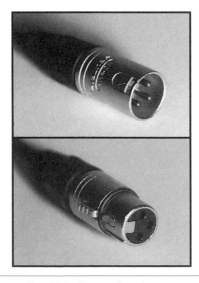

Figure 1.20   XLR Connectors. Top: Male. Bottom: Female.

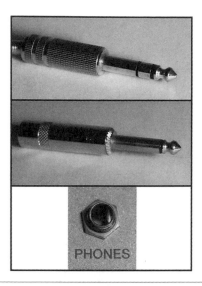

Figure 1.21 Top: A quarter-inch TRS male plug. Middle: A quarter-inch TS male plug. Bottom: A quarter-inch female socket/jack (it could be TS or TRS – there's no way to tell visually, but "Phones" here indicates that it is TRS).

BALANCED AND UNBALANCED CONNECTIONS

Have you ever heard stray taxicab or radio station interference leaking into your sound system or a guitar amplifier? This is usually due to a two-conductor *unbalanced* audio connection between two devices. A *balanced* audio connection requires three-conductor cable and connectors such as XLR and TRS. Balanced connections offer superior rejection of external electrical and electro-magnetic noise and interference, and allow much greater cable lengths to be used. For studio and sound system interconnects, balanced connections are preferred – however, both devices that are connected together have to feature balancing circuits on their respective inputs and outputs. Connecting a TRS cable to unbalanced inputs and outputs offers no advantage. Neither does connecting a balanced output to an unbalanced input, or vice versa – the connection will still be unbalanced and susceptible to noise and interference.

RCA/PHONO CONNECTORS

RCA or *phono* connectors are found on some consumer and prosumer equipment. They are two-conductor, so unbalanced. They are relatively fragile, and do not lock into place – so they are not a preferred method of connection for professional audio systems. CD, DVD and Blu-ray players, turntables, game systems, and other consumer devices usually feature RCA connectors.

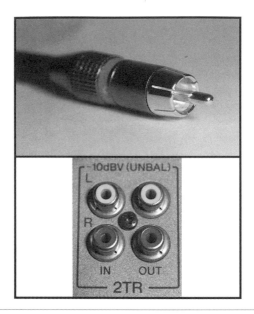

Figure 1.22   Top: A male RCA (or phono) connector. Bottom: Some female RCA connectors.

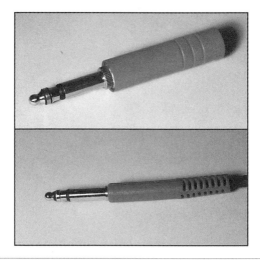

Figure 1.23   Top: A MIL/military connector. Bottom: A bantam/TT connector. Compare their shapes to a quarter-inch TRS connector.

BANTAM/TT AND QUARTER-INCH MILITARY CONNECTORS

Patchbays are used in studios to place the inputs and outputs of the audio equipment in a centralized location – so that they can be hooked up as needed without rewiring the back of the equipment racks. Prosumer patchbays often use quarter-inch TRS connectors. Professional

Figure 1.24 25-pin D-Sub connectors. Top: Male. Bottom: Female.

patchbays use either *MIL* or *bantam/TT (Tiny Telephone)* connections. Both are three-conductor TRS connectors, so can carry balanced signals. The military connector is about the same size as a quarter-inch connector, but is much more robust and secure. Military and quarter-inch TRS patchbay units feature up to 48 connection points per rack-space unit. The bantam connector is not as robust or secure, but has the advantage of a smaller size which allows up to 96 connection points to be put in a single rack-space patchbay unit.

25-PIN D-SUB CONNECTORS

Behind the scenes, in the back of equipment racks, *25-pin D-sub* connectors can be used for both analog and digital multichannel interconnects.

EIGHTH-INCH TRS CONNECTORS

Small, fragile, and generally unreliable, the eighth-inch, or 3.5mm TRS plug, as found on portable music players and earbuds, has no place in professional audio!

1.17 DIGITAL AUDIO CONNECTORS

SPDIF

S/PDIF (Sony/Philips Digital Interconnect Format) is primarily a consumer and prosumer format that can transmit two-channel stereo digital audio data, at up to 24 bit/48 KHz resolution. There is a copper-wire version that uses a single 75 ohm cable and RCA connectors, and an optical fiber version that uses a single optical fiber with *TOSLINK* connectors.

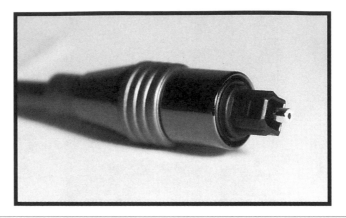

Figure 1.25   A TOSLINK optical fiber connector as used for optical SPDIF connections.

AES/EBU

The original *AES/EBU* format transmits two-channel stereo data, at resolutions up to 24 bit/48 KHz, over a single XLR terminated cable. In addition to featuring sturdy locking connectors, another advantage AES/EBU has over SPDIF, is that it is a balanced connection, allowing much longer cable lengths. AES3 now exists, which supports stereo data at resolutions of up to 24 bit/192 KHz, over balanced XLR, unbalanced RCA, and TOSLINK optical fiber connections.

ADAT LIGHTPIPE

The *ADAT Lightpipe* format uses a single TOSLINK optical fiber to transmit eight channels of digital audio at up to 24 bit/48 KHz resolution. There are also higher sample rate versions:

- SMUX-2 splits 88.2 and 96 KHz data over two fibers; the first carries channels 1 through 4, and the second carries channels 5 through 8.
- SMUX-4 transmits two channels of 176.4 and 192KHz data down a single fiber.

Both the transmitting and receiving devices must be equipped with the appropriate SMUX protocol for high resolution use.

TDIF

TDIF (Tascam Digital Interface Format) is a bidirectional, unbalanced copper-wire format that transmits 8 channels of audio via a 25-pin D-sub cable. Its original specification was for up to 24 bit/48 KHz resolution, but there is now a version that supports up to 96 KHz.

Figure 1.26 MADI connectors. Top: A BNC terminated cable. Bottom: A pair of SC plugs provide bidirectional communication.

MADI

MADI (Multichannel Audio Digital Interface) connections, commonly found on higher-end equipment, but making their way onto less expensive equipment, transmit up to 64 channels of standard resolution audio (up to 24 bit/48 KHz), or a reduced number of channels at higher resolutions. MADI connections can be either copper-wire via 75 ohm BNC terminated cables, or optical fiber terminated with SC type plugs. Cable lengths can be a lot longer than other formats – up to 100 m of copper-wire, or 2000 m of fiber.

ETHERNET TECHNOLOGIES

DANTE transmits multichannel digital audio over inexpensive Ethernet networks and cables. DANTE hardware devices place limits on the number of channels that may be used – for example a DANTE interface may support "32 in x 16 out" operation.

Using Gigabit networks, up to 1024, 24 bit/48 KHz channels (512 in each direction), or 512, 24 bit/96 KHz channels (256 in each direction) can be transmitted in total. When using 100 Mbps networks, 48 x 48, 24 bit/48 KHz operation is possible, or half as many channels at 96 KHz.

CobraNet and *EtherSound* are other Ethernet-based technologies, developed before DANTE.

1.18 DIGITAL AUDIO BASICS

PCM

Most digital recording systems (hardware, software, and plug-ins) use a method known as *PCM* (*Pulse Code Modulation*) to encode and represent audio waveforms. An understanding of PCM will enable you to make more educated decisions as you plan and record projects.

Acoustically, audio is an analog format – its amplitude varies smoothly, with infinite resolution between minimum (silence) and maximum (the point at which the air distorts the waveform); and smoothly with infinite resolution over time. In an analog audio device, a voltage that similarly varies smoothly, with infinite resolution between minimum and maximum amplitudes, and with infinite resolution over time, represents the audio waveform. A digital device is more like a camera – taking snapshots of the audio amplitude at specific intervals of time.

SAMPLE RATE AND FREQUENCY RESPONSE

Figure 1.27 shows an analog audio waveform being sampled by an *Analog to Digital Convertor* (*ADC, or A to D convertor*) in a PCM system. The A to D convertor changes the continuously varying analog waveform into discrete *samples* – measurements of the waveform's amplitude taken at regular intervals of time. The number of samples taken per second is known as the *sample rate*, *sampling frequency*, or *fs*.

The sample rate dictates the highest frequency a system can record. The *Nyquist Theory* states that the sample rate must be at least double the highest frequency to be recorded. This potentially allows for a sample measurement to be taken during both the positive and negative parts of that highest frequency's waveform. If both a positive and negative portion of the waveform could not be stored, the reconstructed waveform, when played back, would contain added erroneous lower frequencies – an artifact known as *aliasing*.

Standard CD sample rate is 44.1 KHz. This means that 44,100 measurements of the waveform's amplitude are taken per second, on both the left and right channels of a stereo signal. The frequency response of this sample rate is up to about 20 KHz – it approaches the capabilities of human hearing.

Given that the best human hearing only extends up to 20 KHz anyway, why would we want to record at commonly available sample rates of up to 192 KHz (and beyond), with frequency responses of up to and beyond 90 KHz? Higher sample rates offer two major benefits:

- They raise the highest frequency that can be recorded.
- They increase the stored resolution and accuracy of the waveform being recorded.

There is also research that shows that although we can't directly hear frequencies above 20 KHz, we can detect their interactions with, and effect on lower frequencies.

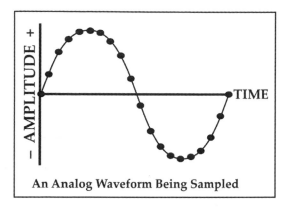

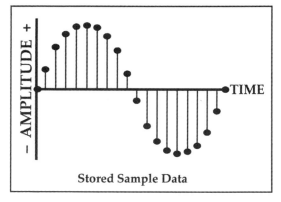

Figure 1.27 Top: The smooth line is the analog input waveform. The dots represent samples – amplitude measurements taken at regular intervals of time. Bottom: The digitally stored information.

According to the Nyquist Theory, higher sample rates should not be necessary to accurately record and reproduce the highest frequency possible for a given sample rate, however technological limitations mean that good quality, higher sample rate converters produce high frequencies that sound smoother, more natural, and less brittle and harsh than lower resolution converters. But – high quality low sample rate converters may still sound better than mediocre quality high sample rate converters!

BIT RESOLUTION AND DYNAMIC RANGE

CD quality audio uses 16 binary digits to represent the value of each sample. This is known as *bit resolution*. An approximate way of calculating the dynamic range of a PCM system is to multiply the bit resolution by six. Each bit allows for a 6 dB increase in dynamic range. Therefore, a 16 bit system offers a theoretical dynamic range of approximately 96 dB. This

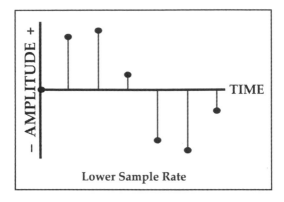

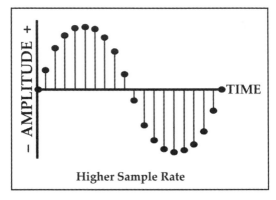

Figure 1.28 Top: At a lower sample rate, less detailed data, and a more approximate version of the sound wave is stored. Bottom: At a higher sample rate a much more detailed data, and a more accurate version of the sound wave is stored.

falls far short of our ear's 130 to 140 dB dynamic range. Most current professional recording systems are capable of at least 24 bit resolution (and many offer 32 bit floating point resolution). Twenty-four bit resolution produces a theoretical dynamic range of about 144 dB. This figure approaches the capability of the human ear. However this is not its primary benefit, as we will hopefully never listen to a playback system so loud that it transfers this range into actual SPL!

Being digital, and non-continuous, the amplitude scale is "stepped" into integer values. A 16 bit system allows 65,536 steps to exist on the amplitude scale. If a sampled amplitude falls between two of those values, it will be rounded to one of the adjacent integer step values. This is a form of distortion known as *quantization error* or *rounding error*. At 24 bit resolution the number of steps on the amplitude scale is increased to 16,777,216. This means that less rounding will occur, and low level details are no longer so close to being masked by the noise-floor of the system. Amplitude values are stored more faithfully, low-level details sound less grainy and metallic, the waveform reconstructed is smoother and more transparent, and a fuller, more precise stereo image is produced.

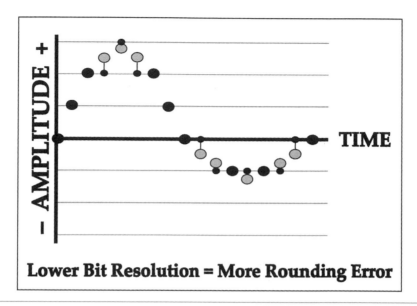

Figure 1.29 At lower bit resolutions there is a greater probability that intended sample values cannot be accurately stored. The grey dots representing the actual input waveform cannot exist at their correct amplitudes and will be rounded up or down to the nearest possible step on the amplitude scale (the small black dots). This is particularly noticeable in low level sounds (the right part of the graph) and low level details contained in louder sounds (the left part of the graph), where the relative percentage change is greater.

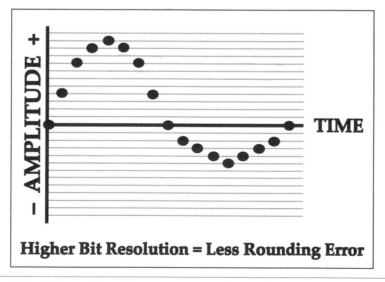

Figure 1.30 At higher bit resolutions there is potentially less rounding, and improved accuracy in both the subtle details of louder sounds (the left part of the graph), and quiet sounds themselves (the right part of the graph).

DO YOU NEED 32 BITS?

Thirty-two bit floating point files don't use the same straightforward bitmapping steps on the amplitude scale as non-floating point formats. Instead, 24 bits are dedicated to storing the amplitude data of the sound wave, and the additional 8 bits to storing where in that number the decimal point occurs. This allows the amplitude to be "floated" above or below the limits imposed by 24 bits of fixed resolution, increasing dynamic range.

This offers little advantage over 24 bits of fixed point resolution when recording – rarely will sound sources, or the technical capabilities of the equipment in the recording chain exceed the capabilities of that resolution. It does mean however, that when processing and manipulating these files digitally (in a DAW for example) the levels can be greatly reduced or increased without the noise, quantization errors, or distortion that would occur at fixed point resolutions, as long as the levels are made sensible prior to the device's convertors.

RECORDING LEVELS

As discussed earlier in this chapter, with the dynamic ranges offered by 24 bit and 32 bit floating point resolutions, there is no need to push dBFS recording level meters all the way to "0," as was more necessary when 12 and 16 bit digital devices were the industry standard. In fact, if you do, and a cluster of samples are captured at digital maximum, even without going "over," distortions can result on playback. It's advisable to leave plenty of headroom so that even unexpected peaks are a few dB below clipping.

Conversely, you do not want to be using only the lowest bits of resolution. Continuously recording at low levels, only lighting the lowest few segments of the level meter, probably means that the track will need to be turned up later, during the mix process. What will be turned up is a grainier low level signal, with significant noise and distortion.

FILE SIZE

Recording at 16/44.1 resolution produces a file size of approximately 5 MB per minute for a mono track. 24/96 files are over 15 MB per minute of mono audio, and 24/192 files over 30 MB per mono minute. Higher resolution files take up significantly more space than lower resolution files, particularly when you multiply by the number of tracks recorded. They also reduce the available track count per hard drive or data hub. *But storage capacities are getting larger and cheaper per GB every day – so it's definitely worth recording at least 24/88.2 files if your system can handle the necessary track count!* It's advisable to record at the best quality available so your work can take advantage of future high quality dissemination formats, and not have a new format reveal the limitations of the initial recording resolution. Also, unless you know you have good quality sample rate conversion algorithms, record at integer multiples of the intended dissemination format's sample rate to avoid potentially degrading non-integer sample rate conversion – which may negatively affect the sound, particularly in the high frequencies.

CHAPTER 2

"Good Sound"

2.1   RECOGNIZING GOOD SOUND

Before even thinking of plugging in and setting up a microphone, it is important to understand what the desirable characteristics (and undesirable characteristics) in sound are. That's why there are some chapters in this book like this one – that don't directly discuss microphones, but discuss things you need to know in order to use microphones to capture the best, most suitable sound possible.

There's no simple answer to the question "what is good sound?" The best answer might be along the lines of "whatever is stylistically and artistically appropriate." Good sound is subjective. One person's ideal guitar sound may be another person's worst nightmare – however that is often related to whether a sound is appropriate to the context it's in, rather than the sound being simply "good" or "bad." But bad sound certainly does exist! Poor quality sound sources, poor quality equipment, bad recording techniques, and poor mixing skills can all result in inappropriate, questionable, or just plain "wrong" sound!

How do you learn to record and mix well? There are basic concepts and skills that should be mastered before developing your own style. Musicians develop their skill sets and individual musical style by listening to other musicians, emulating them, and eventually synthesizing many influences into their own unique characteristics. As a sound engineer or producer, you should similarly find good quality recordings, listen to them, analyze them, and try to emulate them – building up your skills and techniques before eventually developing your own style.

Listening to, and becoming intimately familiar with, a wide variety of musical and production styles will make you more marketable in the industry – if you only listen to hip-hop, good luck when an acoustic folk band shows up for a show or session you're working! Hopefully, like many audio professionals, you can combine your love of great sounding recordings with artists you enjoy musically. Don't just listen to music because you like the style or the artists – when starting to listen critically, it's often easier to concentrate on the sound, and not be distracted by the music, when you're listening to artists and styles you're not a fan of. It's very easy for your love of an artist or band to persuade you that the recording is better than it actually is!

What do you need to be aware of, how should you be listening, and what should you be listening for, in order to identify the desirable characteristics of a recording?

2.2   SOUND REPRODUCTION FORMATS

MONO

A *mono*, or *monophonic* playback system has only one loudspeaker, as in **Figure 2.1**. Mono playback systems include some TVs, bedside alarm clock radios, ceiling type loudspeaker systems in retail outlets (which have many distributed loudspeakers, that are all sent the same

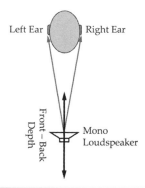

Left Ear   Right Ear

Front – Back Depth

Mono Loudspeaker

Figure 2.1 A mono reproduction system with a single loudspeaker. Sound from the loudspeaker arrives at both ears at the same time (if the loudspeaker is centered). The mono format only allows sounds to be positioned along the loudspeaker's limited front/back axis. The result is a spatially congested image, making mix clarity a challenge.

signal), and speakers on many tablets and mobile phones. Mono systems are one-dimensional. They can offer a sense of front/back depth through the use of creative recording and mixing techniques, but there is no sense of wide space, and all the sounds come from the same location. It is potentially difficult for a listener to clearly hear everything that might be going on in a mono mix, which makes achieving a good mono mix very challenging.

A small nasty sounding mono *Auratone* type loudspeaker is a common feature in many professional recording studios – enabling engineers to anticipate the effects of poor quality, mono sound systems, and make sure their product translates acceptably to them.

STEREO

Stereo, or *stereophonic* systems feature two playback channels – left and right. *Different* signals are sent to each, as shown in **Figure 2.2**. In a stereo loudspeaker system, sound from the left loudspeaker travels to the left ear, *and* the right ear – where it arrives slightly later, changed in timbre due to the extra distance, and filtering/equalization effects of wrapping around the face and head. These delay and EQ effects are known as *HRTFs*, or *head related transfer functions*. Similarly, sound from the right loudspeaker travels to the right ear, and also the left ear – again, slightly delayed and changed in timbre. The sound transfer to each "opposite" ear is known as *inter-aural crosstalk*, and is an essential and desirable component of a stereo playback or monitoring system.

The reason a sound coming from just the left loudspeaker sounds like it's coming from just the left loudspeaker (even though the sound travels to both of our ears) is because our brain uses the HRTF sub-millisecond-level time-delay and the EQ differences of the wavefront's arrival at each ear to determine directionality. We perceive the sound as coming from the direction of the ear at which the wavefront first arrived. This is known as the *Law of First Wavefront*, or *Haas Effect*, or *Precedence Effect*.

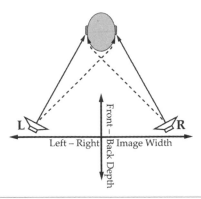

Figure 2.2 A stereo reproduction system uses two channels, each sending its own unique signal. The inter-aural crosstalk between the speakers and each opposite ear (the dashed lines) is an essential component of the format. The path from the left loudspeaker to the right ear is slightly longer than to the left ear, therefore the left loudspeaker's sound arrives slightly later at the right ear, and its tonality is changed as it wraps around the face and head.

If both loudspeakers reproduce an identical sound wave simultaneously, both ears receive the same wavefront at the same time, followed by identical slightly delayed inter-aural cross-talk. The listener perceives this sound as coming from a central location, directly between the loudspeakers – where there is no physical loudspeaker. The illusion of a sound located where there is no loudspeaker is called a *phantom image*.

The stereo format is a two-dimensional format when creative recording and mixing techniques are used:

• There is clearly a sense of left/right directionality, because it is possible to position sounds anywhere between the loudspeakers, and to create the illusion that sound is coming from just beyond the physical loudspeakers.
• It is also possible to create the illusion of front/back depth.
• To a lesser degree, it is possible to create the limited illusion of a third dimension – height.

CHECK YOUR MONO COMPATIBILITY!

Checking your stereo project sounds good in mono – its *mono compatibility* – is very important. You never know what type of system your project will end up being heard on. Cheap TVs, cell phone speakers, elevator music systems, bedside clock radios, and most ceiling speaker systems in shops and stores are all mono systems. The last thing you want is for your mix to sound bad, or for sounds or certain frequency ranges to partially, or in extreme cases, completely disappear when a stereo mix is summed to mono.

||||➡

Most mixing consoles and DAWs have a *mono* button in their monitor section. This sums the stereo mix to mono to check this compatibility. The feature is there for a reason – use it! Significant tone, timbre, or frequency balance (equalization) changes, when a mix is folded down to mono, usually indicate a mono compatibility problem that needs fixing.

SURROUND SOUND

Multichannel surround sound formats, such as 5.1 and 7.1, utilize additional loudspeakers which surround the listener. They offer the advantage of being able to envelop the listener with sound coming from behind and to the side of the listening position. Additionally, a dedicated center channel loudspeaker can take the place of center phantom images, and provide alternate sonic imaging qualities. New formats with height channels are being explored and developed – these truly result in a three-dimensional listening experience. Surround sound formats are beyond the scope of this book, and stereo production should be mastered before attempting any type of surround sound production.

2.3 MONITORING OPTIONS – LOUDSPEAKERS, HEADPHONES, AND EARBUDS

Stereo is the most common consumer listening format, and a pair of studio loudspeakers, called *monitors*, are the preferred listening system when recording, mixing, and mastering in stereo. Boom boxes, hi-fi systems, stereo televisions, car stereos, and the plethora of portable media players (PMPs) such as MP3 players, iPods, and multimedia mobile phones all offer two-channel "stereo" playback. But are all of these devices actually stereo?

Figure 2.2 showed that a stereo system creates inter-aural crosstalk that our hearing system uses to determine the directionality of sound. **Figure 2.3** shows a pair of headphones (or earbuds) on a listener. There is no inter-aural crosstalk in this system – the sound from the left driver goes only into the left ear, and the sound from the right driver goes only into the right ear. The only directional information presented to and processed by our brain is the amplitude difference of the sound between each ear. For this reason, headphones and earbuds should not really be called stereo, despite the labeling to the contrary on the retail packaging! They are in fact *binaural* – featuring two channels, minus the inter-aural crosstalk necessary to make them a true stereo system.

There are several reasons that mixing using high quality, professional loudspeakers is preferable to mixing using headphones:

- Mixes created on loudspeakers translate very well to headphones. Mixes created on headphones do not translate as well to loudspeaker systems.

Figure 2.3 A binaural headphone or earbud system lacks the inter-aural crosstalk necessary to make it a true stereo system.

- "But most of the listeners will be using earbuds anyway." It is perfectly OK, and good, to check a mix on headphones or earbuds. But to create a stereo mix that will best translate to the greatest variety of playback systems, the mix should be crafted on a stereo loudspeaker system. A mix that doesn't translate well to many reproduction systems, or future systems, will have a more limited audience, and a more limited lifespan.
- Headphones do not present the same stereo image or front/back depth that stereo loudspeaker systems are capable of. While a headphone image may be correctly described as more precise and surgical, it is also smaller and more compact. If you are mixing for headphones exclusively, then knowledge of some of the miking techniques discussed later in this book can allow you to incorporate delay-based image steering into your recordings, to add some delay and HRTF-like artifacts into the binaural reproduction system.
- Professional monitor loudspeakers are built to tell the truth, and not to hype specific frequency ranges, or to sound instantly "pleasing" (like most lower cost headphones, and consumer loudspeakers). Professional monitors reveal more problems in your mix or recording than most headphones or consumer loudspeakers. This makes it more challenging to get the sound right on good loudspeakers – but when you do, the results should translate well to a larger variety of playback systems. Most headphones and consumer loudspeakers don't reveal so many details or potential problems – which can lead to unfortunate surprises when a mix is played on a better sound system.
- Many headphones and consumer loudspeakers hype the bass for "instant impact." Professional monitors have a flatter, more linear frequency response in order to more correctly present the sound, and not mask any potential mix issues. This means that a first impression of a professional monitor speaker might be that it lacks bass, and is not as full sounding. If you are new to professional monitors, you need to learn how *your* monitors sound – intimately. Listen extensively to industry-respected, good sounding reference recordings on your new monitors. Recognize the characteristics of good

sound on those monitors, and get used to the balance of the low, mid, and high fre-quencies. *If you do not know and trust how your speakers sound, you cannot reliably use them to craft a mix that will sound good elsewhere.*

There *are* some great sounding (and usually expensive) headphones on the market, and these *can* be used for monitoring, subject to the caveats above. Earbuds however, particularly the cheap stock items that the majority of the public happily use, sound horrible. They either lack real bass, have a highly inaccurate "bass" boost that isn't in a really low frequency range, and their high frequency performance is usually not very good.

EARBUDS – A HEALTH HAZARD?

Earbuds connected to portable media players can produce peak SPLs in the ear canal of up to 127 dBA, depending on the device! The average sustained level is a little below the peak figure, but still well in excess of recommended 85 dBA maximum sound exposure level without hearing protection.

Stock earbuds, and most cheap earbuds, are non-sealing "open" designs that let in extraneous sound so the listener is aware of their surroundings. In noisy environments listeners usually listen at least 6 dB louder than the environmental noise. City traffic is about 85 dB SPL, the noise on a subway train can be over 90 dB SPL, and restaurants and bars can be over 90 dB SPL!

Listening to music at least 6 dB louder than this background noise immediately puts the listener at risk of permanent hearing damage in a short time. Sealing, or "closed" earbuds should promote listening at quieter levels because they block some of the back-ground noise, but many people still end up turning them up excessively loud.

KNOW HOW YOUR MONITOR SPEAKERS SOUND

- If cheap headphones or earbuds are what you are used to listening to, then you will need to retrain your ears by listening extensively on good stereo monitors.
- If you go straight from earbuds to good studio monitors, without learning how the monitors sound, you'll end up recreating the earbud sound on the monitors – and the result will be exponentially worse when your mix is played back on earbuds!
- If you're transitioning to new monitors, it's a good idea to have some respected good sounding commercial mixes spinning continuously, so you can A/B compare the characteristics of your mix to those commercial mixes as you are working.

2.4   COMPRESSED AUDIO FORMATS

Dissemination formats such as MP3, AAC, and Ogg-Vorbis, are *lossy* compression codecs. They reduce (or compress) the audio file size (compared to PCM) by removing audio that the encoder doesn't think will be perceived. As a result, songs can be downloaded faster and more songs fit onto a portable media player (PMP). The process is not transparent though, and more and more detail is removed as the bit-rate is reduced. Lossy compression does negatively affect the quality of the sound.

LOSSY COMPRESSION ARTIFACTS

Some of the many undesirable byproducts of lossy audio compression codecs include:

*   Frequency content discarded throughout the spectrum.
*   Drastic high frequency loss at low bit-rates.
*   MP3's reduction of bass frequencies.
*   Time and phase smearing.
*   Roughness.
*   Ringing frequencies.
*   Swirling and unstable higher frequencies.
*   Loss of transient detail.
*   Flattening of dynamics.
*   Loss of reverberation tails, and reduction of other time-based effects.
*   Stereo image narrowing and blurring.
*   The addition of low-level noise.

Lossy compressed audio formats are not formats an audio professional, or aspiring audio professional, should be listening to when learning what good sound might be, and how to achieve it.

Lossless compression codecs, such as FLAC and Apple Lossless (ALAC), do not suffer from the negative artifacts of lossy codecs, however, they do not offer such large file size reductions.

While iPods and most other modern PMPs can store lossless files of one type or another, or even uncompressed PCM files, the device's cheap convertors and amplifiers, and cheap earbuds mean they're still not an acceptable solution. So, when listening, try to use good quality playback systems, and/or better external conversion of the digital bit-stream from a PMP.

Lossy formats on a PMP or computer, and/or the cheap convertors and amps found on PMPs should not be used for any system evaluation, or to analyze mixes – they do not accurately portray the mix as the engineer intended.

Common Lossy Formats

These excerpts all feature the same musical example, encoded to different formats.

Example 2.1: Uncompressed, raw PCM.

Example 2.2: 256 kbps MP3 (2014 Amazon.com standard).

Example 2.3: The audio *removed*, and *distortions* added by the MP3 encoding in Example 2.2.

Example 2.4: 64 kbps MP3. (This quality and lower are experienced when streaming to mobile devices.)

Example 2.5: 256 kbps AAC+ (2014 iTunes standard).

Example 2.6: The audio *removed*, and *distortions* added by the AAC+ encoding in Example 2.5.

2.5 DYNAMIC RANGE

If you compare a pop or rock recording from the 1970s to one from the late 2000s one thing will probably be really obvious – the latter one is *louder*! The compact disc becoming the most popular dissemination format in the late 1980s, and the availability of the digital limiter in the mid-1990s, prompted competition to have the "loudest" most in-your-face mix – the *Loudness War*. By the late 2000s, the average levels on CDs had become so hot that distortion was apparent on many releases – Metallica's *Death Magnetic* notably attracting negative media attention in 2008.

Some dynamic range compression and limiting are a desirable and essential part of the mastering process – particularly of commercial music. This dynamic control gives recordings extra punch, and can help them play back well on a wider variety of reproduction systems. However, *hyper-compression* – when the peak levels are reduced too much, and end up very close to the more continuous average levels – results in a squashed, gritty, and often distorted sound, that lacks true punch and detail. The transients, the initial attack portions of loud punchy sounds such as the kick and snare drums, are particularly prone to this type of sonic damage. Hyper-compressed mixes are a product of extreme mastering, recording, and mixing techniques. That level of loudness simply cannot be created using more traditional tools and techniques.

Have you ever wondered why your favorite record sounds so different on the radio than on CD? One of the reasons for the loudness war was competition to have the loudest song on the radio. We are easily convinced that something that is louder sounds better. Industry wisdom was that when scanning similar radio stations, a listener was most likely to settle on the one that was louder. Most radio stations employ equalizers, multiband compressors, stereo "enhancers," and aggressive limiters and automatic gain control prior to their transmitter. So in addition to potential hyper-compression during mixing and mastering, the mix is squashed and processed even more by these usually poor-sounding devices and processes.

TURN OFF THE RADIO!

The radio is not a source of good sound. In addition to pre-transmission processing described in the main text, most broadcasters now use automation software that stores music as lossy compressed files, even for analog broadcast. All digital radio is based on lossy compression codecs, and although some sound better than others, current satellite radio formats exhibit audible artifacts because of the lossy data compression used. Streaming internet radio can be even worse! Many of the younger generation stream radio stations or music on their mobile phones – at truly awful bitrates, much lower than computer-based streaming.

Luckily there is a growing trend against extreme hyper-compression, and more and more artists are bucking the trend. Normalization (level matching) technologies found in playback software and hardware are often automatically employed by cloud and streaming services, and media playing computer software such as iTunes. Legally mandated, average level standards are being increasingly imposed on broadcasters. All of this makes hyper-compression less beneficial – the systems turn down tracks with higher average levels, so they won't be any louder than better sounding non-hyper-compressed tracks with lower average levels!

Why does this matter? Products that were a casualty of the loudness war are not desirable to emulate, and in the future will certainly not be considered desirable goals.

To learn, evaluate, and analyze good sound, you need to listen to industry-respected recordings, from uncompressed or lossless source formats.

Dynamic Range Processing

These excerpts are all the same musical example, with different amounts of dynamic limiting applied during mastering.

Example 2.7: No limiting applied. The dynamics are as they came off the mixer output.

> ## Dynamic Range Processing (continued)
>
> **Example 2.8**: Moderate limiting. About 6 dB of gain reduction on the loudest peaks, allowing the gain and average levels to be turned up by 6 dB. The mix is much louder and powerful, yet maintains most of its punch and clarity.
>
> **Example 2.9**: Loudness war, hyper-limiting. Over 12 dB of gain reduction on the loudest peaks, allowing the average levels to be made over 12 dB louder. The mix sounds distorted, and the impact and power of the kick and snare drum transients are destroyed.

2.6   WHAT ABOUT DISTORTION?

Is distortion bad? Well…yes. And no.

Distortion as a result of digital recording levels being too high, digital mix bus levels being over-hot, clipping processors or plug-ins – yes, that's bad. But as discussed earlier, gentle overloading of analog circuits and magnetic tape can produce pleasing effects. What would the sound of an electric guitar be without gentle, moderate, and severe forms of analog distortion, and digital pedal or processor emulations of those characteristics? What would bands such as Nine Inch Nails sound like without deliberate bit-crushing digital distortion?

Distortion is an essential part of some instrument sounds! A clean DI'd guitar track is usually out of place, inappropriate, and just does not work in a heavy rock or blues context – a stylistically appropriate guitar sound has either gentle distortion on the attacks of the notes, or more aggressive, continuous, self-compressing distortion throughout the notes. The loudspeaker cone of a guitar or bass amp distorts the electrical audio signal fed into it, even if all distortion knobs are set to "off." Non-linearities in the cone's behavior are technically distortion, and produce the sound's unique character. The rotating horn in a Leslie speaker distorts an organ's output waveform, and again, this distortion *is* the instrument's sound and character – without it, a B3 just wouldn't be the same!

Gentle distortions are why one piece of gear sounds different to another, and can be used to give sounds a little extra character. Moderate or severe forms of distortion can be used for creative effect, giving elements of a mix hyper-character, grit and grunt when needed.

Once you have learned how to create clean, technically perfect mixes, carefully applied distortion can be a very powerful and effective tool. As part of the recording chain, it is fair to say that any accidental digital distortion, or much more than gentle analog distortion, is undesirable. You cannot undo distortion, so even if you want to use distortion effects creatively in your mix, it's better to track and record "clean," and add distortion in a controlled way as part of the mix – in context, when you know how much is needed.

Distortion – Friend And Foe

Example 2.10: Inappropriate distortion on an instrument track. The first section of this example is analog distortion caused by overloading the mic preamp. The second half is digital distortion caused by clipping the inputs (or outputs) of a digital device, DAW, or plug-in.

Example 2.11: A clean, undistorted guitar track. It is bland, and lacks character.

Example 2.12: The slight distortions of the guitar amp cabinet loudspeaker color the sound and make it more characterful.

2.7   WHAT IS A GOOD RECORDING?

Musicians practice scales as a prerequisite to finding their own style. A similar prerequisite for an aspiring audio professional would be learning to make simple, technically and artistically correct recordings prior to exploiting more creative stylistic techniques. "Technically correct" means free of any undesirable technical artifacts. So what makes a technically good recording?

- Good sounding sources and musicians are a prerequisite.
- Appropriate microphone choice.
- Good mic placement and mic techniques.
- No noise or distortion problems created by incorrect or inappropriate use of any of the equipment in the recording and mixing chain.
- Good balances and use of the stereo soundstage.

"Artistically correct" means that the recording and mixing styles are appropriate to the project, and musical style.

By understanding how to capture, process, and mix sound using equipment technically correctly, you learn to:

- Use the equipment to control the sound.
- Really hear the effect of more creative, artistic use of the equipment.
- Anticipate how creative processing may benefit a project you're working on.

BUT IT'S ABOUT THE MUSIC, NOT THE RECORDING!

Let's not forget one important thing – the music creates a hit song, *not* the recording! Many hit records are not technically perfect – there may be minor engineering mistakes and errors because a great musical performance trumps a little distortion on a killer vocal take!

2.8 ACCURACY

When learning to record and mix, one characteristic to aim for is *accuracy*. Is the recorded sound a faithful reproduction of the instrument or singer? If acoustic musicians are professional and used to playing together, they know how to blend themselves. You, the recording engineer simply need to capture their performance appropriately. The recording room, mic choice, and mic placement are huge factors that impact the characteristics of a recording. Accuracy is unachievable if you place the wrong mic in the wrong position on an instrument in a bad room – all you can do is wrestle the sound somewhat into shape as part of the mixing process.

Great sound sources, a good sounding room, the right microphones, and good mic technique will capture sounds that mix themselves more. Getting the initial recording right results in a better, quicker, and easier mix.

Inappropriate Recording Techniques

Example 2.13: A vocal recorded in a room that is too live and reverberant for the project's style.

Example 2.14: A vocal recorded in a more suitable, drier vocal booth.

Example 2.15: Drums, recorded in a room that is too dry. The sound is small, compact, and lifeless.

Example 2.16: Drums, recorded in a live drum room. The sound is bright, punchy, and exciting.

2.9 NON-NATURAL SOUNDS AND BALANCES

Having discussed the importance of accuracy in a recording, it has to be admitted that most pop and rock music is not about overall accuracy – it's about achieving a sound that is stylistically and artistically appropriate. A good example of this is the sound of a modern rock drum set – the recorded kick, snare, and tom tom sounds are quite different to how they sound naturally from a normal listening position. Microphone and production techniques are exploited to make those sounds larger than life, phat, and in-your-face. They are *not* necessarily accurate, but they *are* certainly stylistically and artistically desirable.

In real life, most singers would not be heard above the naturally much louder drums, guitar, and bass amps of a typical rock band. Recording equipment allows the engineer to create non-natural balances so the singer is heard clearly. Effects such as compression and reverb are used creatively during mixing, to improve the way the sounds work as a recording. The balance and mix of sounds and effects we're used to hearing in pop music has little to do with natural balance, but everything to do with style.

"Accuracy" in pop music involves capturing the actual source material in a way that allows construction of stylistically appropriate sounds. If you are not familiar with either the natural sound of the instruments being recorded, or the stylistic goals of the type of project you're working on, how can you record appropriate tracks and create a good mix from them?

It is important to listen, listen, and listen to industry-respected recordings of styles you might one day be called to work on.

2.10 WHAT ARE THE ELEMENTS OF A GOOD MIX?

Regardless of musical or production style, there are some fundamental characteristics that are essential and common to any good mix. They include:

- Appropriate frequency balance.
- Clarity and intelligibility.
- Effective use of the stereo image, and stereo imaging concepts.
- Effective use of soundstage depth, and front/back imaging concepts.
- Appropriate focus and amplitude balance.
- Good use of processing and effects.

2.11 FREQUENCY BALANCE

A mix should have appropriate amounts of low, mid, and high frequency content. A *real time analyzer (RTA)* is a tool that can be used to visually show frequency content. **Figure 2.4** shows an RTA plot of a great sounding mix. The RTA is set to average out the frequency content over fairly long intervals of time, and to respond fairly slowly. If the RTA shows instantaneous readings, it jumps around too much, becomes difficult to interpret, and is dissimilar to human hearing (which has a tendency to determine frequency balance based on longer-term averages).

An "ideal" frequency curve, based on current mixing trends, is for a slight hype in the low end, relatively "flat" content into the mid range, and a gentle roll off up into the highest frequencies.

- If a mix doesn't have enough bass it will sound thin and lacking in power.
- Not enough mid range, and it will sound distant, thumpy, sizzly, and lack diction and clarity.
- Not enough high frequency content, and it will sound dull.

Visual tools are just tools to help train or confirm what the ear is hearing – your trained ear should *always* be the final judge.

A good way to confirm that your mix is on the right track is to have a respected, good-sounding mix available for playback, and to frequently and quickly switch to, and A/B it with

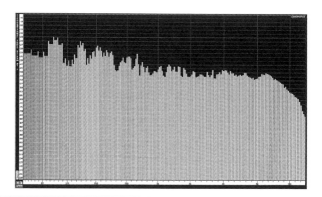

Figure 2.4 An RTA plot of a great mix. Note the relative "flatness" of the middle of the plot, with a gentle rise in the bass (on the left), and a rolling off of the high frequencies above about 6 KHz.

your mix in progress. The commercial mix will probably be louder and more "in-your-face" because it has been mastered, but you should listen to frequency content, not overall loudness.

Your choice of microphone, the position you put it in, and the room you record in are just a few of many variables that impact the frequency balance of the sounds you record. It's essential that you record a sound that will give you the frequency content you need of that sound source in the mix.

SOME ESSENTIAL FREQUENCY CHARACTERISTICS TO LEARN TO IDENTIFY

- 150 Hz and below: Is the low frequency content of the kick and bass guitar/bass line boomy and undefined, tight and full, or small and compact sounding?
- 150 to 400 Hz: Does too much of the low-mid frequency range cloud the mix and make it too thick and muffled? Or does the mix lack fullness and body because there is too little of this frequency range?
- 400 to 500 Hz: Too much of this frequency range can give the mix a confused, boxy sound. Try banging a cardboard box with a stick, or talking into a cardboard box to get an idea of this quality!
- 600 to 800Hz: Not quite a nasal sound, but like talking into a toilet roll tube. Too little of this frequency range, and many sounds lack definition. Too much of this range results in a honky sound.
- 1 to 1.6 KHz: A lot of nasal, diction, and definition characteristics are contained in this frequency range. Too much of this range can result in a thin, nasal, AM radio, megaphone-like sound. Not enough, and a "smile curve" type of EQ can result, where the mix lacks power and sounds distant.

- 2 to 3 KHz: Probably the ugliest sounding frequency range! Too little of it and the smile curve effects described above can result. Too much, and your mix could have a very cheap sounding, thin, tinny timbre.
- Around 4 Khz: "Not quite high frequencies" but "not quite mid frequencies"! Too much can give a harsh edge to instruments such as horns, guitars, drums, and cymbals. Too little of this frequency range can reduce a mix's clarity, particularly of vocals.
- Around 8 KHz: "Proper" brightness and high frequencies. Too little content in this range makes mixes dull and lifeless. Too much, and the mix can become over splashy, too bright, or too sibilant.
- Above 12 KHz: This range contains the "sprinkles" – the magic dust that can give your mix "air," and a sparkly sheen. Too little of this frequency range and the mix can sound flat and unexciting. Too much, and the mix will be too sizzly.

Figure 2.5 shows an RTA plot of a mix with an inappropriate frequency balance. The low and high frequencies are too loud, and the mid-range too quiet. This mix will have a boomy, bright, and sizzly sound that lacks definition. This is what is commonly referred to as the *smile curve* or *loudness curve* sound, and is commonly dialed in by many consumers on their equalizers, or by pressing the "loudness" button on some playback devices. It can be instantly pleasing because it hypes the extreme frequency ranges our ears are less sensitive to, particularly when listening at lower volumes. But at higher volumes, it creates an inappropriate frequency balance.

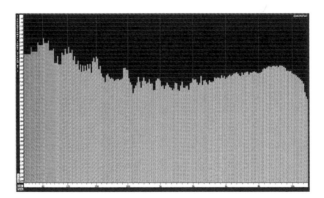

Figure 2.5   An RTA plot of a mix with too much low and high frequency content. Note the areas of "smile curve" hype in the low (left) and high (right) extremes.

Figure 2.6 shows the RTA plot for a mix that is lacking in bass and high frequencies. It will sound thin, AM radio like, and similar to cheap earbuds! If you only listen on earbuds, then this is the type of sound you might think is desirable – because it's the way you're used to hearing things. If you do think cheap earbuds sound good, invest in some good loudspeakers,

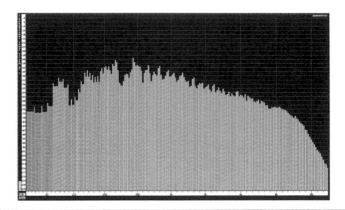

Figure 2.6 An RTA plot of a mix that is lacking low and high frequencies. The prominence of mid frequencies produces a thin, AM radio, or cheap earbud sound.

throw away the earbuds, and re-train your ears to recognize the characteristics of a good mix on good loudspeakers – before you record or mix anything else!

Mix Frequency Balances

Example 2.17: A mix with a good, frequency response, similar to Figure 2.4.

Example 2.18: A mix with "smile curve" EQ. Too many lows and too many highs create a mix that lacks definition, similar to Figure 2.5.

Example 2.19: A mix with too much mid-range lacks highs and lows. The mix sounds thin, like many cheap earbuds, similar to Figure 2.6.

2.12 CLARITY AND INTELLIGIBILITY

Every element in a mix should be able to be heard clearly, or appropriately to its artistic function. Clarity and intelligibility are products of many things, including:

- Overall frequency balance: If the overall frequency balance of the mix is incorrect, then that will negatively impact the listener's ability to hear everything appropriately in the mix.
- Frequency content of the individual elements in the mix: By nature of the format, a stereo mix places many constituent sounds in a relatively small space – the space between the loudspeakers, or between the headphone drivers. When sounds are positioned on top of each other, or in close proximity to each other, they become more

difficult to accurately interpret, and their frequency contents sum together to form a new, combined frequency balance.

- Spatial positioning and panning: By panning sounds to different positions we physically separate them, making them clearer and improving the clarity of a mix – as well as making it spatially more interesting to listen to.

The individual sounds or tracks in a mix might sound great when listened to in isolation, but when put together the sound can become muddled and unclear. Equalization (EQ) can be used to fix this. The unnecessary, or less important frequency components of a sound can be attenuated (de-emphasized) so that more important components of *other* sounds can occupy that frequency space. This enables both sounds to be heard more easily because they are no longer "fighting" with each other in that same overlapping frequency range.

EQ-ING FOR CLARITY – GUITARS AND VOCALS

PROBLEM: A distorted electric guitar and vocal may both have a lot of frequency content around 2 KHz. They both get in the way of each other in this essential vocal diction and intelligibility frequency range. Neither is clear.

WRONG SOLUTION: Turning one up just obscures the other more, and/or makes the track too loud.

CORRECT SOLUTION: The guitar is less important musically, and also has a greater amount of other beneficially usable frequency content than the vocal – it has its body at lower frequencies, and brightness at around 5 KHz. An EQ attenuation around 2 to 3 KHz on the guitar can set it back in the mix a little, and make that frequency space available to more essential vocal diction and intelligibility frequencies. The problem is solved without turning anything up.

EQ-ING FOR CLARITY – KICK DRUM AND BASS GUITAR

PROBLEM: Kick drums and bass guitars frequently "fight" due to overlapping low frequency content. If a frequency range is congested, then all elements competing in that range lose.

SOLUTION: Attenuating the kick drum in a frequency range above its fundamental pitch (its "boom") can de-clutter frequency space that the bass can then occupy and be more clearly heard. De-emphasizing the bass, around the frequency of the kick drum's fundamental boom will allow the beef and boom of the kick to be heard more clearly.

Clarity Issues

Example 2.20: A mix lacking clarity. A product of poor mixing skills, this mix does not utilize the stereo image, and EQ is not effectively used to separate the elements of the mix.

Example 2.21: The clarity of the previous mix is improved through effective EQ, and positioning sounds more spatially throughout the entire stereo soundstage.

2.13 MUSICAL ARRANGEMENT

Like many things discussed in these early chapters, this has nothing to do with microphones or mic techniques, but the musical arrangement of a song can be the difference between a mix and song that works and sounds great, or one that doesn't reflect either the band or you as an engineer favorably! The clarity of a mix and the transparency of the sounds in a mix can often be improved by reducing the number of instruments playing simultaneously, or by changing an instrument's part so it is not playing in the same range as another instrument. Musical arrangements should ideally be cleaned up in preproduction meetings well before any mics are set up in the studio. The best mics in the world, good-sounding instruments, and amazing musicians won't help you produce a great mix if the musical arrangement is poor.

Depending on your relationship with the musicians, and your role in the sessions, you may be able to suggest instrumentation and arrangement changes. Even if a band insists on tracking everything (the same way they thrash through a song at a local bar gig), the mixer or DAW has *faders* and *mute* buttons! Just because something is recorded, doesn't mean it has to be used. Taking tracks out of the mix, or turning unimportant tracks down, can improve the clarity and focus of an otherwise cluttered, muddled, and over-busy mix.

If the band or producer is adamant that everything has to remain in, try to find time to do an extra mix, as you would prefer it – even if it's on your own (unpaid) time. Both can be presented to the client. You never know, they might like the stripped down version – and if not, you have a better mix for your resume, demo disc, or professional satisfaction! Regardless, good musicians and good people will be impressed that you cared enough about their project to go the extra mile.

2.14 THE STEREO IMAGE

A good mix really takes advantage of the space between the loudspeakers. Leaving all the sound sources panned centrally, parked on top of one another, does not effectively use this space – it's boring, and things are difficult to hear and comprehend. Having sounds come from different locations in the stereo image not only makes the mix more interesting to listen to, but it also means that sounds can have their own spaces – we can hear each element of the mix more clearly, and the clarity and intelligibility of the mix is improved.

Chapter 5 of this book discusses the stereo image extensively.

2.15 FOCUS AND AMPLITUDE BALANCE

Poor amplitude balance between the elements in a mix will negatively affect frequency balance and clarity. For example, if the bass is turned up too loud it will obscure the kick drum, guitars, and keyboard sounds. It will also make the mix generally too boomy, and lacking in mid frequency punch and high frequency brightness.

Amplitude balance is dependent on frequency balance – a good amplitude balance cannot be obtained until a good frequency balance has been worked out between all the tracks. But a good frequency balance is reliant on the amplitude balance of the tracks! Everything is dependent on what you've done to it, what you've done to everything else, and what you haven't yet done to everything else! Every time you change an amplitude or EQ setting, you have to go back and re-evaluate its effect on every other track or channel you've already worked on. You must be prepared to rework every other track or channel every time you change something!

This sounds like an impossible process, but a common approach might be to:

1. EQ a sound so it sounds good by itself. Or better yet, EQ and balance (channel fader) a small group of related tracks so they sound good together. Don't get too hung up on how an individual soloed track sounds – even though something sounds amazing by itself, it probably won't fit in the complete mix, and may cause other elements to disappear!

2. Add and balance another track, or small group of related tracks – not all of the mix elements, but just more. EQ and balance them so they work with the track(s) worked on previously.

3. Listen carefully to ensure the previously worked on tracks still sound good since the addition of the new tracks. Also, if a new track just isn't clear, or "popping" the way it should, the cause could be some of the previously worked on tracks getting in its way. Go back and further refine the EQ and amplitude balance of the previously existing tracks that need it so the new combination of tracks all work together.

4. Return to step 2 and add more tracks into the mix.

But what is a good amplitude balance?

You need to be familiar with the typical amplitude balances of whatever style of music you're working on (or may unexpectedly end up working on). The desired sound and amplitude of the kick drum and bass in a jazz setting are very different to their respective sounds and levels in a rock project. The only way to learn what is desirable in a particular musical or production style is to listen to industry-respected recordings.

Additionally, a mix needs focus – a focal point. What is the most important element of the mix? In vocally driven music it is of course the lead vocal. If the lead vocal cannot be heard and clearly understood, either because of poor frequency balance, clarity, or amplitude balance problems, the mix has failed.

Prior to the 1980s, vocals were generally louder in the mix than they are today. One current trend is to mix vocals more on par with other elements, rather than having them "on top." In some mixes, the vocals can actually be quite quiet, but due to their frequency content and the arrangement of the other instrumental tracks around them, they are clearly identified as the focal point. It's harder to mix in this contemporary way, due to the collisions of similar frequencies in the vocal and other instruments that are used at similar amplitudes to the vocal. In addition to more creative EQ, effective musical arranging, and the careful selection of sounds in the mix, the source recording needs to be made with this production aesthetic in mind.

In pop and rock music, the drums drive the rhythm of most songs – particularly the kick drum and snare drum. Usually they are mixed at about equal levels, and of equal focus to the lead vocal (or for dance music they are often the loudest elements in the mix). If the drums are too quiet, the mix will lack rhythmic drive. If the bass is too quiet the mix will lack a solid foundation and "bottom."

There are different ways to develop a mix:

1. Some engineers start with the drums, add the bass, add the rhythm section, and then park the focal point, usually the vocals, on top.
2. Other engineers start with the focal point, and then mix the other instrumentation in around it.

No method is right or wrong. *You* have to develop a process that works for you, and the type of product you are producing. For novice engineers, I suggest mastering the first method before moving on to the second. One thing is guaranteed though – you will end up with very different results using each of these methods – and if your usual method is the first, you should definitely give the second a go! Different projects, music, or production styles will benefit from these different approaches.

2.16 PROCESSING AND EFFECTS

Compression and reverb are like audio "glue" and "makeup." Compression can be used to tighten individual sounds, or to give them power and punch. It can also be used gently on the master output bus to apply a bit of glue that gels the whole mix together. Reverb, like real makeup, can smooth over slight blemishes on individual tracks, and generally make things more pleasing.

We usually hear acoustic musical sounds in a room or hall – an enclosed space of some kind. That space (unless it is the open air) imposes its reverberant characteristics on the sound. Some recording studio environments are acoustically dead and dry – particularly iso-booths and home studios treated with acoustical absorption products. When a microphone is positioned relatively close to a sound source in an acoustically dry environment, the recording lacks the spatial reverberation that we are used to hearing – so artificial reverb can be used to put that sound source back in a more characterful space.

The choice of reverb character is very style and tempo dependent – and it's true that pop music mixing styles have become relatively dry sounding these days. But that doesn't necessarily mean that no effects are used – short room characteristics, as opposed to long swishy halls, are often used, and early reflections can be exploited instead of reverb tails.

Drums sound dull and like the life has been sucked out of them without the sound of a bright reflective room around them. This is why the best professional recording studios have dedicated drum rooms that are relatively reflective – so excitement and energy does not have to be artificially added. Vocals and solo instruments usually sound smoother, and more professional and polished after the addition of some reverb. A common reverb applied to an entire mix, either during the mixing or mastering stage of production, acts like "acoustic glue," gelling the entire band together in a similar environment.

Delays, choruses, flanging, distortion, and a multitude of other creative effects are powerful production tools that should also be used when making an artistically creative recording. Mixes without processing and effects are not as interesting as they otherwise could be!

Processing and Effects

Example 2.22: A dry vocal, no processing.

Example 2.23: Compression makes the vocal more even, a little fuller, and bigger sounding.

Example 2.24: The addition of a short, early reflection-based reverb, increases the size and power of the vocal.

Example 2.25: A longer reverb tail acts like makeup, putting a professional sheen on the performance.

Example 2.26: The addition of a stereo delay creates a much more interesting image and effect.

2.17 SONG STRUCTURE AND ARRANGEMENT

Rarely does having all the musicians thrash away on the same riff or rhythm incessantly for an entire song produce an interesting record that a listener wants to listen to repeatedly. A great record is all about drawing the listener in – to do that there must be flow, development, tension, and release:

- BORING: A verse of vocal and full instrumentation followed by chorus of the same full instrumentation. In terms of intensity, the song hasn't gone anywhere and has nowhere to go.
- INTERESTING INTENSITY AND TEXTURAL CHANGE: Having only the drums, bass, and keyboard in the mix for the verse, before adding the guitars for the chorus.

A great band, made up of experienced musicians who are good arrangers, usually orchestrates itself. Different musicians and musical parts will come in and out effectively, and they will naturally pitch their parts so that they aren't in similar octaves or frequency ranges. Mixing is a lot easier when a band does this for you!

Other bands, whose regular performances might be thrashing away at a local bar or club, might need some production assistance in order to get their songs (which may well be acceptable alongside the other distractions of the live performance environment) to translate and work well as *recordings* – where the sole focus is the music. If the guitar and keyboards are playing material that is too similar, it may be beneficial to suggest that one of the musicians tries something a little different. This could be as subtle as changing the synth sound, slightly varying the rhythm of a part, changing the octave, or even not playing that section.

How much you, the engineer, can suggest to the band musically depends on your relationship with the performers – and whether there is an actual producer present. If there is a producer, you should keep your mouth closed, and not have an opinion even when asked! If you are hired because of your relationship with the musicians, and you are respected for your opinions, then it would be appropriate to educate the band, and shape their performance into a better recording.

2.18 MAKING A GREAT RECORD

A GREAT PERFORMANCE VS THE BEST TECHNOLOGY

Time for a reality check!

The best equipment, and recording and mixing techniques can't turn a poor performance, or bad sounding instruments, into anything other than a "slightly improved" version. And intonation processing software can only do so much before it turns the vocal into a "robot voice"!

It is very frustrating trying to record and mix bad sounding instruments or singers! Corrective EQ can only do so much, and only fix certain problems – for example, a poorly tuned drum set, drum set rattles and buzzes, loudspeaker cone noises, or wrong inflections in the vocal performance *cannot* be fixed in the mix. If you find yourself spending a long time struggling to fix one specific problem, it could be caused by issues not related to recording or mixing. Solutions?

- Locate better sounding instruments.
- Exercise producer skills and coax, guide, and nurture the performer(s) to a confident performance.
- (Or get better performers!)

WHAT DO YOU REMEMBER ABOUT YOUR FAVORITE SONG?

Is it the pristine vocal sound recorded with a very expensive high end condenser microphone? Or is it the catchy hook and the words – which were captured with a cheaper dynamic mic, because that's what was plugged in when the engineer decided to hit the record button "just in case"?

For audio people it's probably (and hopefully!) a combination of both. But for most consumers, it's usually the latter. Of course, better equipment (a great mic, and a great pre-amp) mean better sound, and that has to be desirable – but the fact of the matter is that many top selling records have been recorded on less than the best equipment, and do sometimes exhibit technical problems that are easily overlooked in the context of a great musical performance.

While "we'll fix it in the mix" is certainly a myth, the goal of 100 percent technical perfection does have to be balanced with knowing when a magical and unrepeatable musical performance has been captured.

About Microphones...

IN THIS CHAPTER:

3.1   THE MICROPHONE

There are *many* different microphones on the market for good reason – each model sounds different. Put another way, different mics make the source sound different. Selecting the right microphone is part of the art of recording – a mic's characteristics should complement the sound source being recorded, and capture the most appropriate sound for the mix.

A microphone changes sound waves (variations in air pressure) into electrical waveforms (variations in voltage). A mic's *capsule* contains the diaphragm assembly. The *diaphragm* is a very thin flexible membrane that moves corresponding to the sound wave energy that it is exposed to. A mic is a transducer that changes acoustical energy into electrical energy.

Mics are the critical first stage of the recording chain. After the microphone, the sound is represented and manipulated as electricity. The sound quality of a recording is limited by the weakest link in the recording chain. There is no way that subsequent electronic manipulation can make up for inappropriate mic choice or poor mic technique, so it is essential to understand the different types of microphone available, and the characteristics of each.

3.2   END ADDRESS OR SIDE ADDRESS?

Most microphones fall into one of two address types:

- *End address* mics, such as the one shown in the top of **Figure 3.1**. "On axis," "the front," or 0° is literally the front "pointy" end of the mic.
- *Side address* mics, such as the one shown in the bottom of **Figure 3.1**, are addressed from the side, as the name suggests. Usually the front is the side with the company logo on it – but always read the product manual to determine this!

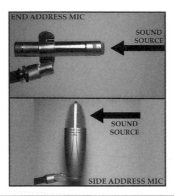

Figure 3.1 Top: An end address mic. Bottom: A side address mic.

Neither of these types are better than the other – they just lend themselves to different orientations, which affects function, ease of set up, and visual aesthetics.

3.3 DIRECTIONALITY AND PICK-UP PATTERNS

The *directionality*, *pickup pattern*, or *polar response* of a microphone determines how well it picks up sound coming from different directions. This is usually visually represented in a two-dimensional diagram – but remember that mics are placed in three-dimensional environments, so the following diagrams should be interpreted as representing both the horizontal and vertical planes.

CARDIOID MICROPHONES

Cardioid mics are most sensitive to sound arriving *on-axis*, from directly in front of the mic. They are still relatively sensitive to their sides (and above and below), at 90° and 270°, and have a *null point* (the angle of least sensitivity, or most rejection) at 180°, directly behind the mic, as shown in **Figure 3.2**.

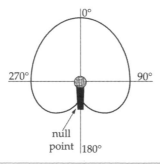

Figure 3.2 The pick-up pattern of a cardioid mic. The further the pick-up pattern plot is from the center of the crosshairs of the graph, the more sensitive the mic is to sound coming from that direction.

HYPER-CARDIOID MICROPHONES

Hyper-cardioid mics, as shown in **Figure 3.3**, are less sensitive to sound coming from the sides (and above and below) than cardioid mics – although they do still exhibit some pickup from the sides, above, and below. This makes them more directional – they do focus more on sound directly in front, and reject more *off-axis* sound than a cardioid mic. An unavoidable trade-off of the hyper-cardioid pattern is an area of slight sensitivity at 180°, directly behind the mic. This means the null points are 35° to 45° displaced from the rear of the mic.

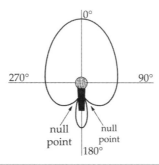

Figure 3.3   The pick-up pattern of a hyper-cardioid mic.

OMNIDIRECTIONAL MICROPHONES

Omnidirectional mics pick up sound coming from all directions more evenly, and are typically represented by a graphic resembling the shape in **Figure 3.4**. However, *all mics become more directional at higher frequencies* – so it is still important to point an omnidirectional mic in the right direction, on-axis to the sound source. An omnidirectional mic will pick up more *spill* (sound from adjacent sound sources, not really intended to go into the mic) and off-axis room reflections than a directional mic. This additional spill may or may not be desirable – it depends on the sound source, its role in the mix, the room, the type of project, and the desired production and mix style. Omni mics have a more open and transparent sound than directional mics, and can generally be positioned closer to sound sources than directional mics, without sounding boomy or muddy.

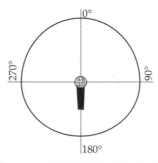

Figure 3.4   The pick-up pattern of an omnidirectional mic.

WIDE-CARDIOID MICROPHONES

Wide-cardioid mics are less directional than cardioids, but more directional than omnidirectional mics. They favor sound coming from the hemisphere in front of the microphone, and are more equally sensitive to sounds coming from the sides (and above and below). Their null point is the region directly behind the mic. **Figure 3.5** shows the polar pattern of a wide-cardioid mic. Their sound tends to be a balance of the openness of an omnidirectional mic, with some of the directional control of a cardioid mic.

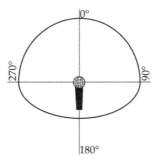

Figure 3.5   The pick-up pattern of a wide-cardioid mic.

BIDIRECTIONAL MICROPHONES

Bidirectional mics, also called *figure-8* mics, favor sound sources in front of *and behind* the mic capsule. They strongly reject sounds coming from the sides, above, and below – as shown in **Figure 3.6**. The extreme rejection of sound coming from the sides, above, and below the mic is a major benefit of this polar pattern. If there are desired sound sources behind the mic, the rear pick-up can be advantageous, but if the sound sources or spill coming from behind the mic are not desirable, the rear pick-up is problematic.

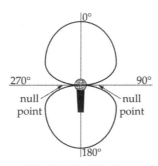

Figure 3.6   The pick-up pattern of a bidirectional mic.

> ## SINGERS! DO NOT CUP THE MIC WITH YOUR HAND!
>
> All *directional* mics achieve their directionality by allowing sound waves to enter the rear of the capsule. Covering the back, or rear vents of an end address mic, or the rear portion of a side address mic, prevents this and makes the microphone more omnidirectional. Cupping drastically changes how the mic sounds – it will become thin and nasally. On a live concert stage, feedback potential is increased because a cupped mic is picking up sound from all directions.

SHOTGUN MICROPHONES

Shotgun mics are rarely used in the recording studio, but are certainly used in television, film, broadcasting, live sound, and location/field sound recording. The capsule of a shotgun mic is at the back of a long tube which has small cut-outs along its length. A shotgun mic is very directional, with a very narrow forwards facing pick-up pattern, and much less off-axis sensitivity than any other type of directional mic. The longer the tube, the more directional the mic is. **Figure 3.7** shows a typical shotgun mic and its pick-up pattern.

3.4 DYNAMIC MICROPHONES

A *dynamic microphone* features a thin, lightweight, usually circular diaphragm, which moves backwards and forwards when excited by the sound waves that travel towards it, as shown in **Figure 3.8**.

Attached to the rear of the diaphragm is a coil of wire. Surrounding the coil is an immovable magnet. As the diaphragm moves backwards and forwards, the coil moves in the magnetic field. This causes a small amount of electricity to be induced in the coil of wire, the polarity

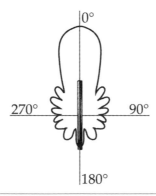

Figure 3.7 A shotgun mic and its pick-up pattern.

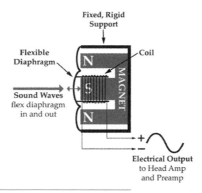

Figure 3.8 A cross section of a dynamic mic capsule.

of which is determined by whether the coil is moving backwards or forwards. This small electrical voltage is an analog of the sound wave that was picked up by the diaphragm. It is the same waveform, but in a different form – electrical voltage rather than acoustical energy. A head-amplifier in the mic raises this voltage to a mic level signal, which then goes down the mic cable, and is amplified further by either a mixing console or an outboard pre-amp.

Dynamic mics are relatively rugged – they withstand both sonic and physical abuse better than other technologies. For this reason, they tend to be the go-to mics for loud sound sources and for situations where the mic may be at risk of being physically damaged. For example:

• Inside a kick drum.
• A couple of inches away from a guitar or bass speaker cabinet.
• In danger of being dropped by a singer on a live performance stage.
• In danger of being hit by a fast moving drum stick.

Generally, dynamic mics have relatively poor *high frequency response*, *sensitivity*, and *reach*. They struggle to pick up the top octave of sound, and often impose a somewhat distorted or colored character on higher frequencies. They are not the best choice for sound sources with essential high frequency content (cymbals, hi-hats, acoustic guitars, etc.), nor if you want the brightest, crispest, smoothest, or most detailed high frequencies in your recording. The reason for this is that the diaphragm has to be made thick and strong enough to support the weight of the coil of wire attached to it, and it also has the added mass of the coil attached to it. This means that the diaphragm is not able to move as fast as it otherwise might, and it has more inertia – it is less able to stop and reverse direction to accurately represent the sound waves hitting it. It also takes more energy to set this heavier, less flexible diaphragm in motion, meaning that a very quiet sonic impulse (or the low level details within a louder sound) may not be strong enough to make the diaphragm respond – so those details will not be captured in the recording.

A dynamic mic would be a poor choice when recording quiet low-level sounds, such as acoustic string instruments or the sound of a pin dropping, or when a highly detailed recording containing all the subtle nuances of the sound is desired. Dynamic mics are like "low megapixel" cameras – they give an overall impression, but lack details and fine textural information.

Reach refers to a microphone's ability to pull sounds in from a distance. Because of their poor sensitivity, dynamic mics do not have good reach. They need to be close to a sound source. This makes them good for use in environments where there are lots of adjacent sound sources spilling into the mic – such as on a live performance stage, or within a compact miking environment such as a drum set. But they are a poor choice for anything not closely miked – for example, they do not make good room or distance mics in the studio, or classical concert hall recording mics.

WHEN TO USE DYNAMIC MICROPHONES

In typical rock studio type recording, dynamic mics are frequently used on loud sound sources that do not have essential upper high frequency content, and which can often benefit from the slight compression and phattening of the sound caused by the mic's sluggish response, for example:

- Kick drums.
- Snare drums.
- Tom toms.
- Guitar and bass cabinets.

3.5   CONDENSER (CAPACITOR) MICROPHONES

Condenser microphones, also called *capacitor mics*, offer better high frequency response, and improved sensitivity and reach compared to dynamic mics. A diagram of a condenser mic capsule is shown in **Figure 3.9**.

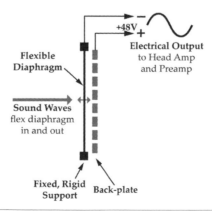

Figure 3.9   A cross section of a condenser mic capsule.

The usually circular diaphragm of a condenser mic does not have a coil attached to it, allowing it to be made thinner, and has much less mass than a dynamic mic's diaphragm. A condenser mic's diaphragm is coated with a very thin layer of electrically conductive metal particles – just a few microns thick – a process known as *sputtering*. Because it is so thin, the sputtered layer does not impede the diaphragm's ability to move, but it does allow a small amount of electricity to flow across the diaphragm.

ABOUT SPUTTERING

Gold is usually used for sputtering diaphragms – it oxidizes very slowly, giving a mic a potentially long lifespan. If iron were used, most of it would fall off as rust particles in a very short time! A "gold sputtered diaphragm" is nothing unusual in a condenser mic – more than 99 percent of condenser mics use gold sputtered diaphragms. Despite the hype some manufacturers give the process, gold sputtering is the norm.

A few very high-end microphones feature titanium sputtered diaphragms. Titanium is lighter, stronger, and oxidizes even slower than gold – giving the mic more performance stability, and an even longer service life.

Behind a condenser mic's diaphragm is a *back-plate*. This is a rigid metal plate, with many holes drilled through it. The holes allow the air between the diaphragm and back-plate to displace more readily as sound waves cause the diaphragm to move backwards and forwards relative to the fixed back-plate. A steady direct current (DC) polarizing voltage, known as *phantom power*, is applied to the back-plate – by engaging a button on the mixing console or pre-amp. As the distance between the back-plate and moving diaphragm changes, the capacitance changes, and those fluctuations become the output signal. The resulting modulating voltage is an electrical representation of the incoming sound waves, and is then amplified to an AC mic level signal by the head-amp in the mic, and transmitted down the mic cable, before being amplified to line level by the pre-amp the mic is plugged into.

The thinner, lighter, and more flexible diaphragm in a condenser mic can change directions and move faster and more easily that the thicker, heavier, "diaphragm plus coil" in a dynamic mic. This gives condenser mics the ability to pick up high frequencies more accurately – most condenser mics can efficiently pick up all the way to 20 KHz, and some to 30 KHz, 40 KHz, and even 50 KHz and beyond. It also means that very quiet sounds, and the low-level details contained within louder sounds, are picked up by a condenser mic. Condenser mics also have much better reach than dynamic mics – they pick up sound (including spill and room sound) from much further away.

WHEN TO USE CONDENSER MICROPHONES

Condenser mics are preferred when:

- A sound source contains essential high frequencies.
- The sound source is quiet.
- A very accurate and detailed recording is desired.

Good condenser mics are generally more expensive than dynamic mics. They are also much more fragile and need to be handled and used with care. Wind and air gusts can perforate diaphragms, and physical shock can damage capsules. *Windscreens* should be employed when condenser mics are used outside or in the presence of moving air currents, and *pop filters* should always be used between the mic and a singer close to the microphone.

Condenser mics are the high-megapixel camera of microphones – they pick up all the details, which is often a good thing. But don't forget, some sounds can benefit from the slightly obscured coloration of a dynamic mic.

DIAPHRAGM SIZE

Condenser mics are additionally categorized by the diameter of their diaphragm:

- Small diaphragms are approximately ½ inch or smaller.
- Large diaphragms are approximately 1 inch or greater.

Generally, small diaphragm condenser mics have a more extended high frequency response than large diaphragm condenser mics – although there are many large diaphragm mics that are very capable in this regard. Small diaphragm condenser mics are generally more "accurate" and exhibit less coloration than large diaphragm condenser mics.

Large diaphragm condenser mics commonly have "bigger characters" and a tendency to "hype" the sound. They make things larger than life – which is often desirable. They generally exhibit more coloration than small diaphragm condenser mics, so could be described as less accurate, but more characterful.

Large diaphragm mics are generally quieter than small diaphragm mics – they make less hiss and background noise. Additionally, more acoustical energy is captured by the diaphragm and converted into electricity, therefore less (potentially noisy) gain in the mic's amplifier and mic pre-amp is required.

There are several manufacturers making microphones with smaller quarter inch diaphragms that have frequency responses up to 50 KHz and beyond. Their trade-off is that they are noisier – the mic itself produces more hiss and noise. They often also require more pre-amp gain compared to a large diaphragm microphone. Higher quality, quieter pre-amps are necessary in order to get enough clean gain out of these mics, without adding the noise of poor quality pre-amplification to the mic's own noise.

ELECTRET MICROPHONES

Electret microphones are similar to condenser mics, but instead of requiring an external polarizing voltage to be applied to the diaphragm and back-plate, they use a permanently charged back-plate, diaphragm, or capsule surface. Their head-amps (in the mic) do require either phantom power or battery power, depending upon the mic. Because this voltage does not have to be 48 V, compact 9 V or 1.5 V batteries are commonly used. The current drain is very low, so the batteries do last a long time.

Electret mics can be used wherever a condenser mic is a good choice, with the exception of very quiet sound sources. In terms of performance, some electret mics come close to condenser mics, but most have an inferior frequency response, and are noisier.

3.6 RIBBON MICROPHONES

A *ribbon microphone*'s capsule features a folded "ribbon" of aluminum, anchored at the top and bottom, surrounded by a magnet, as shown in **Figure 3.10**. As the ribbon moves backwards and forwards as it is excited by sound waves, its motion within the magnetic field causes electricity to be induced into it.

In order to allow the ribbon to move quickly (as required to resolve high frequencies), and easily when slight pressure changes excite it (in order to resolve subtle details), the diaphragm

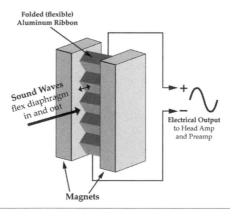

Figure 3.10 A cross section of a ribbon mic capsule. The ribbon is fixed and anchored at the top and bottom (not shown in this diagram). The magnet does not touch the flexible ribbon.

is very thin. Because of this, historically, ribbon mics have been very fragile – wind gusts, plosives (the rush of air from the mouth associated with "p" "b" and "t" type sounds), and physical shock could cause the ribbon to stretch, perforate or tear, requiring an expensive re-ribboning. Some modern ribbon microphones are more durable and, taking some precautions, can be used on stage and in front of loud amp cabinets.

Phantom power can also damage or destroy the ribbons in many *vintage* ribbon mics, but most *modern* ribbon mics will not usually be damaged by it – some even *require* it in order for their internal amplifiers to function. However, ribbon elements *can be damaged* if phantom power is short-circuited – which *will happen* if quarter-inch, bantam/TT, or MIL patchbay connections between the mic pre-amp and the mic are plugged or unplugged with phantom power turned on, or there is a short in a mic or patchbay cable. If, in a home or project studio, there is no patchbay in use and all mic connections are XLR, phantom power typically presents no danger to modern ribbon mics – but do make sure by reading the manual first!

If in any doubt – keep ribbon mics away from live concert stages, away from phantom power, and away from singers unless pop shields are used!

Some condenser mics have a slightly harsh and brittle high frequency character. In contrast, ribbon mics have a smooth and silky high frequency character. Many ribbon mics are also exploited for their "vintage" character – they are a little "darker and rounder." Other ribbon mics have more extended and flatter frequency responses.

No longer manufactured, and much less common than conventional ribbon mics, *printed ribbon microphones* feature a helix-shaped aluminum ribbon printed on a polyester film diaphragm, surrounded by magnets, front and back. These designs combined the sonic characteristics of ribbon mics with the durability and end-address designs of dynamic mics in a form that did not require phantom power – which was not as commonly available as it is on equipment today. Like ribbon mics, printed ribbon mics can be either bidirectional, or omnidirectional – but not both.

IS THERE SIGNIFICANT SPILL FROM BEHIND THE MIC?

Most ribbon mics are bidirectional. It is important to consider this when positioning the mic.

Some ribbon mics have slight sonic differences between their front and rear pick-ups. So do not assume the "front" has to be the front – the characteristics of the rear of the mic may suit some sound sources. In some designs, the rear portion of a ribbon mic's capsule is closed up, making it an omnidirectional mic.

Vintage ribbon microphones, and modern recreations of vintage designs, have very low electrical output. This means that they need a lot of gain from the mic pre-amp. The cheap pre-amps found in many budget to mid-range mixing consoles and interfaces, don't have enough gain to get good signal levels from these mics – and if they do, they become very hissy and noisy. A necessary and essential investment alongside this type of mic would be some high quality, clean, quiet, and high-gain mic pre-amps.

In contrast, some modern ribbon mics feature higher gain amplifiers in the mics themselves. This means they do not need such a high-gain pre-amp – so the mic *can* be used with less than top-of-the-line pre-amps. These active mics are more expensive than their classic counterparts, but you're paying part of the expense of an otherwise necessary and costly pre-amp when you buy the mic. These active designs *do* typically need phantom power to power the internal amplifier.

WHEN TO USE A RIBBON MICROPHONE

Ribbon mics are commonly used when:

- A smoother, rounder, warmer representation of high frequencies is desired, or a sound that is very bright and shrill needs "mellowing."
- A "vintage" character is desired.
- The extreme side rejection of a bidirectional pattern would be useful, minimizing spill from sources to the sides, above or below the mic.
- Huge proximity effect is beneficial. Or when you want a warm, full sound from a foot or two away.
- You want the ability to quickly rotate the mic 180°, and exploit the potentially different backside character of the mic.
- High SPLs, moving air currents, and physical shocks *will not* be a threat to the mic!

3.7 TUBE (VALVE) MICROPHONES

Guitarists have long favored the subtle harmonic distortions, sonic character, and warmth of *tube* or *valve* electronics in their amplifiers. Tube, or valve microphones, use sonically colorful tube amplification circuits instead of more modern, reliable, and stable solid-state head-amplification stages. This tube amplification colors the sound of the condenser capsule with sonic fullness, musical warmth, and smooth silky high frequencies.

Original, classic, vintage tube mics, built using very high quality materials and tubes were expensive. Faithful modern recreations of these classic designs are *very* expensive! There are also many cheaper tube mics on the market. To keep the price down, some very cheap mics use poor quality modern tubes and components – so assuming a tube mic is always better than a regular condenser mic is not correct. A classic tube mic will cost $5,000 to $10,000. There's just no way a $200 copy/clone/rip-off is going to have the same qualities, or automatically be the right choice, just because it's a tube mic!

Additionally, due to the high degree of coloration a tube mic produces, it is not necessarily the best choice for all sound sources or production styles. If a sound source is already very thick and warm sounding, the additional coloration added by a tube mic may be too much. But if a sound source is a little thin, and needs some warmth, body, or "phatness," a tube mic could provide useful "sonic makeup."

As a tube ages, its characteristics can change – negatively affecting its performance and sound. Tubes do need replacing. Tubes are fragile, and physical abuse will damage them – so care must be taken when setting up and tearing down. Tube circuits also tend to be noisier than solid-state electronics, so tube mics are noisier – making them less suitable for recording very quiet sound sources.

For rock music, the coloration, warmth, "phatness", and "bigness" characteristics of analog tape have long been favored over digital recording systems by many engineers. With the demise of analog tape, and prevalence of digital recording systems, some stylistically desirable sonic colorations are missing from the recording chain. In recent years there has been renewed interest in tube technology, and modern tube mics, tube pre-amps, and tube and tape saturation plug-ins have been developed to add analog coloration to digital recording systems.

3.8   OTHER MICROPHONE TECHNOLOGIES

LOUDSPEAKER CONE MICROPHONES

For decades, recording engineers have experimented with reverse wiring loudspeaker cones into mic inputs, and exploiting the very colored sound that such a large and heavy loudspeaker cone "diaphragm" produces. Nowadays, commercial products are available to do the same, as shown in **Figure 3.11**.

Figure 3.11   A commercial loudspeaker cone mic on a kick drum.

Loudspeaker cone mics do not produce a very detailed sound – they lack high frequencies, and usually sound boomy, bassy, and mushy! Their sound is not usable alone. However, their huge beefy bottom end can be blended with the detailed sound of a high quality traditional mic. Is the resulting sound accurate? No, not really – but a desirably huge, beefy, modern recorded kick drum sound is a non-natural, engineered sound anyway!

BOUNDARY MICROPHONES

A boundary microphone (trademarked "PZM" by Crown) features a very small condenser mic capsule mounted above, and facing down towards a sound reflective boundary plate, as shown in **Figure 3.12**. Sound takes two paths to the mic capsule:

1. Directly into it.

2. Reflecting off the boundary plate up into it.

A regular mic picking up both direct and reflected sound, the reflected sound arriving at the capsule momentarily after the direct sound due to the extra distance it travels, would usually exhibit audible comb filtering – the sound would be "phasey." Because of the extremely small distance between a boundary mic's capsule and the boundary plate – usually less than 0.050" – the sound waves remain in phase throughout the audio frequency spectrum. Boundary mics are not commonly used in music recording, but they are common in theater, conferences, and broadcasting.

Boundary mics should be mounted flat, on large, hard surfaces. The larger the surface area of boundary the mic is mounted on, the better its low frequency response. A surface of at least several feet square is necessary for good bass response. Most boundary mics have a hemispherical pick-up pattern – like the "front half" of an omnidirectional pick-up pattern. Directional boundary mics (cardioid, or hyper cardioid) also exist, which reject sound coming from behind the mic to varying degrees. Hemispherical boundary mics tend not to color off-axis sounds in the way that other types of mic do. This means that sound sources placed around the entire front hemisphere of microphone will be picked evenly, and that off-axis reflected sound (such as reverb) will be picked up more neutrally and accurately than they would be by other types of mic.

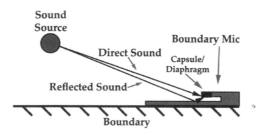

Figure 3.12 A cross section of a boundary mic capsule.

WHEN TO USE A BOUNDARY MICROPHONE

Common uses for boundary mics include:

- Mounting inside pianos – on the lid, which acts as the necessary boundary.
- Mounting on walls for room and drum mic applications.
- Mounting on the front of stages for theater, where the movement of performers and stage floor reflections would cause phase problems with other mic technologies.
- On desks and tables when phone and video conferencing.

Although they are not expensive, boundary mics can produce great results when set up correctly and tweaked with a little EQ.

LAVALIER AND HEADSET MICROPHONES

Lavalier, *lave*, *lapel*, or *tie-clip* mics are very small mics that usually clip on to clothing. They are used to capture voices in the broadcasting, motion picture, and corporate sound industries. For theater productions they can be inconspicuously mounted on an actor's forehead, cheek, or in their hair. Condenser and dynamic models are available, with directional or omnidirectional patterns. Some models are have fairly flat frequency responses, others have a boost in the high frequencies to compensate for mic positions where high frequencies are naturally attenuated – under a layer of clothing, under a person's hair, or away and behind the mouth (head and cheek positions). Headset mics position the capsule directly in front of the mouth, so generally sound better than lave mics – but they are much more conspicuous.

Lavalier and headset mics are not the best sounding or quietest mics available, so they are not generally used for studio recording.

CLIP-ON DRUM AND INSTRUMENT MICROPHONES

Many manufacturers now make dedicated drum and instrument mics featuring integrated clip systems to mount them directly to drums and instruments. These mics are primarily designed for the live sound industry, and not serious studio recording. While easy to position, they do not sound as good as stand mounted studio models, are generally noisier, and mechanical vibrations transmitted through the mounting clips affect the sound. Some manufacturers make instrument mounting clips for their conventional mics – but for the best sound, with maximum isolation from undesirable mechanical vibrations, and maximum freedom to adjust the mic's position, a proper mic stand should be used with a good studio mic.

PARABOLIC MICROPHONES

Not used in the recording studio, but frequently seen capturing distant sounds at televised sporting events, *parabolic mics* feature a condenser mic capsule mounted in a plastic "saucer" about 60 cm (2 ft) wide (similar to a small satellite dish). Parabolic mics are very directional, the dish giving them a very narrow "beam" pick-up.

Different Microphone Technologies

Example 3.1: A vocal, recorded with a dynamic microphone.

Example 3.2: The same singer, recorded with a small diaphragm condenser microphone.

Example 3.3: The same singer, recorded with a large diaphragm condenser microphone.

Example 3.4: The same singer, recorded with a tube microphone.

Example 3.5: A kick drum recorded with a single kick mic.

Example 3.6: The same kick drum recorded with the same kick mic *and* a loudspeaker cone mic.

3.9 PHANTOM POWER

Phantom power is a steady DC current, usually sent by mixers and pre-amps, down the mic cable to power condenser microphones (and other mics requiring power for their head amplifier). Not all phantom power supplies are created equal though! True phantom power is +48 V DC. If a piece of equipment is labeled "phantom power" rather than "+48 V," it can be an indication that it does not be send the full 48 V – and possibly as little as 12 V or less! Most high quality mics do require the full 48 V to perform close to specification. Some mics can run on these lower voltages, but others will become noisier, and their high frequency response will be impaired.

Not all mixers have phantom power switches on all channels – they might be switchable in groups of four, six, eight, or globally. Phantom power presents no danger to dynamic mics – it can be turned on, and will have no effect on them. As previously discussed, some ribbon mics will be damaged by phantom power, others can tolerate it, and some actually need it – so do double-check! Tube mic power supplies may or may not be damaged by phantom power – so it's best to check with the manufacturer.

By far the safest thing to do is to not send phantom power to anything that doesn't actually need it. If your mixer switches phantom in blocks, you may be able to group your mics together in "phantom required" and "phantom not required" blocks.

3.10 PROXIMITY EFFECT

Proximity effect is a boost of low and low-mid frequencies that occurs when a directional microphone is close to a sound source. As a general rule, the more directional the mic is, the more pronounced its proximity effect. This means that bidirectional mics have the most,

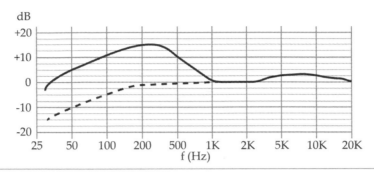

Figure 3.13   The dotted line below 1 KHz represents the flatter low frequency response of a directional mic when it is used in the "free-field" (at a distance of more than a couple of feet). The solid line represents the low frequency boost of *proximity effect*, when the mic is used in the "near field" (up close).

hyper-cardioids a little less, cardioids a little less again, and wide cardioids the least. Proximity effect can boost frequencies as high as 400 to 500 Hz, with the amount of boost increasing as the frequency gets lower – the amount of boost usually peaks somewhere between 100 to 200 Hz.

Figure 3.13 contains a frequency response chart that shows the *near-field* (up close) characteristics of a directional mic, with its associated proximity effect, and the *free-field* (at a distance) characteristics, which are free of proximity effect.

Radio DJs, many announcers and emcees, and some singers use proximity effect deliberately to make themselves sound bigger, beefier, and boomier than they do naturally. Generally however, *proximity effect is a bad thing in the context of a busy music mix*, and a frequent reason for muddy, confused mixes is low and low-mid frequency congestion. In many recording situations, particularly smaller rooms or home/project studios, this frequency congestion quickly becomes a problem because of the predominant and close-up use of cardioid and hyper-cardioid microphones – both of which exhibit proximity effect when used close to a sound source. Backing a singer or instrument off the mic by a few more inches can really reduce proximity effect problems.

Some mics, including hand held vocal mics, are built to mitigate proximity effect. This means that they sound great, and not boomy, a few inches from a sound source – but start sounding thin and tinny if they are too far away. If you do have to work with directional mics very close to sound sources, research their characteristics and apply equalization to undo the proximity effect if necessary.

Proximity Effect

Example 3.7: A voice recorded accurately, or "flat," from 45 cm (18 in) away.

Example 3.8: The same voice recorded from 8 cm (3 in) away. Boomy proximity effect can be heard.

3.11 FREQUENCY RESPONSE

Frequency response is a measure of how effectively a microphone is able to pick up different frequency ranges. There are several different ways of expressing frequency response, and the level of detail and usefulness of the quoted specification usually corresponds to the type, price, and quality of the mic.

"20 TO 20 KHZ"

Many cheaper mics simply state a range of frequencies. Unfortunately this supplies little useful information. Microphones pick up extreme low and high frequencies less well. This simple specification doesn't tell us how much less sensitive the mic has become at either extreme. Yes, the mic may pick up 50 Hz and 15 KHz, but it is probably doing so much less effectively than it picks up 2 KHz – you just don't know from this uninformative specification.

"20 TO 20 KHZ ±3 dB"

Some mics quote an effective frequency range *and* a tolerance. This is more useful. It tells us that at 20 Hz and 20 KHz, the mic is 3 dB ("slightly") less sensitive than its average response between those extremes, and that within the quoted frequency range its sensitivity to a particular frequency could vary by up to 6 dB – it could pick up *frequency A* 3 dB hotter than average, and it could pick up *frequency B* 3 dB less well than average. When looking at this type of specification, the smaller the tolerance, the flatter and less colored the mic's sound is – which can be a good thing. However this still does not tell us where those areas of higher and lower than average sensitivities are.

GENERIC FREQUENCY RESPONSE GRAPHS

Frequency response graphs, such as those found in product literature and manuals, are much more useful. As shown in **Figure 3.14**, these are plots of frequency (x-axis) against a dB scale of relative sensitivity (y-axis), showing how a mic picks up the entire frequency range of an on-axis sound source. While a flatter mic might pick up a much more accurate picture of a sound, it does not mean it's necessarily the most suitable or flattering mic for every application.

SERIAL NUMBER SPECIFIC FREQUENCY RESPONSE PLOTS

The electronic components in a microphone are all built to specific tolerances. Tighter tolerances mean more identical behavior – and that multiple mics of the same model will sound more similar. But the fact of the matter is that multiple mics of the same model and vintages can sound a little, or even quite different, depending upon the tolerances they are built to. So, a generic plot printed in the product manual is not necessarily a completely accurate indication of the performance of the mic in your possession.

More expensive, higher quality microphones often include custom, individual, serial number specific frequency response plots for each mic. For professional recording engineers

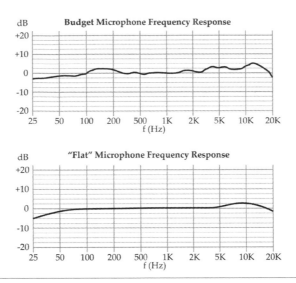

Figure 3.14 Top: A frequency response graph for a low budget microphone. The plot is not "flat." It has some peaks in its response where the mic is more sensitive – hyping that particular frequency range. Bottom: A "flat" microphone has a much more even, linear response to all frequencies in its effective pick-up range.

this is valuable information. If you are buying multiple mics for stereo or multichannel arrays, then the mics should be closely matched. *Matched pairs* can be purchased from many manufacturers. They usually cost a little more than buying two unmatched mics because of the extra testing and analysis required to match up the closest pairs – but for serious stereo pair work, this is money well spent.

3.12 OFF-AXIS RESPONSE

All microphones, regardless of their pick-up pattern, become more directional at higher frequencies, and more omnidirectional at lower frequencies. The plots shown earlier only show how a microphone responds to sound coming from directly in front of it, on-axis. In a multi-mic recording situation, or any live sound situation, there is also spill – unintended sound from adjacent sound sources reaching the mic off-axis from the sides or behind. Off-axis, a directional mic is much more sensitive to low frequencies than high frequencies. An omnidirectional mic is slightly less sensitive to high frequencies coming from the sides or behind. This means that off-axis spill can be colored, boomy, or muddy, due to the lack of high frequencies that give the sound intelligibility and clarity. This colored spill causes a cumulative buildup of "mud" in projects recorded with predominantly cardioid and hyper-cardioid mics.

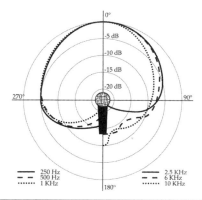

Figure 3.15 A mic's directional sensitivity is shown for different frequencies, each plotted hemispherically.

A major difference between cheaper and more expensive, higher quality mics is the quality of the off-axis pick-up. A higher price point usually correlates to a more linear, better sounding off-axis response which produces better sounding spill – and less mud and mush builds up in a recording because of the spill.

High quality microphones also come with frequency response charts that show the mic's directional sensitivity at different frequencies, as shown in **Figure 3.15**. These charts are not serial number specific.

Similar to the pick-up pattern diagrams discussed earlier, 0° represents the mic's response to on-axis sound coming from directly in front, and the farther away each line is from the center of the crosshairs of the diagram, the more sensitive the mic is to sound coming from that direction. The closer to the center of the crosshairs each line gets, the less sensitive the mic is to sound coming from that direction. Different line styles represent different frequencies. A frequency's plot is only shown on half the diagram in order to allow additional frequencies to be shown on the other side – but remember, the mic not only exhibits symmetrical pick-up on the left and right, but also in three dimensions, above, below, and around the mic.

Off-Axis Response of a Cardioid Microphone

Example 3.9: A voice recorded at 0°, on-axis.

Example 3.10: The same voice recorded at 90°, off-axis.

Example 3.11: The same voice recorded at 180°, in the mic's null point.

3.13 FLAT MICROPHONES VS VOCAL MICROPHONES

Microphones with a "flatter," more accurate frequency response are generally preferred for instrument, classical orchestra, and choir recording. *Diffuse field* mics, built for very distant use, are not completely flat, but have a slight rise in the high frequencies to compensate for natural high frequency attenuation over distance – this also avoids distant reverberant pick-up in a large concert hall sounding too dark or muddy.

Vocal mics are typically quite "characterful." This means they are not "flat," but that they hype and boost some frequency ranges – there are usually one or two *presence peaks* in the 3 KHz to 10 KHz range, shown in **Figure 3.16**. Presence peaks are areas of increased response and sensitivity to bring the intelligibility and diction of a voice "forwards" in the mix.

Depending on the voice being recorded, microphones with a relatively low frequency presence peak (3 KHz to 5 KHz) can sometimes sound a little harsh, *or* they can help with projection and "cut" – but they are not suitable for all vocalists. For more critical recording studio work, a higher frequency presence peak (around 8 KHz) produces a brighter, more shimmery "studio" type sound. Presence peaks can also conflict with *sibilance* – the sizzle of "S" and "T" sounds. If a voice is very sibilant, a presence peak in the same frequency range as the sibilance can unpleasantly over-exaggerate it.

No two voices or instruments sound the same, and ultimately the specific voice or instrument being recorded determines the character of the mic necessary. A mic that makes one artist sound great, may not work well on another. The only way to determine which mic brings out the most pleasing characteristics of any sound source is to experiment and try different mics and placements.

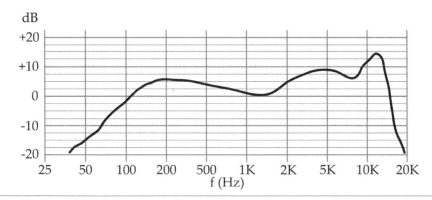

Figure 3.16 The frequency response graph of a mic with two presence peaks: A wide one at about 4 KHz, and a more narrow one at about 11 KHz.

3.14 LOW FREQUENCY RESPONSE

Directional mics do not pick up very low frequencies as well as omnidirectional mics. This may seem counter-intuitive considering the low frequency boosting characteristics of proximity effect, however it is important to remember that proximity effect only occurs *when the mic is close to the sound source*, and that this unnatural boost is inaccurate and can cause frequency balance issues that make the sound muddy and confused.

At frequencies below about 50 Hz, even when used up close, the frequency response of many directional microphones falls off quite sharply. There's another very powerful octave of sound below 50 Hz! Additionally, when used a distance from a sound source, the low frequency response of directional proximity effect compensated mics falls off dramatically below 200 Hz.

Omnidirectional mics do not exhibit proximity effect. This means that their low and low-mid frequency response will be the same regardless of the distance they are from the sound source. Also, and importantly, their low frequency response extends down to lower frequencies than directional mics. A good omnidirectional mic will have a flatter, more even frequency response down to 30 Hz, 20 Hz, or below! This means that it will really pick up the subwoofer shaking low frequencies of orchestral bass drums, string basses and bass guitar speaker cabinets. Most directional mics will not pick up the same depth, and if they are used up close that depth will be masked by proximity effect.

Low Frequency Response

Example 3.12: Distant cardioid drum room mics.

Example 3.13: Distant omnidirectional drum room mics in the same room.

3.15 LOW FREQUENCY INSTRUMENT MICROPHONES

In recent years, more and more microphones for bass and low frequency instruments have become available. These are typically dynamic mics, and their frequency response is heavily contoured to make sound sources like basses and kick drums more instantly appealing. Generally this means that the low frequencies and some higher frequencies are hyped, and there is a big cut in the mids. These mics can produce excellent results, however they have such exaggerated characters that they tend to either really work or really *not* work with a particular instrument or drum – there's little middle ground.

It is always preferable to get a great sound by selecting the right mic, and put it in the correct position on a great sounding instrument – rather than to use console or DAW equalization to compensate for preventable and avoidable deficiencies. It can be beneficial to use a frequency contoured low frequency instrument mic rather than equalize a flatter mic into shape if you're using low quality EQ circuits or plug-ins. But, if the EQ curves built into this type of mic are not exactly what is needed for a specific situation, you don't want to have to use EQ to undo the effects of the mic, and then apply further desirable corrections. A more generic, flatter mic may not sound as instantly "big" as a low frequency instrument mic, but you may be able to get better results by using some good EQ to tweak the flat mic into shape.

Low Frequency Instrument Microphones

Example 3.14: A kick drum recorded with a general-purpose dynamic mic.

Example 3.15: The same kick drum recorded with a low frequency instrument dynamic mic.

3.16 SENSITIVITY

Microphone *sensitivity* is a measure of a mic's electrical output, when it is placed in a sound field of a specific SPL, usually 94 dB SPL. Most manufacturers quote sensitivity as the number of millivolts the mic produces for this reference level (which can be expressed as *mV/Pa*, or *mV per 10 µbars*). When sensitivity is expressed in one of these formats, higher numbers are usually more desirable – the higher the quoted number, the less pre-amp gain will be required to bring the mic's signal up to line level, minimizing any noise potentially introduced by lower quality pre-amps. A mic with a spec of 29.8 mV/Pa has a higher output than a mic with a spec of 5.6 mV per 10 µbars.

Some manufacturers express sensitivity in a "−dB" format, and others in the older level standard of a 74 dB SPL input level, 1 µbar, or 0.1 Pascal – those three units are identical. The 94 dB equivalent is expressed as *dB re 1V/Pa*, and the 74 dB equivalent as *dB re 1V/µbar*. Expressed these ways, microphones with greater electrical outputs will have smaller negative numbers – so for recording very quiet sound sources, a mic with a rating of −31 dB re 1V/Pa would be preferable to one with a rating of −45 dB re 1V/Pa.

To compare two mics, when one quotes sensitivity as "−dB" to a 94 dB equivalent, and the other as "−dB" to a 74 dB equivalent reference level:

94 dB reference equivalent = 74 dB equivalent − 20 dB

74 dB reference equivalent = 94 dB equivalent + 20 dB

Greater sensitivity potentially means less noise will be created by the mic pre-amp, because less gain will be needed – but it does not necessarily mean that the mic sounds better.

3.17 SELF-NOISE AND EQUIVALENT NOISE RATING (ENR)

Self-noise and *ENR* are the same thing – a measure of the background noise (hiss and rumble) that a mic makes itself. Specifically, it is a measure of the sound pressure level required to create an output level the same as the noise the mic outputs when it is surrounded by silence. Self-noise is usually quoted as a dBA figure. Good quality modern mic pre-amps and digital recording systems can be very clean and quiet, and are able to resolve the smallest sonic details, so self-noise can be very important – particularly if quiet sounds are being recorded, because the self-noise correlates to the lowest extreme of a mic's dynamic range.

Self-noise is only quoted for condenser microphones, where it is a measure of the noise created by the head-amp in the mic itself. This noise is usually greater than the noise introduced by high quality console or outboard pre-amps, and can be audible when the gain is turned up high to record quiet sound sources. Most of the noise in dynamic and ribbon mics is created by the electrons moving within the coil or ribbon. Because the output voltage of these mics is much lower and more gain is needed on the pre-amp or console, the noise generated by the pre-amp is louder than the self-noise of the mic itself. This makes self-noise irrelevant, but makes having good quality, quiet, high gain pre-amps very important.

Self-noise figures can be as low as 5 dBA for modern large diaphragm condenser mics. Small diaphragm mics tend to be a little noisier, at 12 to 18 dBA. Very small diaphragm mics are usually noisier still, with specs between 22 and 27 dBA. Self-noise in the upper 20s can definitely cause problems when recording quiet sources, or recording from large distances. If you know that you are going to record quiet sources, or do classical orchestral or choral recording, low self-noise figures are important, and mics with lower self-noise figures are definitely preferred. But for most rock, pop, and loud instrument recording, self-noise figures are less important than the actual sound of the mic. Using noisier mics as drum overheads for example, would present no problem – not a lot of gain is required due to the high SPL of the sound source, so the self-noise would be insignificant.

3.18 SIGNAL-TO-NOISE RATIO

Directly connected to self-noise, the *S/N ratio*, or *SNR* of a microphone is a measure of the amount of signal output, compared to the level of mic-induced noise present, when the mic is in a 94 dB SPL sound field. Higher numbers indicate better performance.

The following equations are useful to convert between self-noise and SNR, if you are trying to compare a mic that has only a self-noise spec with a mic that has only an SNR spec:

$$\text{SELF-NOISE} = 94 - \text{SNR}$$

$$\text{SNR} = 94 - \text{SELF-NOISE}$$

3.19 MAXIMUM SPL

If a mic is overloaded by being put in front of a sound source that is too loud, it will distort. *Maximum SPL* is a measure of the SPL that produces a slightly distorted output from the mic – usually quoted for 0.5 percent THD or 1 percent THD (total harmonic distortion). Although it is dangerous to listen to sounds above 100 dB SPL for any length of time, and a drummer may sit in a sound field of greater than 110 dB SPL when playing, the actual SPL a couple inches from a drum can be in excess of 130 dB SPL! So high SPL capable mics are definitely necessary!

Condenser mics often have *pads* (labeled "–10 dB," "–20 dB," etc.), which attenuate the mic's sensitivity so they can be exposed to louder sound sources and not overload their internal electronics or the pre-amp they are plugged into. Maximum SPL figures are quoted for all pads on the mic engaged.

Some pre-amps and mixing consoles have pad buttons, but with a mixer or pre-amp pad it is still possible to overload the microphone itself. If you are recording a very loud singer (or other sound source) with a condenser mic and are hearing distortion, but all your pre-amp, input and output levels look good – it's probably the mic distorting. Engaging the mic's pad should fix the situation – as long as the sound source is not in excess of the mic's maximum SPL level.

You should be very cautious when using ribbon mics in loud sound fields, or close to sound sources you don't think are too loud – an SPL louder than the recommended maximum can destroy the ribbon by stretching or tearing it.

3.20 DYNAMIC RANGE

A microphone's dynamic range is the span of sound pressure levels over which it will effectively pick up sound. It is the difference between sound being buried and masked by the mic's self-noise, or the diaphragm's inability to resolve low level sonic impulses, and the onset of distortion at the mic's maximum SPL. Greater dynamic range specs are usually desirable.

3.21 TRANSIENT RESPONSE

Transients are the first few peaks of the attack of a sound. They contain a lot of important data that our brain uses to identify the sound. Sounds typically described as having important transient details include percussion instruments (drums and pianos) and plucked string instruments (particularly acoustic guitars). To record these sounds with the most accuracy, transparency and "zing," a mic with good *transient response* is desirable. The diaphragm of the mic needs to be able to move fast and change direction easily to respond to positive and negative transient peaks, and the subtle nuances contained within them.

Dynamic mics, with their heavier, more sluggish diaphragms, cannot respond fast enough to accurately capture initial transients, so the attacks of sounds become compressed and subtly distorted. In terms of accuracy this is undesirable, but compressing the amplitude of the initial and loudest peaks of a sound means that pre-amp gain needs to be turned up more to achieve good signal levels – increasing the sound's average level. This results in a less transparent, but bigger, phatter, and more powerful sound that can be desirable for rock drums, electric guitars, and basses.

Manufacturers making condenser mics with ultra-small diaphragms usually do so because their design philosophy emphasizes the extended high frequency response *and* improved transient response that is only possible with ultra-small diaphragms. Many (regular) small diaphragm mics are respected for their transient response. There is no specification for transient response though. It's not as simple as "the smaller the diaphragm, the better the transient response" – the head-amp electronics in a mic also have an effect on transient response. Some manufacturers purposefully design and promote the "fast response" of their mic's electronics. If you are unable to audition a mic before purchasing it, the best way to judge its transient response is to read non-biased, reputable professional reviews.

Transient Response

Example 3.16: Acoustic guitar, recorded with a small diaphragm condenser mic known for its good transient response.

Example 3.17: The same acoustic guitar, recorded with a small diaphragm condenser mic with less good transient response.

3.22 POP FILTERS, WINDSCREENS, AND DEAD CATS

Pop filters are essential when recording the human voice (singing or speaking) from within a couple of feet, with the talent aiming at the microphone, as shown in **Figure 3.17**.

Figure 3.17 A correctly positioned pop filter, with a few inches of distance between the singer and the filter, and the filter and the microphone.

Plosives are created when a burst of air associated with B, D, G, K, P, and T sounds leaves the mouth. If this air current hits a mic's diaphragm, it can cause loud pops and distortions, and potentially damage the diaphragm. Studio condenser mics do not usually have protection from these stray air currents. A *pop filter* is an acoustically transparent material or perforated metal screen positioned between the talent and the mic. It diffuses the plosive's airflow, and prevents it from directly hitting the diaphragm. In order to work properly, a pop filter needs several inches distance between it and the talent, *and* it and the mic.

Most musical instruments do not propagate plosive air currents, so pop filters are unnecessary. If a studio vocal mic is positioned at least 6 inches above or below the singer's mouth, and at least a foot away, making sure the singer does not sing "into" it but "across the top" of it, the plosives are directed away from the diaphragm and a pop filter may not be necessary.

Commercial pop filters with gooseneck mounts can be purchased relatively inexpensively. Alternatively a pop filter can be made for minimum expense using pantyhose and a wire coat hanger.

WINDSCREENS

A *windscreen* is a foam cover that is put directly around a microphone's capsule, as shown in **Figure 3.18**. In addition to the boom of plosives, loud low frequency rumbles are produced when a wind current flows over or into a mic's diaphragm. Depending upon their severity, a windscreen will reduce or eliminate these artifacts. Windscreens should be used when a mic is unavoidably positioned in the air stream from an HVAC duct, or when using mics outdoors where wind is unavoidable.

Figure 3.18 A mic with and without a windscreen.

Windscreens do affect a mic's high frequency response, so should only be used when necessary in the studio. When recording singers in a recording studio, pop filters are preferred over windscreens, because they are more acoustically transparent.

WIND MUFFS/DEAD CATS

Wind muffs, or *dead cats*, are used in high wind conditions in the motion picture, television, and broadcasting industries. They are commonly seen on the end of mic booms and fishpoles. A highly directional condenser mic is mounted inside the muff, sometimes in its own foam windscreen within the muff. The muff is made of artificial fur, and designed to minimize wind noise but remain acoustically transparent.

In the music production industry, about the only time wind muffs are used is on exposed condenser mics at outdoor events in windy conditions – not in studio recording situations.

3.23 SHOCK MOUNTS

Vibrations traveling through the floor (a singer's foot movement, mechanical HVAC vibrations, trucks driving by, low frequency sound waves, etc.) can travel up microphone stands and into the mic where they manifest themselves as low frequency rumbles and booms. In a live recording or concert stage situation, a mic stand can get knocked or bumped, causing a loud boom. Shock mounts, as shown in **Figure 3.19**, are elastic suspension mounts that mechanically isolate the mic from the stand. Most vibrations traveling through the mic stand are absorbed by the elastic material, and do not reach the microphone. Shock mounts are generally specific to the microphone in use, and are essential for serious studio and location recording.

Figure 3.19 Mics in their shock mounts.

ABOUT MIC STANDS

- Always use a good, sturdy mic stand.
- Always loosen clutches and joints before trying to adjust the stand – you won't wear it out so quickly.
- Always set the legs up properly. Center columns of tripod stands should *not* be touching the floor – the rubber feet on the ends of the legs isolate the stand (and microphone) from vibrations in the floor.
- Mic stands should not touch other mic stands, and mic stands should not touch any part of any instrument. Any physical contact can cause vibrations, buzzes, and booms to get into the mics and your recording.
- Make sure all joints and clutches are tight – mechanical movement in the stand will be heard as clunks and bumps through the mic.
- Ensure the stand is not going to be knocked or bumped by anyone – even with the best shock mount, some mechanical energy will get to the mic and cause booms.

3.24 MIC PRE-AMPS

Selecting microphones and mic techniques to best match the characteristics of the sound sources and the desired mix is an art form. If that didn't present enough variables to worry about, different mic pre-amps also add different colorations to the sound. While the cheap pre-amps found on budget mixers have certainly improved in recent years, they still tend to sound harsh and unrefined compared to the higher quality circuits found on professional consoles and outboard preamps.

There are three common categories of pre-amp sound:

- In-your-face, and "aggressive" or "assertive." These characteristics can really bring a sound forward, and help it stand out in the mix.
- Warmer, fuller, and phatter. Common characteristics of tube-based circuits, these pre-amps make things sound bigger and smoother.
- Transparent. A pre-amp with this character is designed to impart little of its own flavor, and simply report the characteristics of the microphone and what it's picking up.

Of course, these are generalizations, and you should read product literature and unbiased reviews to help you select pre-amps to meet your needs. In a small home or project studio, a few high quality outboard pre-amps as front-end to a DAW recording system are a great investment, allowing you to bypass the lower quality pre-amps found in cheap mixers and audio interfaces.

SATURATE ME!

Some tube mic pre-amps offer adjustable amounts of *drive* or *saturation*. The more saturation dialed in, the more the tube is overloaded so that its behavior becomes increasingly non-linear – and its characteristic distortions are produced. Some solid-state pre-amps feature variable harmonic distortion cicuits. "More" of these types of coloration is not always "best" though, and it's important to keep the original sound in mind, and what sound will be most beneficial to the mix. *You can't undo overdone saturation artifacts.*

The traditional location for pre-amps (whether they are in a console or interface, or are external outboard units) is in the control room. The drawback of this is that very long runs of mic cable are usually needed. How long mic cables can be before the audio quality degrades depends not only on the quality of the cable, but also the circuits each end of the cable plugs into. 60 m (200 ft) snakes are common in live concert sound systems, but undesirable for critical recording. High frequencies can be attenuated by poor quality cable – and you may not always know what cable (or how much of it) you are plugging into if it's hidden behind a wall plate or snake box. For critical recording, the best advice is to keep the mic cable runs as short as possible.

If long cable runs are unavoidable there are two other options:

Remote control pre-amps put the amplifying electronics in the recording room, near the microphones – so the mic cables can be kept as short as possible. Balanced analog line level signals (which are less susceptible to interference and degradation than mic signals) then run the distance to the recording equipment. The pre-amp's gain, phantom power, polarity, and any other adjustable parameters it may have, are operated remotely from the control room, using a control box or computer software. The pre-amp and remote are usually connected together using some kind of inexpensive data cable.

Digital snake systems locate the pre-amp electronics *and* analog to digital converters in the recording room near the mics. The audio is transmitted to the control room as digital data, over copper wire data cables or optical fibers, and the cable runs can be well over 100 m (300 ft). The long data cable run (for the audio and control data) is *much* cheaper and lighter than a traditional copper wire snake would be – but the drawback is that all the pre-amps in the system are the same, and not as good as top quality outboard pre-amps. Not the preferred option for critical recording, most digital snake systems were developed for the live sound industry, and are proprietary systems designed to interface with manufacturer specific devices.

YOU'RE ONLY AS GOOD AS YOUR WEAKEST LINK!

There's no point in having top of the line monitor speakers if you have poor quality microphones or pre-amps! *Your recording chain is only as good as its weakest link.* Purchasing high quality *front-end* first (the input devices) allows you to upgrade your *back-end* (the mixing and playback system) at a later date, but still have great sounding material originally captured. Having poor quality mics or pre-amps means you are capturing potentially poor sound, which can't be turned into great sound later no matter how good your monitors are. In fact, great monitor speakers will just magnify the deficiencies of poor mics or any other devices in the recording chain.

Great mics and some great pre-amps connected to a good quality audio interface will enable you to capture better sound.

Mic Pre-amps

Example 3.18: A vocal recorded through a budget mixing console pre-amp.

Example 3.19: The same vocal and mic, recorded through a professional mixing console pre-amp, known for its warmth and fullness.

Example 3.20: The same vocal and mic recorded through a boutique outboard pre-amp, known for its punch and aggressive qualities.

3.25 WHAT MIC TO USE?

Generic characteristics of microphones and pre-amps can be anticipated – but that's as far as any science goes! Recording is an *art form* because of the myriad variables in the recording and mixing chain that allow the engineer to create the sound of the final product.

Good, unbiased product reviews are a great place to start when deciding what mics to use or purchase. Stay away from manufacturer publications, and catalogs with "reviews" that are really sales pitches published by manufacturers and retailers. The following summarized information should help you make initial mic choices:

USE DYNAMIC MICS WHEN:

- The sound source is very loud.
- The sound source contains no essential real high frequency content.
- Amplitude and transient compression characteristics are desired.
- A "smudging over" of details is not problematic.

Common recording studio applications include: kick drum, snare drum, tom toms, guitar, and bass amplifiers.

Stage and live sound applications include: other drum percussion instruments, horns, and vocals.

USE SMALL DIAPHRAGM CONDENSER MICS WHEN:

- Accuracy, details, and maximum resolution are desired.
- The sound source contains essential high frequency content.
- The sound source has important initial transients or sharp, percussive characteristics.
- The bigness and "hype" of a large diaphragm condenser mic is not desired.

Common recording studio applications include: drum overheads, hi-hat, other percussion (particularly transient or bright sizzly instruments), acoustic guitar and other plucked string instruments, horns and other wind instruments (when accuracy is preferred over hype and color), bowed string instruments, and pianos.

Stage and live sound applications are similar, but more care must be taken when using relatively fragile condenser mics on stage. Additionally, the mic's extra sensitivity and reach can increase feedback potential.

USE LARGE DIAPHRAGM CONDENSER MICS WHEN:

- A big, full, hyped sound is desired.
- A detailed recording with good high frequencies is desired.
- The slightly warmer and/or smoother sound of many large diaphragm mics will be beneficial to the sound source and mix.

Large diaphragm mics tend to be studio workhorses – they are the generic go-to mic for many uses.

Recording studio applications include almost anything where a big, bold, detailed representation is desired: vocals, horns and wind instruments, string instruments, acoustic guitars and other plucked string instruments, drum overheads, room mics, and pianos. They are becoming increasingly popular as guitar and bass speaker cabinet mics.

On stage and for live sound they need to be used with care. Their cost, size, and weight make them less popular, but with knowledge of how to keep feedback at bay they can be used on quieter stages – jazz or folk shows perhaps, for vocals, strings and acoustic guitars, horns and wind instruments, speaker cabinets, and pianos.

USE RIBBON MICS WHEN:

- Their smooth, less "sizzly" high frequency qualities are desired.
- Their good transient response is desired.
- Extreme rejection of sounds coming from the sides (and above or below) is desired (and if the ribbon mic is bidirectional, there is no spill coming from directly behind the mic).

Typical studio applications include: vocals (with a good pop filter), drum overheads and room mics, acoustic guitars, electric guitar cabinets, horns, strings and other orchestral instruments, and piano.

They are less commonly used on stage due to their fragility, but professional touring acts do sometimes use them.

USE TUBE MICS WHEN:

- A big, phat, warm sound is desired. Maybe the source sound is a little thin or harsh, and needs warming up?
- Warmth and thickness are more important than sizzle and fine detail in the very high frequencies.

Common studio uses include: vocals, horns, thin sounding guitar and bass cabinets, and other acoustic instruments that need some "sonic makeup."

DIRECTIONAL MICS ARE BENEFICIAL WHEN:

- Spill from sound sources behind the mic needs to be minimized – use a cardioid mic.
- Spill from sound sources to the sides and towards the rear of the mic (but not at 180°) needs to be reduced – use a hyper-cardioid mic.
- The least pick-up to the sides (and above and below) the mic are desired (but there is no spill coming from behind the mic) – use a bidirectional mic.
- Room reflections need to be de-emphasized, as is typical in potentially bad sounding, acoustically untreated (or incorrectly treated) small rooms – use cardioid or hyper-cardioid mics.
- Proximity effect is desirable to "beef up" a sound.

OMNIDIRECTIONAL MICS ARE BENEFICIAL WHEN:

- Their more open, transparent sound is desired.
- Their better, more linear low frequency response is desired.
- Close miking is necessary, and their lack of proximity effect mud is desirable.
- A good sounding room produces desirable reflections that will give a sound excitement and energy. In many typical homes, small room recording situations, omnidirectional mics are generally not used, because the room characteristics are unfortunately problematic.
- A less "point source," and more organic and blended image is desired – and can be achieved through effective use of the better sounding spill an omni mic picks up.

3.26 THERE'S MORE TO IT THAN SPECIFICATIONS!

A lot of this chapter has discussed specifications, and you *should* use mic spec sheets to help identify mics with characteristics beneficial and complementary to the sound sources and projects you're recording. But while specifications *are* an indicator of technical performance, they *are not* an indicator of perceived sonic performance or how a sound will work within the context of a mix. The *actual sound* of a microphone is much less easily quantifiable and is a combination of its technical specifications and many other characteristics that are impossible to quantify numerically.

A mic with stunning technical specs may just not work well on a given sound source – it might exaggerate characteristics in an unflattering way. A noisier, less sensitive mic may make a specific singer sound stunning, even though its technical specs are not as good! What is more important? Having a sound that works aesthetically, or having a more technically clean and less noisy signal to work with? Most engineers would sacrifice technical specs for the *right* sound! A slight technical sacrifice isn't going to stop a record becoming a hit!

PRACTICAL EXERCISES

Record identical sound sources (a voice or an instrument) using the following techniques. Record a minute or two of each to different tracks on your DAW. Adjust the pre-amp gain to achieve identical levels for each example.

1. A directional dynamic mic from a distance of at least 1 foot.

2. The same directional dynamic mic from a distance of just a couple of inches.

3. A small diaphragm directional condenser mic from a distance of at least 1 foot.

4. The same small diaphragm directional condenser mic from a distance of just a couple of inches (with a pop filter for vocals).

5. A large diaphragm directional condenser mic from a distance of at least 1 foot.

6. The same large diaphragm directional condenser mic from a distance of just a couple of inches (with a pop filter for vocals).

7. An omnidirectional mic from a distance of at least 1 foot.

8. The same omnidirectional mic from a distance of just a couple of inches (with a pop filter for vocals).

9. Using mics of different polar patterns move the sound source around the mic as you record.

10. Then try similar things with tube mics and ribbon mics if you have them.

Listen to each example. How do they sound different?

- How do the near and far positions sound different?
- How do the near and far positions of the omnidirectional mic compare to the directional mic?
- How does the timbre, level of detail, and intimacy of the sound compare between the dynamic, small diaphragm condenser, and large diaphragm condenser (and ribbon and tube mics if you have them)?
- How does the off-axis sound differ between a cardioid and omnidirectional mic? What happens to the sound as you move more off-axis on a cardioid mic?

EQ Basics

4.1   WHAT IS EQ?

Equalization, or *EQ*, is available on every mixing console and in every DAW. At some point during most recording and mixing projects, EQ will probably be necessary. This chapter is included in this book because EQ is such an intrinsic part of the recording process, used to complement the mic techniques discussed later.

EQ changes the relative frequency balance of a sound. It allows different frequency ranges to be boosted or attenuated by variable amounts. EQ traditionally works by manipulating the relative phase and timing of frequency bands, causing boosts or attenuations of those frequency ranges. Because the temporal (phase) integrity of the audio is changed, EQ should be considered a relatively destructive process – and its use avoided if there are other solutions.

Different analog EQs, using different circuitry, and different EQ plug-ins *sound different*. (Although some EQ plug-ins sound remarkably identical to each other because they use the same underlying algorithms.) There are certainly some cheap EQs available that sound bad because of the extra artifacts they color the sound with. Conversely, there are also (usually expensive) EQs available that impose very desirable side-effect characteristics on the sound!

4.2   LAST RESORT, AND CREATIVE MIX TOOL

Because the relative phase of a sound's frequency content is changed as part of most EQ processing, it is best to consider EQ a "last resort," and not a go-to tool. When recording or tracking, you, the engineer, should aim to capture the best, most desirable sound possible. "It sounds OK…. It's not quite right, but we'll EQ later," is *not* a professional way to approach recording. Positioning a suitable mic where it makes the instrument sound good *is* a professional way to approach recording!

Corrective EQ i*s not* a substitute for good sound sources, good mics, good mic technique, or a great sounding room to record in. The characteristics and frequency content of a recorded acoustic sound source can be changed significantly by using different microphones, different mic techniques, and even different sound sources, as a preferable natural acoustic alternative to EQ. If something doesn't sound right when it is being tracked, the problem should be identified and fixed, by changing one or more of those variables. Aside from minor tweaks, it is rarely possible to "fix it in the mix."

EQ *is* a creative tool that should be used to achieve clarity in a mix – assuming great sounding tracks were recorded in the first place. The stereo soundstage is the space-compressed environment between the loudspeakers, into which many sound sources are placed. Most loud or important sounds are panned on top of each other in the center, where they compete for physical and frequency space. While building up a recording layer by layer, it is impossible to anticipate what specific EQ or timbre each element will need in order to sound good *together* – this will only be evident when they are all at appropriate mix balances and pan positions.

CASE STUDY: FIX IT BEFORE YOU RECORD

A common problem that should be fixed before pushing the record button is a miked bass guitar (or any other sound source) that sounds too boomy and muffled, and lacks real pitch definition and clarity. Possible solutions include:

- Moving the mic further from the sound source to reduce proximity effect.
- Using a less muddy sounding mic.
- Dialing in an alternate sound on the bass amp.

CASE STUDY: EQ IT AS YOU MIX

If the bass sounded great in isolation while tracking, but is obscuring the kick drum in the mix, then EQ *should* be used while mixing, to make those sounds work together.

CASE STUDY: SOMETIMES YOU JUST HAVE TO...

Of course, not all recording situations are ideal. Sometimes, you have to deal with a bad snare drum for example, and no matter what mic and technique is used, it just doesn't sound as good as a snare drum should – but the recording has to happen. In this situation, if EQ helps, then yes, *use it* for corrective reasons. It's not an ideal situation, but "the show must go on!" But don't rush to this conclusion before exploring all other potential solutions though.

4.3   CAN YOU EQ SPILL?

When evaluating a sound, channel, or track for EQ treatment, make sure you are listening to the source sound itself, and are not distracted by any spill in the background. A tom tom mic will pick up lots of distant tinny sounding snare drum spill. This mid range spill should not be EQ'd out. The tom tom has desired frequency content in that same range and the tom tom will become dull, and lack definition and punch if the snare spill is EQ'd down. Just about the only kind of spill that can be reduced a little by using EQ is extreme low or high frequency spill in a frequency range that the actual desired sound source does not occupy – for example cymbal splash leaking into a bass mic, or bass guitar boom leaking into an acoustic guitar mic.

In large room recordings, polar patterns, mic placements, and sound barriers can be explored to minimize spill. If spill is unavoidable yet undesirable and unworkable, tools such as gating, or silence stripping in a DAW, may help.

ABOUT SPILL

Spill is not always the enemy, and for some musical and recording styles it should be embraced as an essential part of the sound and mix. A mix devoid of any spill sounds ultra-clean, and possibly too sterile for some projects. A mix which embraces good sounding spill can sound organic, wholesome, and united.

4.4   EQ FILTERS

An EQ circuit is known as a *filter*. Different filter types affect different frequency ranges in different ways. Several types of filters are commonly found on mixing consoles, outboard gear, and as plug-ins.

SHELVING FILTERS

A *low shelf filter*, as shown in **Figure 4.1**, allows frequencies *below* a specified *cut-off frequency* to be boosted or attenuated by up to ±15 to ±18 dB or more. The maximum amount of boost or attenuation depends upon the specific circuit or plug-in being used. The amount of boost or cut can be anywhere between maximum cut, through 0 dB (no change) to maximum boost.

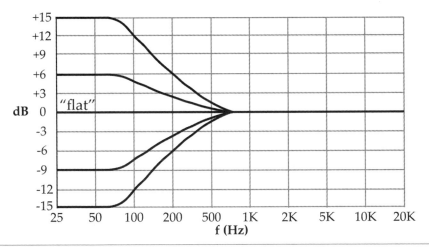

Figure 4.1   The straight line at "0 dB" on the y-axis represents "flat," or "no change" – the filter has no effect on the sound, and nothing is boosted or attenuated. The largest "uphill" plot as you read to the left, represents the maximum boost of +15 dB, below the cut-off frequency of 100 Hz in this example. The largest "downhill" plot as you read to the left, represents the maximum attenuation of –15 dB below the cut-off frequency. The other plots represent some possible intermediate settings of +6 dB and –9 dB – but remember it is possible to boost or cut by *any* amount between no change and the maximum boost/cut values.

CUT-OFF POINTS

The *cut-off frequency*, or *cut-off point* of a filter is the frequency at which it is 3 dB less than maximally effective. The filter in **Figure 4.1** is described as operating below the "−3 dB" cut-off point, which is 100 Hz.

SLOPES

It is impossible to build a filter that operates like a brick wall – doing nothing to frequencies above 100 Hz, but immediately being maximally effective below 100 Hz. That type of filter would be musically unusable anyway! All filters have a *slope* – a range of frequencies over which they become increasingly effective. Even though the filter in **Figure 4.1** is described as having a cut-off point of 100 Hz, its slope means that it *does* affect a broad range of frequencies well above 100 Hz.

A *high shelf filter*, as shown in **Figure 4.2**, allows frequencies *above* a specified cut-off point to be boosted or attenuated by anywhere between minimum and maximum values.

Shelving filters are often switchable between a couple of different cut-off frequencies, or they are *sweepable* – meaning that the cut-off frequency can be smoothly moved up and down over a range of frequencies. This allows a low shelf filter to boost or cut below a cut-off point of 60 Hz in order to focus on the weight and thump of a kick drum or bass guitar, or that same filter might be swept up to 250 Hz in order to attenuate low and low-mid frequency proximity effect build-up.

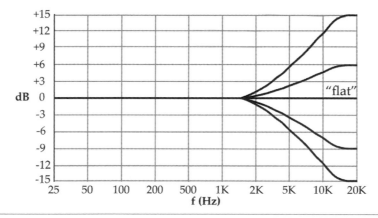

Figure 4.2 A high shelf filter. The maximum boost of +15 dB, above the cut-off point of 10 KHz is represented by the largest "uphill" plot as you read to the right. Note that the −3 dB point, the cut-off point, is at 10 KHz and the filter's slope affects frequencies well below this. The largest "downhill" plot as you read to the right, represents maximum attenuation. Any amount of boost or cut between these minimum and maximum values is possible.

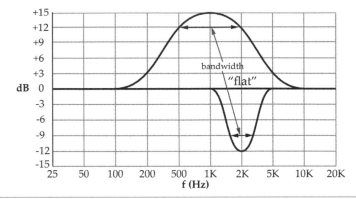

Figure 4.3   A sweepable and bandwidth adjustable peak/notch filter, showing two of an infinite number of possible settings – a wide +15 dB boost around 1 Khz, and a narrow -12 dB attenuation around 2 KHz.

If a shelving filter has a switchable or sweepable cut-off frequency, it will usually have two controls:

• A gain knob to dial in the amount of the boost or attenuation.
• The switch to select, or knob to sweep the cut-off frequency.

Low shelf filters are the default low frequency (LF) EQ circuit, and high shelf filters the default high frequency (HF) EQ circuit on most traditional equipment and EQ plug-ins.

PEAK/NOTCH FILTERS

As pictured in **Figure 4.3**, *peak/notch filters* allow a range of frequencies *around* a center frequency to be boosted or attenuated by any amount up to ±15 dB or ±18 dB or more, depending upon the equipment or plug-in. Mid frequency (MF) equalization filters are always peak/ notch filters.

Peak/notch filters may also be sweepable – which allows them to really focus on an issue. Additionally, they may have a *bandwidth* control, allowing them to affect a wider range of frequencies for broader, more "musical" tonal changes, or a very narrow range of frequencies for more surgical problem solving. The bandwidth controls on many hardware EQ sections often use icons to represent narrow and wide filter widths. Some plug-ins use *Q* or *Quality Factor* indications of bandwidth.

BANDWIDTH, OR "Q"

Q, or Quality Factor, is an indication of a peak/notch filter's musical bandwidth. It is calculated using the following equation:

$$Q = center\ frequency\ /\ bandwidth$$

Just about all EQ filters are *constant Q* filters, meaning that they affect a similar musical bandwidth (or number of musical octaves) as the filter is swept up and down. A bandwidth of 100 Hz in the low frequencies represents a wide bandwidth – over an octave if it is centered around 100 Hz, giving it a Q factor of 1. Frequency is a non-linear, exponential scale, and higher octaves are made up of a much larger numerical frequency range, so to retain a Q factor of 1 when centered around 1 KHz, the same filter must have a bandwidth of 1000 Hz.

- Higher Q factor numbers mean that the filter is narrower, and affects a smaller frequency range.
- Lower Q factor numbers mean that the filter is wider, affecting a broader frequency range.

If the bandwidth of the filter above stayed at a constant 100 Hz, it would have a Q factor of 10 if it was centered around 1000 Hz. This would be a *constant bandwidth* filter – but they are musically useless, so not found on audio equipment.

LOW CUT FILTERS

Also known as *high pass filters* or *HPFs*, *low cut filters* are sometimes found as part of an EQ section or plug-in, or as part of the pre-amp section of a hardware device. In the recording studio they are more of a technical problem solving filter and less of an artistic or musical filter than shelving or peak/notch filters. As shown in **Figure 4.4**, low cut filters *roll off*, or progressively attenuate frequencies below the cut-off frequency, by a fixed amount.

Many HPFs only have an *in/out* button to turn them on and off. Some are sweepable, with an additional frequency control. Some, particularly plug-ins, offer adjustable slopes.

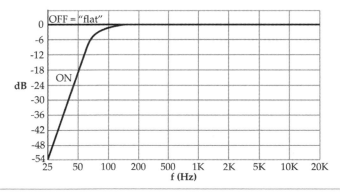

Figure 4.4   This low cut filter severely attenuates below a cut-off point of about 80 Hz when engaged. No boost is possible. The filter is either "in" or "out" of circuit – either fully effective, or "off."

> **MORE ON SLOPES...**
>
> - A 6 dB/octave HPF with a cut-off point of 100 Hz will attenuate 50 Hz by −6 dB and 25 Hz by −12 dB.
> - An 18 dB/octave HPF also set at 100 Hz will attenuate 50 Hz by −18 dB, and 25 Hz by −36 dB, making the very low frequency content much less audible.

HPFs can be used to remove the rumbles and booms caused by mechanical or HVAC sources, or some proximity effect build-up – although proximity effect usually extends up into higher low mid frequencies which HPFs do not affect.

4.5   ANALOG VS DIGITAL EQ

A couple of frequent observations made by engineers transitioning from analog EQ to digital EQ, are that:

- Many digital EQs require more significant boosts or cuts than they're used to making, in order to hear a difference.
- "Character" is missing from many digital EQs.

Many popular analog EQs have sonic characteristics that set them apart from other more "transparent" EQs which just "do the job" without imposing much of their own signature on the sound. Regardless of which design philosophy is used, a good analog EQ really has an obvious effect on the sound when a very small boost or cut is dialed in. In order to perceive a similarly obvious change on many digital EQs and plug-ins, a significantly greater amplitude change often has to be dialed in.

This doesn't mean that all digital EQs are bad! Character arguments aside, it just means that you should be prepared to make more significant changes when using some digital EQs. Analog devices are a function of their circuitry, while digital EQs are a series of mathematical equations meant to exhibit similar changes. There are many plug-in recreations of classic vintage analog EQs and the reviews of these products are generally favorable – however it is an accepted fact that while the plug-in versions of analog devices come close, they *do not* sound the same as the original analog devices. Digital EQs though, can offer a level of precision, control, and linear behavior that analog devices cannot.

DAW USERS AND EQ

Even though most digital EQs and plug-ins don't sound the same as the best analog circuits, it is definitely worth upgrading from the stock EQ plug-ins found in many DAWs, and investing in some with specific characters beneficial to the musical style and projects you're working on.

If you are a DAW or digital console user using good analog EQ for the first time, don't be surprised by the smaller EQ gain changes needed!

In books and magazines, a lot of interviews with engineers and producers cite EQ changes in the ±3 to ±5 dB range. Many of those figures are referring to changes made by users of analog EQ. In terms of impact, ±3 to ±5 dB on a classic analog EQ needs something like ± 6 to 8 dB on a stock DAW EQ – so don't be afraid to use a little more than you might read about.

Ever noticed that there seem to be more knobs, buttons, and greater control ranges in plug-ins compared to analog devices? Most hardware devices offer less flexibility because more control or increased control ranges cost more money. So a hardware unit is more focused on what you actually need 99 percent of the time! It costs nothing to add more controls or control ranges to plug-ins, but this can make the best sounding ranges and settings harder to find.

4.6 ADDITIVE VS SUBTRACTIVE EQ

It is preferable to use EQ subtractively wherever possible. This means turning down frequency ranges that contain, or are causing problems, and *not* turning up frequency ranges around the actual problem area.

PROBLEM: A vocal recorded with the singer close to the mic is going to exhibit proximity effect build-up in the lows and low-mids.

POOR SOLUTION: As shown in **Figure 4.5**, turning up the high-mid EQ to increase "cut," "presence," "intelligibility," and "bite." In addition to turning up potentially desired characteristics, this additive EQ also turns up whatever noise and spill there is in that frequency range.

BETTER SOLUTION: The problem is *not* that there aren't enough high-mids, but that there is an overabundance of low-mid frequencies causing congestion that obscures the high-mid details. Scooping out the lows and low-mids, as shown in **Figure 4.6,** targets the problem directly. Using this approach, noise, spill, gremlins, and undesirable EQ artifacts have not been unnecessarily boosted – so the sound, and mix, will remain cleaner and clearer.

BEST SOLUTION (FOR NEXT TIME): Position the mic more appropriately, and/or use a different mic, to capture a less muddy and boomy sound in the first place!

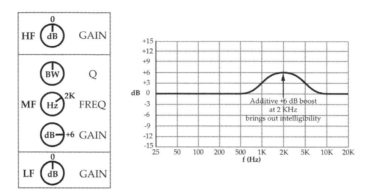

Figure 4.5 Additive EQ to boost the "cut," "presence," "intelligibility," and "bite" of a vocal which has too much proximity effect clouding up the lower frequencies is not the best solution to a muddy vocal problem.

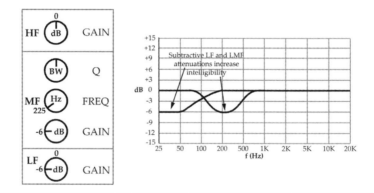

Figure 4.6 Subtractive EQ targets the problem directly, and attenuates the proximity effect boost of the lows and low-mids without boosting noise or spill, or leaving that excess frequency content present to cloud up a mix.

IDENTIFYING A PROBLEM FREQUENCY RANGE

An effective way to identify a potentially problematic frequency range is to:

- Create a large boost in an EQ filter – at least +10 dB.
- Sweep the frequency control around until the nastiness *really* jumps out.
- Return the gain control to "0" for a time, to re-familiarize yourself with the original sound.
- Reduce the gain of the problem frequency to correct the problem.

4.7 THE FEWER FILTERS THE BETTER

Because EQ can negatively impact the technical integrity of the sound, use as few EQ filters as possible. It is usually easier for novice engineers to hear the effects of an EQ boost than it is to hear an attenuation, and a common mistake is to turn up many frequency bands instead of attenuating just one or two. Some of the reasons for this common error are:

- Our ears have a very poor memory – it is difficult to *really* remember how something sounded 30 seconds ago. After making some EQ adjustments it's easy to forget the specific problem that needed fixing.
- Our ears are easily fooled into thinking that something sounds "better" simply because it sounds different.
- Making something louder fools our ears into thinking it sounds "better." Boosting some frequency content certainly makes the sound louder, but "louder" does not always mean "better"!
- Turning a certain frequency range up might make the sound more instantly appealing, and then turning up another frequency range might add another instantly appealing characteristic. But this approach has little to do with locating and fixing the actual problem!

The effect of an EQ curve created by boosting multiple filters, similar to the top diagram in **Figure 4.7**, can be better created by attenuating the only non-boosted frequency range instead, as shown in the bottom diagram. The attenuation approach is preferable because:

- It targets the specific problem frequency band.
- It uses fewer filters, adding less potential technical degradation to the sound.
- It is subtractive, meaning less undesired signal is amplified.

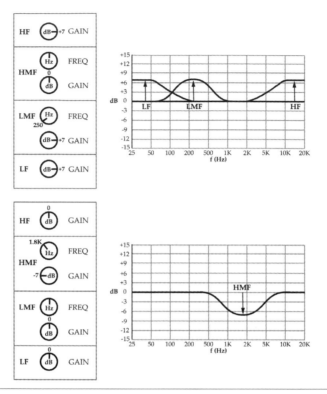

Figure 4.7   The "see-saw" effect of EQ means that similar results are better achieved by attenuating the only non-boosted frequency band in the top diagram, as shown in the bottom diagram.

ADDITIVE EQ

While subtractive EQ is generally preferred, there are certainly times when additive EQ is necessary – after all, there's a reason the gain knobs boost as well as attenuate! Sometimes a sound does need an extra boost in a certain frequency range to make it pop. If a vocal track needs a little extra "air" in the top end, it's best to do it with only one filter – a couple of dB boost above 10 KHz on the high shelf filter. Using one filter additively is simpler and cleaner than turning down the LF, LMF, and HMF to achieve a similar result subtractively.

Some plug-ins have many more filters than the usual three or four found on a hardware mixer EQ section – so it's very easy to end up with multiple adjacent frequency bands turned similarly up or down. If two or three adjacent bands overlap, and are boosted or cut similarly, it would be simpler and more logical to use only the middle of those filters and to widen its bandwidth.

4.8   HOW MUCH TO EQ?

Do whatever the sound and mix need. But – if you're working with great sounding source tracks, it's a good idea to question situations where changes greater than 6 dB are made when using analog EQ, or about 8 dB when using digital EQ. Sometimes large changes are necessary, but use 6 to 8 dB as a red flag to remind yourself to double-check that such a large change is really necessary.

4.9   WHEN TO EQ?

Minor tweaks to fit a sound into the mix are best done as part of the mixing process. It is bad to EQ the sound as it is recorded, and then have to try to undo and create slightly different EQ during mixing.

If after trying all the other methods preferred over EQ (discussed throughout this book) some minor EQ is still necessary in order to capture a great sound, it can be better to EQ it as it goes into the recording system, rather than during mixing. This is particularly true when the problem is an overabundance of a particular frequency range, commonly low frequencies, that can take up headroom, resulting in lower average signal levels and gain structure issues when lots of corrective EQ is applied during the mix.

4.10 GOLDEN RULES OF EQ

- EQ is a last resort, and not a go-to process in lieu of other solutions. *Don't be lazy while tracking!*
- EQ subtractively whenever possible.
- Use as few filters as possible.
- EQ additively if it means using fewer filters that way.
- Do not EQ to remove spill – it will probably negatively affect the desired sound source.
- Double-check that any EQ changes of more than 6 dB are really appropriate and necessary.
- Never use EQ to make something louder. A common novice error is turning up the low and high shelf filters to produce a "smile curve" if a sound seems too quiet. If EQ seems to make something "louder," it was probably too quiet in the first place – use the fader to correct balance issues before using EQ to fit the sound in the mix.

PRACTICAL EXERCISE

Record some vocals with a directional mic at different distances (ranging from a few inches away to a couple of feet away). Record each to a different DAW track. Remove proximity effect from the closer recordings using subtractive EQ. Listen to the EQ'd closer tracks and the un-EQ'd more distant tracks, and compare the following:

- The timbral and tonal frequency content differences.
- The reflected room sound/ambience differences.
- The differences in proximity, and sense of distance perceived.

CHAPTER 5

Stereo Imaging

IN THIS CHAPTER:

5.1   THE STEREO SOUNDSTAGE

A stereo loudspeaker system allows sounds to be positioned in the *soundstage* pictured in **Figure 5.1**. A good, clear, interesting music mix usually uses much of this space between, and around the loudspeakers. This chapter will familiarize you with the stereo soundstage and different imaging concepts so that you can more effectively exploit the space in your recordings, and use mics and mic techniques to record the sound the mix needs, rather than trying to "force" inappropriately recorded sounds into a mix using electronic processing.

Remember that this soundstage is specific to stereo *loudspeaker* systems – and *not* headphones, as discussed in **Chapter 2**.

5.2   PHANTOM AND DISCRETE IMAGES

The pan control on a mixer or in a DAW is used to steer and position sound between the left and right loudspeakers. Modern panners are continuously variable from the left, through the central space between the speakers, and to the right.

The perceived location of any single mono channel, panned anywhere except hard left or hard right, is an illusion known as a *phantom image* – there is no physical loudspeaker where the sound appears to be located. Phantom center images have a unique character because of the comb filtering and frequency cancellation (above 5 KHz) produced when each speaker's direct sound combines with the inter-aural crosstalk from the "opposite" loudspeaker at each ear. This is not something you have to consciously think about though while recording and mixing – but it does make creating a mix based on phantom center images very challenging!

Discrete, single loudspeaker images are produced when a sound is hard panned exclusively to the left or right loudspeaker. The ear closest to the loudspeaker reproducing the sound receives direct sound, and the other ear receives only inter-aural crosstalk – neither

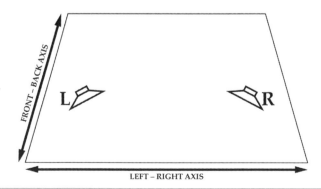

Figure 5.1   A 2-D representation of the effective stereo loudspeaker soundstage. Sounds can be positioned within this space.

ear receives both direct *and* time-delayed inter-aural crosstalk as is the case with a non-hard panned phantom image. Discrete single loudspeaker images have very different sonic characteristics to phantom images due to the lack of these frequency cancellation effects. They are:

• Clearer.
• More focused.
• More precise.
• Tighter.
• Timbrally more assertive.
• Arguably "smaller."

Phantom images are:

• Slightly "larger."
• Less focused.
• Arguably a little weaker sounding.

5.3 IMAGE WIDTH

MONO POINT SOURCES

A single (mono) microphone or channel produces a narrow, focused, *point source* image, which although panned somewhere in the soundstage, has no width or spread. Mono point-source images can be panned by any amount to the left or right:

• Centered.
• A little off center.
• Almost to one side or the other.
• All the way to one side or the other.

Panning many mono point sources throughout the left/right soundstage produces an interesting and wide stereo image, with many discrete details and distinct points of sound spaced throughout it.

SPREAD IMAGES

Spread images are produced by stereo mic arrays (discussed later in this book), by synthesizers and keyboards with a stereo output, and by stereo reverb and effects units. Spread images have *width* – they take up left/right space. A spread image is a single unified stereo source, panned to take up space – sound comes from throughout its width. A spread image can be:

• Narrow – only a little wider than a point source mono image.
• Wide – taking up nearly, or all of the space between the loudspeakers.
• Symmetrically panned – the pan controls are equal but opposite from the center position.

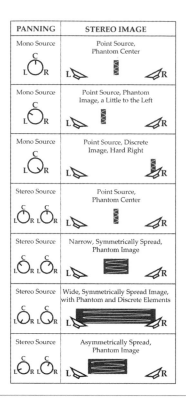

Figure 5.2 Pan positions and the images they create.

- Asymmetrically panned. For example, a stereo synth sound panned so it takes up the left side of the soundstage, or a stereo organ sound panned so it takes up the right side of the soundstage, or a stereo synth sound panned 60 percent L and 20 percent R, or a stereo organ sound panned 30 percent L and 70 percent R.

Figure 5.2 shows some possible stereo imaging concepts and the pan positions that achieve them.

Stereo Image Width and Panning Concepts   @

*Examples 5.1 through 5.7 correspond to **Figure 5.2**.*

Example 5.1: A mono point source, panned centrally.

Example 5.2: A mono point source, panned slightly left.

Example 5.3: A mono point source, panned hard right.

> ### *Stereo Image Width and Panning Concepts (continued)*
>
> **Example 5.4**: A stereo source, both channels panned centrally, produces a mono phantom center.
>
> **Example 5.5**: A narrow spread image, panned symmetrically.
>
> **Example 5.6**: A wide spread image panned symmetrically.
>
> **Example 5.7**: An asymmetrically panned spread image.
>
> **Example 5.8**: An image that is too wide. Sounds can be clearly identified and located in the left and right extremes of the image, but a blurry "hole" is created in the middle where it's difficult to precisely identify and localize sounds.
>
> Listen to these examples on both loudspeakers and headphones to hear how the sense of space sounds different on both reproduction formats.

5.4 BEYOND THE LOUDSPEAKERS

As shown in **Figure 5.1**, it is also possible to create the illusion that sound is coming from just beyond the physical spacing of the loudspeakers. This can be achieved using a variety of methods of varying predictability:

- Context. A widely panned stereo source may appear to be super-wide depending upon what else is going on at the same time, and what other imaging concepts it is being contrasted with.
- Out of phase content. A wide stereo sound source that has a significant amount of de-correlated information in each channel can appear to extend beyond the physical position of the loudspeakers. Big room/hall reverbs are a good example of this. Reverb, generated electronically by a reverb processor or plug-in, or captured acoustically with microphones at the time of recording represents width and space. It exists to be perceived as width and space, and is made up of random reflections, delayed and filtered so that some of the left channel information is out of phase with the right channel. When listened to on stereo loudspeakers, the out of phase content can push the image slightly beyond the loudspeakers.

5.5 DEPTH CONCEPTS

In addition to the left/right axis, the stereo format allows us to create the illusion of a front/back perspective. Sounds can appear to be positioned from slightly in front of the loudspeaker plane, to well behind the loudspeakers – as shown in **Figure 5.1**. Different techniques and concepts can create the illusion of depth in a mix:

- High frequency attenuation: As sound sources get further away from the listener, the air the sound is traveling through naturally absorbs some high frequency content. So one way to create the illusion that a sound is positioned behind the loudspeakers, further away from the listener, is to gently roll off some high frequencies. Conversely, the brighter and crispier a sound is, the more "up front" and "in-your-face" it usually appears.
- Reverb: In a natural acoustic environment (a room, concert hall, etc.) we hear a sound source close to us as mainly direct, *dry* sound – there is much more dry sound than reflected, *wet*, reverberant content. A far away sound source is experienced as predominantly wet, reverberant content – and very little dry, direct sound. The addition of reverb can create the illusion that a sound is pushed behind the loudspeakers. The effect can be magnified by adding a little high frequency attenuation to the source sound (and manipulating the pre-delay of the reverb).
- Amplitude balance: A contextually quieter sound can also be interpreted as being further away. But, it is also possible to have a very quiet sound appear to be forwards in the mix due to its frequency content and (lack of) associated reverb.
- Sound can appear to be forward of the loudspeakers because it is bright and relatively dry. Or, a reverb with a longer pre-delay can be used so the reverb is more detached from the dry sound. The "up-front-and-in-your-face" factor can also be increased with good volume automation and compression, to make the sound more consistent.

Context is also a powerful contributor to front/back imaging:

- If a mix contains sounds which have good frequency balances, and contrasting reverbs (with fairly similar reverb times) and wet/dry balances are applied to different tracks, the contextual illusion of front/back depth will be much more effective. Be careful though – large differences in reverb time can create interesting effects and sound stylizations in a mix, but too much variety can also destroy the concept that the band were playing together, and turn the mix into a collection of distinct instruments playing the same song, but not together.
- If similar and abundant reverb is added to most of the elements in a mix, reverb becomes a less effective way of pushing sounds back.
- If the entire mix is timbrally dark and mellow, high frequency attenuation will be less effective at pushing sounds back.

In a multi-track production, these characteristics can be adjusted electronically during mixing. The focus of this book though, is that they can also be adjusted acoustically while recording – through the use of creative mic techniques. The result is very different, and much more organic and natural, than using electronic processes or effects during mixing.

> ## Depth Concepts
>
> **Example 5.9**: A bright, dry sound appears forwards in the soundstage.
>
> **Example 5.10**: Gentle high frequency attenuation, and the addition of reverb, pushes the same source sound back behind the loudspeakers.
>
> **Example 5.11**: The same instrument, recorded with a more distant mic technique naturally moves the sound to the rear of the soundstage.

5.6   THE ILLUSION OF HEIGHT

It is also possible to create the illusion of height in a stereo mix. The perception of height is the hardest dimension to control and predict. As a huge generalization, it might be said that brighter, swishy, more sizzly high frequency sounds can "float" above the bulk of the mix – but it's all a matter of context.

5.7   STATIC AND DYNAMIC PANNING

A stereo mix with most elements panned center has two drawbacks:

- A probable lack of clarity due to too many sound sources with overlapping frequency content competing for the same physical space.
- It is boring and uninteresting to listen to! The stereo soundstage exists to be used – it makes the sonic experience more expansive and keeps listeners returning for another listen to see what else they can notice.

Static panning occurs when the pan controls are adjusted and remain unchanged throughout the mix – each sound source stays in the same place for the entire song. Some sound sources should be panned away from the center to improve clarity and interest. In a hypothetical mix, the lead vocal might be panned center, the electric guitar panned to the left, and the acoustic guitar to the right, and they stay in those locations for the entire song.

Dynamic, or *animated panning* involves moving and changing a sound's position, actively, as it is sounding:

- *Fly-bys*: Sounds heard transitioning through the stereo image can be very effective. Used too much, or inappropriately, moving pans *can* be distracting, but a moving fly-by of a swishy sound or a percussion effect, in to the measure before the chorus can create a spectacular lead in to the next section of the song!

- *Auto-panning*: An auto-panner is a device or plug-in that automatically moves a sound between a left and right location at a speed and movement style set by the engineer. It is easy to over-use, but continuous auto-panning has been used very effectively on solos and sound effects on countless rock and pop records.
- *Ping-pong panning*: A musical "question" phrase panned centrally, followed by a musical "answer" that alternates between being panned left and right; or two parts that fairly rapidly alternate left/right. There is no smooth movement from one pan position to the other, just a repeating bounce, or *ping-pong* between them. If a recording has musical material conducive to this effect it can really expand the width of a mix and be interesting ear candy to draw listeners further into the mix.

Prior to mixing consoles with automation, engineers had to physically move the pan controls at the correct time, live, during mixdown – usually requiring a few engineers for big mixes, a lot of practice, and a few mistakes before getting it right! With automation and DAW systems, panning movement has become easy – draw it in or record the automation, edit it once and the system will recreate that movement perfectly each and every time.

Panning Concepts

Example 5.12: A mix with static panning only.

Example 5.13: A mix in which some elements move around dynamically.

Example 5.14: A mix featuring elements of antiphonal, side-to-side, question/answer panning.

5.8   IMAGE SYMMETRY

Stereo image symmetry and physical balance are desirable in a mix. If there are too many elements or too much amplitude on one side of the stereo soundstage, the image becomes lopsided and unbalanced. The following principles can help achieve a good, balanced stereo image:

- Divide sound sources of similar role and function equally between the two sides of the stereo soundstage:
  - If a guitar part is panned to the left, it is usually best to balance it with something similar on the right – otherwise the image will be left heavy. Another guitar part, or perhaps a piano part, can be panned to the right to create this symmetry.
  - Percussion sounds are great to pan around – they very effectively create width and stereo interest. A shaker, used quietly and panned left, balanced with a triangle or clave, also used quietly but panned right, will instantly open up and widen a mix.

- Stereo image balance does not have to be created by an identical instrument, but the musical functions of the two should be similar – a big distorted guitar on the left would *not* be appropriately balanced with a backing vocal on the right!
- Balance amplitudes between both sides of the stereo image. You do not want the mix to end up with hotter levels on one side, due to asymmetrical panning or too many instruments of similar function panned to the same side.
- Both simultaneous symmetry (sounds happening at the same time) and antiphonal symmetry (subsequent sound events alternating sides) can be very effective, as long as the side-to-side alternation is not so slow that each event is perceived as asymmetrical static panning.

A common issue with music that builds up in layers as the verses and choruses progress, as a lot of pop music does, is that the reduced instrumentation of the first verse lacks enough layers of activity to create a balanced image. Subtle double tracking of rhythm parts (see **Chapter 13**), and layering slightly different and opposingly panned keyboard sounds are some strategies to avoid this. More obvious double trackings and sound layering can be saved for later sections of the song.

Image Symmetry

Example 5.15: A symmetrically balanced mix.

Example 5.16: An unbalanced, asymmetrical mix.

5.9   USE ALL OF THE SOUNDSTAGE!

The biggest, most interesting and expansive mixes use all of the available soundstage – there is sound located:

- Front and center.
- Behind the speakers.
- Extreme left and right.
- Between the phantom center and left and right speakers.

A mix that contains only center panned channels, plus additional mono channels panned hard left and hard right, will appear to have holes in the image between the center and extreme left and right.

Great mixes also exploit a variety of imaging concepts simultaneously. For example:

- Narrow, point-source images can be surrounded by wide symmetrically panned spread images.
- Narrow, point-source images can be framed by different narrowly panned spread images on each side.

There is no single "correct" mix. Wide, expansive, pointillistic mixes can be created by panning many narrow point sources throughout the soundstage. Less precise, but equally, if not more, expansive and immersive mixes can be created by panning multiple stereo sources differently throughout the soundstage. The stereo soundstages of two contrasting mixes are plotted in **Figure 5.3** and **Figure 5.4**.

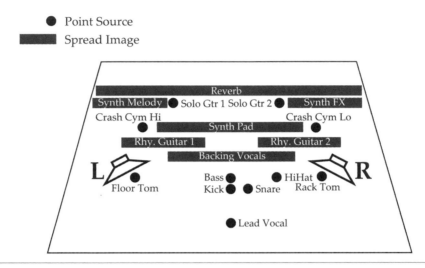

Figure 5.3   A bigger, more expansive mix that utilizes the entire soundstage and multiple imaging concepts.

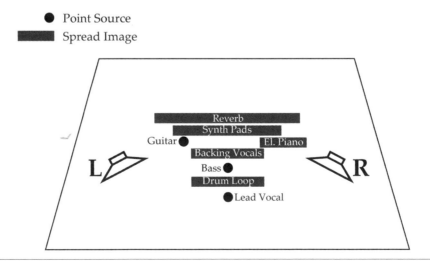

Figure 5.4   A mix that uses the soundstage more conservatively.

5.10 HOW TO LISTEN

In order to properly perceive the sound of a stereo loudspeaker system it is essential to sit in the *sweet-spot* – located by creating an equilateral triangle between the loudspeakers and the listening position, as shown in **Figure 5.5**.

If you sit too far forwards, the stereo image will appear too wide and have a tendency to portray a hole in the center of some sounds. You will compensate for this by not panning aggressively enough and the result will be a mix that is too narrow.

If you sit too far away from the loudspeakers the stereo image will appear too narrow to you. You will compensate and create a mix that is too wide with too much extreme panning.

If you sit off-center, the *law of first wavefront* dictates that the image will steer towards the loudspeaker closest to you and appear asymmetrically balanced and too heavy on that closest loudspeaker. Your mix will be too heavy in the opposite loudspeaker when listened to correctly.

It is also important to have symmetrical room geometry on each side of the monitor speakers – the angle of the walls and the materials used. Asymmetry in control rooms can contribute to imaging problems.

Remember that headphones and earbuds are not technically stereo, despite what their packaging says, and they present a much more one-dimensional image in a plane between the drivers on each of the listener's ears. So, as discussed previously, headphones and earbuds are not recommended for stereo mixing.

5.11 REALITY VS RECORDING

A recording is not a reflection of reality. Surround sound environments greater than 5.1 can come close to recreating reality, but stereo just can't. A recording is always a fold-down or reduction of something happening in a much larger space. Collapsing many microphones, channels, tracks, or sound sources into a two-channel reproduction system creates the challenge of making the mix clear and intelligible. Fully exploiting the stereo soundstage will help the

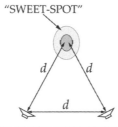

Figure 5.5 The correct listening position, sitting in the "sweet-spot." All d distances should be identical.

clarity and intelligibility of each component sound source by positioning them in their own unique physical space. The more that panning and the soundstage are explored and used in a mix, the easier it becomes to achieve clarity in the mix.

Exploitative use of the soundstage may not be natural or faithful to an artist's set-up when performing, however that is less important than making a product that works well as a recording.

PRACTICAL EXERCISE

1. Sitting in the sweet-spot between a good pair of stereo monitors, analyze some commercial mixes and make soundstage diagrams similar to those in this chapter.

2. Identify different imaging techniques used in those mixes, and note:

   a. What makes the mix clear and gives it good clarity?

   b. What makes the mix interesting and immersive to listen to?

3. Listen to the same mixes on good headphones and see if you get the same sense of space and imaging.

4. Use these observations and techniques in your own mixes!

C H A P T E R   6

Stereo Microphone Arrays

6.1   MICROPHONE ARRAYS

A microphone *array* is a collection of microphones that function together as a unit in order to capture the physical width of a sound source, and portray it as having width between the loudspeakers or headphones. *Minimalist* mic techniques can use as few mics as there are loudspeaker channels in the recording or dissemination format – so two mics are the minimum required for a stereo mic array. More mics can be used, but there are several standard techniques that should be understood and mastered before embellishing them and adding extra mics.

Matched microphones are strongly recommended for stereo techniques. There can be slight sonic differences between mics of the same make, model, and vintage – due to tolerances and differences between the components each mic is made from. *Matched pairs* undergo additional testing by the manufacturer in order to pair together mics of as similar performance as possible. This usually costs a little more than buying two individual mics, but you're paying for this testing and the better, more accurate stereo images that will result!

HOW OUR EARS PERCEIVE DIRECTION

Our ears use three methods to determine the perceived location (the *localization* or *directionality*) of a sound source:

- Amplitude differences between the ears: A sound is perceived slightly louder in the ear that it is closest to. This is a more significant indicator of the directionality of frequency content above about 800 Hz.
- Time arrival differences between the ears: The ear that the sound source is closest to hears the sound slightly before the opposite ear, which is slightly further away. Our brains calculate directionality from the sub-millisecond time difference between the wavefront's arrival at each ear. This is a more significant indicator of the directionality of frequency content below about 800 Hz.
- Our anatomy EQ's the sound as it travels around different parts of the face and head to get to each ear.

Put together, these three phenomena create *head related transfer function (HRTF)* effects.

6.2   XY COINCIDENT PAIR TECHNIQUES

A *coincident pair*, or *XY array*, uses two cardioid or hyper-cardioid microphones positioned so their capsules are as close together as possible. The mics are arrayed between 90° to 130°, with their pickup patterns crossing in front of the array, as shown in **Figure 6.1**. The array as a whole is aimed at the center of the sound source, putting each mic 45° to 65° off-axis from

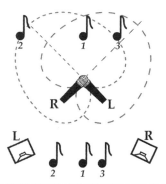

Figure 6.1 An XY coincident pair of microphones. Sound sources are shown at various positions in the array's pick-up and their perceived playback locations are shown between the loudspeakers.

pointing directly forwards. The mics must not touch, acoustically shade, or interfere with each other. If they touch, mechanical vibrations and buzzes can result. If a microphone is physically "in the way" (in line of sight to the sound source) of the other mic, frequency response and phase inaccuracies can result.

How does this technique work?

Sound source "1" in the figure comes from the center of the sound source and is equally off-axis and equidistant to both microphones. This means that both mics pick up identical sound at the same time. When the mics are panned hard left and hard right on a stereo loudspeaker system, both loudspeakers reproduce the same sound at the same time. Identical direct sound and inter-aural crosstalk arrive at each of the listener's ears creating a phantom center image directly in-between the loudspeakers (assuming the listener is sitting in the sweet-spot).

Sound source "2," located far to the left of the array's pick-up is also equidistant to both mic capsules – so both mics pick up the sound at the same time, and on playback both loudspeakers reproduce the sound at the same time. However, compared to sound "1," this sound source is more on-axis to the left mic, and beyond 90° off-axis to the right mic. The left mic picks up a greater amplitude of sound with better frequency balance than the right mic, so the sound is reproduced louder and more clearly in the left loudspeaker than the right loudspeaker. This localizes the sound to the left when we listen from the sweet-spot.

Sound source "3," located "somewhat" to the right of the array's pick-up area, is again equidistant to both mic capsules – so whatever sound is picked up by each mic will be reproduced at the same time by both loudspeakers. This sound source is on-axis to the right mic, and less than 90° off-axis to the left mic. A slightly greater amplitude and slightly better frequency balance is picked up by the right mic than the left mic, so the sound is reproduced slightly louder and a little more clearly in the right loudspeaker. This localizes the sound somewhat to the right when we listen from the sweet-spot.

The reproduced locations of the sounds are not as widely spaced as the original sound source.

Time arrival differences are powerful indicators of directionality, but because the microphone capsules of an XY coincident pair are as close together as possible, this technique produces no time arrival differences for sounds coming from *any* location. XY techniques only resolve and recreate directional information as amplitude differences between the two mics and loudspeakers. A mic's off-axis response alone does not come close to replicating complex HRTF effects – so directional information and image localization is arguably compromised using XY techniques.

General characteristics of XY coincident techniques include:

- Narrow, compact images due to the lack of time arrival cues, and a lot of overlap of each mic's pick-up due to their positioning so close to each other.
- Potential for muddy sound due to the significant amount of each mic's colored off-axis pick-up – no mic is actually pointed on-axis towards the center of the sound source. Cheaper directional mics, with their inferior off-axis coloration exaggerate this problem. The increased price of more expensive directional mics is justified by the benefits of their improved off-axis frequency response in this context.
- Good mono compatibility! With no time arrival differences between the capsules there is no phase cancellation or comb filtering when they are summed together for mono playback.
- The perceived stereo image can be widened by increasing the angle of incidence between the mics – however, this puts each mic further off-axis from the center of the sound source the array is pointed at. This makes the center of the image muddier – particularly if the mics have poor or colored off-axis response.
- Using hyper-cardioid mics instead of cardioid mics decreases the overlap of the pickup patterns and unclutters the center of the image, making the image wider. However, sounds coming from the center of the source are now effectively more off-axis to each hyper-cardioid mic's more directional pick-up – so they are picked up with greater off-axis coloration and slightly less amplitude.

This list of mainly negatives might suggest that XY coincident pair techniques are of limited usefulness. Not so! Where mono compatibility is a major concern, or if an expansively wide image is not desired, the technique can work very well. With some sound sources, and in some rooms and concert venues, XY coincident pair techniques produce more pleasing results than other techniques. It is hard to predict exactly how different stereo arrays will sound on different sources or in different rooms, so do be sure to try XY coincident pair techniques!

Mic Arrays and Stereo Images

The same drum set is recorded throughout this chapter.

Example 6.1: A single mono overhead microphone, centered on the drum set.

Example 6.2: An XY coincident pair of overheads, centered over the drum set.

6.3 BLUMLEIN PAIR TECHNIQUE

A *Blumlein pair* is a coincident array of bidirectional microphones crossed at 90°. Each mic is displaced 45° from the center of the sound source, as shown in **Figure 6.2**. This array works in a similar way to an XY coincident pair – it *is* a coincident pair after all. There are no time arrival differences between the coincident capsules, so as with XY coincident pair techniques, only amplitude difference information is recorded and reproduced on playback.

Bi-directional microphones *really* reject sound sources positioned to their sides. This results in a lot less overlapping pick-up between the mics. Blumlein pairs can produce very natural, realistic images that are wider, more spacious, and lack the narrow mono tendencies of XY coincident pair techniques. Mono compatibility remains excellent because there are no time arrival differences between the two mics. Again though, no microphone is directly on-axis with the center of the sound source.

Sound from behind the microphones will be picked up due to the bidirectional mic's rear pick-up lobes that are as equally sensitive as the forward pick-up lobes. This can be useful in a good sounding natural acoustic – room reflections and reverb can really energize the sound! But it can be problematic if the room sound is not desirable or there are sources of unwanted spill, or walls or ceilings too close behind the mic array.

Mic Arrays and Stereo Images

Example 6.3: A Blumlein pair of overheads, centered over the drum set. You can hear more of "the room."

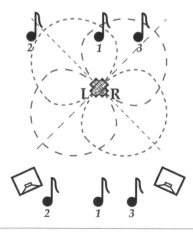

Figure 6.2 A Blumlein pair of microphones. Sound sources are shown at various positions in the array's pick-up, and their perceived playback locations are shown between the loudspeakers.

6.4 NEAR-COINCIDENT PAIR TECHNIQUES

A *near-coincident array* uses two directional microphones with the capsules positioned a small distance apart. The mics face away from each other, resulting in less overlap of their pick-up patterns than an XY coincident array. The angle of incidence between the mics is usually between 90° to 110°, as shown in **Figure 6.3**.

How does this technique work?

A sound coming from the center of the sound source labeled "1" in the figure, is equally off-axis and equidistant to both microphones. Therefore, both microphones pick up identical sound at the same time. With the mics hard panned, both loudspeakers reproduce identical sound simultaneously. Each of the listener's ears receives identical direct sound and identical inter-aural crosstalk, causing a phantom image to be perceived in the center, directly between the loudspeakers.

Sound "2," located far to the left of the array's pick-up area, is *not* equidistant to both mic capsules. It is closer to the left mic, which picks up the wavefront a fraction of a millisecond before the right mic – so the left loudspeaker reproduces it first. Additionally, this sound is on-axis to the left mic and beyond 90° off-axis to the right mic – so it is reproduced louder and with no off-axis coloration by the left loudspeaker.

Sound "3," located somewhat to the right of the array's pick-up area, is also not equidistant to both mic capsules. The right mic picks up the sound slightly before the left mic, so the right loudspeaker reproduces it slightly before the left loudspeaker. This sound source is on-axis to the right mic, and quite off-axis to the left mic, so the sound is reproduced with slightly more amplitude and less off-axis coloration by the right loudspeaker.

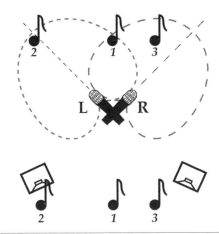

Figure 6.3 A near-coincident pair of microphones. Sound sources are shown at various positions in the array's pick-up, and their perceived playback locations are shown between the loudspeakers.

The distance between the mic capsules allows important time arrival information to be recorded and reproduced.

Characteristics of near-coincident techniques include:

- A wider, clearer stereo image than XY coincident techniques – often more closely matching the original sound source.
- A less muddy and confused sound due to the reduction in common off-axis pick-up between the mics.
- Sources in the center of the image might still be slightly muddy due to their off-axis position – no mic is pointed directly at the center of the sound source. However, the reduced pick-up pattern overlap between the mics decreases this tendency.
- A slight decrease in mono compatibility because the small time arrival differences between each capsule can cause some phase cancellation and comb filtering when the mics are summed together for mono playback. The mono compatibility decreases dramatically as the distance between the two capsules increases.
- The perceived image can be made wider or narrower by increasing or decreasing the angle of incidence between the mics, but as with an XY coincident array, increasing this angle puts each mic further off-axis with the center of the source the array is pointed at, further muddying the center image sound, particularly if the mics have poor, colored, off-axis response.
- Using hyper-cardioid mics instead of cardioid mics will widen the image, however any sound coming from the center of the source will be more off-axis to each mic and consequently picked up with increased off-axis coloration and slightly less amplitude.
- It may be possible to decrease the angle of incidence when using hyper-cardioid mics and maintain a similar image width to using cardioid mics – with the advantage of the hyper-cardioid mics being less off-axis to the center of the sound source.

This list of mainly positives makes the technique seem an always preferable alternative to XY coincident techniques. But when mono compatibility is a major concern, or an expansively wide image is not desired, XY coincident techniques may still be preferable. It's important to use the "mono" monitoring button before recording, to see if much sound does disappear, or if any strange phasey comb-filtering artifacts are heard when the image is summed to mono. Slight adjustments to the spacing and angle of incidence can reduce these artifacts and increase mono compatibility.

Specific near-coincident pair techniques include the following:

ORTF

Developed by the Office de Radiodiffusion-Télévision Français, the *ORTF* technique uses two cardioid mics set at an angle of 110° with the capsules spaced 17 cm (6.7 in) apart. With capsule spacing similar to the ears on your head, this technique produces a satisfying, transparent stereo image with relatively good mono compatibility.

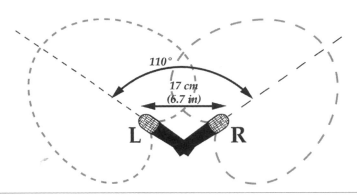

Figure 6.4   An ORTF array.

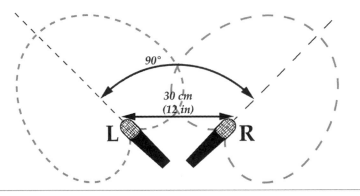

Figure 6.5   A NOS array.

NOS

Developed by Netherlands Radio, the *NOS* technique uses two cardioid mics set at 90° to each other with the capsules 30 cm (12 in) apart. Due to this wider spacing, mono compatibility is not as assured as with an ORTF array but due to the narrower angle of incidence between the mics, they are less off-axis to the center of the sound source. The increased phase differences introduced by the wider spacing results in a slightly bigger and more immersive image than a typical ORTF image.

DIN

Standardized by the German Deutches Institut Für Normung organization, the *DIN* technique positions two cardioid mics 20 cm (7.8 in) apart, angled at 90°. The mics are not as off-axis as in an ORTF array, but are spaced slightly further apart. The spacing is significantly less than in a NOS array. This results in a good balance of time arrival and amplitude differences that is particularly effective at shorter distances.

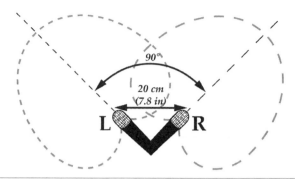

Figure 6.6   A DIN array.

Near Coincident Mic Arrays

Example 6.4: A ORTF near-coincident pair of overheads, centered over the drum set.

Example 6.5: A NOS near-coincident pair of overheads, centered over the drum set.

Example 6.6: A DIN near-coincident pair of overheads, centered over the drum set.

6.5   SPACED PAIR (AB) TECHNIQUES

In *spaced pair* or *AB* techniques, two microphones which face directly forwards are positioned with their capsules 40 to 60 cm apart (15 to 24 in), as shown in **Figure 6.7**. *Omnidirectional* microphones are generally used for spaced pair techniques – but there are many applications, such as drum overheads, when spaced directional mics can be used.

Sound source "1," located centrally, travels the same distance to each microphone – the sound arrives at each mic simultaneously at the same amplitude. Both loudspeakers then reproduce this sound at the same time and at the same amplitude creating a phantom image centrally located between the loudspeakers.

Sound source "2," located to the extreme left, travels a significantly shorter distance to the left mic than to the right mic, so the left mic picks it up a millisecond or two (and even several milliseconds with more extreme mic spacing) before the right mic. This sound source is also slightly quieter when it arrives at the right mic because the right mic is further from it than the left mic, but in most cases this amplitude difference is trivial. On reproduction, the left loudspeaker propagates the sound the same number of milliseconds before, and possibly just slightly louder than the right loudspeaker.

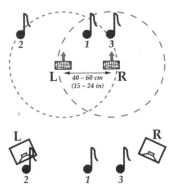

Figure 6.7 A spaced pair of microphones. Sound sources are shown at various positions in the array's pickup, and their perceived playback locations are shown between the loudspeakers.

Sound source "3" is picked up by the right mic slightly before the left mic, and is fractionally louder in the right mic. Therefore the right loudspeaker reproduces the sound slightly before, and slightly louder than the left loudspeaker.

Time arrival information is the primary indicator of directionality in spaced mic techniques. Mic spacing of approximately 50 cm (20 in) creates a maximum time arrival difference of approximately 1.5 ms between the mics, which produces a natural listening experience for a listener in the sweet-spot of a stereo pair of loudspeakers.

A suitably spaced AB mic array can capture an image that very closely matches the natural acoustic image, or pleasingly expands it.

General characteristics of AB spaced pair techniques include:

- A wide, expansive stereo image created solely by time arrival information. The image is not necessarily the most focused or precise, but it is the most *enveloping*.
- If the mic spacing is too wide, sources in the center can lack definition and focus.
- As the spacing between the mics is widened, longer than natural time arrival differences are generated, and the image becomes weaker and made up of "ghostly" separated left/right components with a "hole" in the center where nothing can really be localized.
- The relatively large time arrival differences between the mics make this the least mono compatible stereo technique. It is vitally important to check for phasing and comb filtering before recording, and to adjust the array spacing subtly to minimize any issues – although it will probably be impossible to remove all mono compatibility artifacts.
- The perceived image width can be increased or narrowed by increasing or decreasing the spacing between the mics – but don't go too wide on a close sound source (the image will have a hole in the middle), or too narrow when the mics are further away (the image will become too mono).

- Using directional mics instead of omnidirectional mics decreases common overlap, widening the stereo image, but it also positions centrally located sound sources more off-axis to each mic, subjecting them to off-axis coloration. Directional mics will, however, minimize the pick-up of undesirable room sound and sources of spill to the rear of the mic array.
- If a wide sound source such as a symphony orchestra, choir, or large drum set is being recorded, it is possible to augment a spaced pair with a third, center mic, and position the left and right mics equidistantly wider than if they were just a pair. This extra center panned information can either aid mono compatibility by adding common sound to both loudspeakers, or further decrease it by adding a third time displaced signal to the mix – it is entirely situational, depending on the spacing and relative balance between the mics.

Spaced Mic Arrays

Example 6.7: A spaced pair of omnidirectional overheads, 50 cm (20 in) apart, centered over the drum set.

Example 6.8: A widely spaced pair of cardioid overheads, each mic positioned over the edge of the drum set's width.

6.6 MS (MIDDLE-SIDE) TECHNIQUES

In all of the stereo techniques previously discussed, left and right microphones were present – and each were routed discretely to their respective loudspeaker (for a full width stereo image). An *MS* array, as shown in **Figure 6.8**, is significantly different. It doesn't pick up left/right information. Instead, MS techniques use a forward facing microphone (most commonly a cardioid mic, but it could be any polar pattern) to pick up the center, or *middle (M)* information, and a bidirectional microphone turned sideways at 90° to pick up *side (S)* information (which is a combination of the sounds coming from the left and right sides of the array).

The S mic is a single mic capsule with a single combined output of the sum of the sound waves hitting its front and rear – there is *not* a separate left and right capsule or output.

Sound source "1," in the center of the array's pick up, is only picked up by the M mic – it is in the null point of the S microphone.

Sound source "2," to the left, is picked up by a combination of both the M mic and the S mic. Its polarity in the S mic is normal because it is "in front" (+) of that mic.

Sound source "3," to the right, is also picked up by both mics, but its polarity in the S mic is reversed because it is "to the rear" (−) of that mic. It is also louder in the M mic and quieter in the S mic than sound source "1" because of its position relative to each mic's axis.

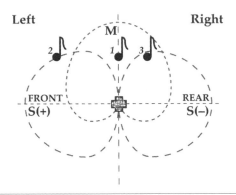

Figure 6.8   An MS array.

CONVERTING MS TO LR STEREO

In order to be reproduced on stereo loudspeakers (or headphones) an MS array needs to be *matrixed* (or decoded) into stereo using a sum and difference matrix.

Raw MS tracks can be recorded and then matrixed to stereo at a later time, or matrixed prior to the recording device to record the derived L/R stereo tracks. If you record raw MS tracks you *should* monitor a matrixed L/R stereo form of the signal in order to check the array is working properly and that the matrixed image is desirable. To record L/R stereo tracks a hardware matrix is necessary after the mic pre-amps and before the recording device. Hardware matrixes usually have few controls, and possibly only one – an S level control which varies the level of the S+ and S− signals that are combined with the M signal – to adjust the image width. Matrixing is also possible on a mixing console or in a DAW.

THE SUM AND DIFFERENCE MATRIX

The left side of an MS mic array's pick-up, as shown in **Figure 6.8**, is a combination of the M mic and normal polarity sound picked up by the front of the S mic (S+).

$$LEFT = M + S+$$

The right side of the mic array's pick-up is a combination of the M mic and polarity reversed sound from the rear of the S mic, (S−).

$$RIGHT = M + S-$$

Those equations simplify to:

$$LEFT = M + S$$
$$RIGHT = M - S$$

LEFT is the *sum* of the M and S mics, and RIGHT is the *difference* between the M and S mics.

MATRIXING IN A DAW

- Label the "M" track, pan it center, and put the fader at unity.
- Duplicate the S track.
- Label the original track "S+" and pan it hard left.
- Label the duplicate track "S−," polarity reverse it, and pan it hard right.
- Put both the S+ and S− faders at −∞, then group them together so that they are always at exactly the same level when you move them.
- With the S+ and S− faders at −∞ the image will be mono because all you are hearing is the center panned M mic. Increase the width of the image by increasing the level of the S+ and S− faders. Decrease the stereo width by decreasing the level of the S+ and S− tracks.
- Once the desired stereo image has been achieved, group together the M and both S faders so that their relative balance (and the stereo image produced) stays identical if you adjust their overall level.
- If you adjust any pre-amp, plug-in, or gain controls related to these three channels you will have to re-balance the M and S channel levels to maintain the stereo image.
- Any insert effects (EQ or compression, etc.) should be applied to the matrixed L/R stereo signal by routing the outputs of the M, S+, and S− tracks to a group or aux track (instead of the main stereo outs) and applying them on that track.

MATRIXING ON AN ANALOG MIXING CONSOLE

Matrixing on a mixing console requires three channels: M, S+, and S−. "Y-cabling" the S signal into two channels is not recommended because all faders, even supposedly identical ones, do not perform exactly the same throughout their travel. Maintaining an identical level of the S+ and S− channels is essential, and simply visually matching fader positions is not accurate enough.

- Label the "M" track, pan it center, and put the fader at unity. Adjust the gain to achieve good input levels. (The level of the M fader can also be below unity if you are balancing the array's level with other sources in the context of a larger mix.)
- Mute the M channel.
- Label the first S channel "S+," and connect the S signal to its input. Adjust its gain to achieve good input levels. Pan it hard left.

- Connect the S+ channel's post-fader Direct Out (or similar individual post-fader output) to the line input of a third channel, labeled "S−." Polarity reverse this channel and also pan it hard left. (Yes, *left*, the same as the other channel. For now.)
- Put both the S+ and S− faders at unity. You will not move the S− fader from unity, so put some board tape over it so it does not get accidentally knocked.
- Adjust the S− gain control until the two S channels cancel out as much as possible. When maximum cancellation is achieved both the S+ and S− channels are amplitude matched.
- Pull down the S+ fader to −∞.
- Pan the S− channel hard right.
- Unmute the M channel.
- Gradually creep up the S+ fader to increase the S component in the signal and widen the stereo image. Reduce its level if the image gets too wide. Do not adjust the S− channel – it has already been calibrated to the S+ channel and its feed is after the S+ fader, so the S+ fader effectively adjusts it as well.
- If you change the level of the M track at any time you will have to adjust the S+ track by exactly the same amount in order to maintain an identical stereo image.
- You could route the M and both S faders through a stereo group fader (and not directly to the L/R output fader) and have a simple way to control the level of the matrixed image in your mix.

The level of the S component in the matrix should not be as high as the M signal. The S faders will not need to be run at unity if the S input levels are trimmed to be similar to the M input levels – they will commonly be at least 6 dB lower than the M fader when producing a good stereo image. If there is too much S component in the image, a strange phasey "hole" develops in the center – activity is heard on the left and right extremes but not throughout the width of the image.

MS technique has a very different sound to the other stereo techniques discussed in this chapter. It produces a very precise image in which it is easy to pinpoint the location of specific sound sources. It is criticized by some for being too "surgical" and not as impressively immersive or enveloping as near-coincident or spaced techniques – which trade MS's localization accuracy and focus for slightly less accurate "smeared" images that are bigger and more instantly impressive.

MS technique is completely mono compatible – more so than any other technique discussed. If the stereo image is summed to mono, the S+ and S− signals cancel out completely (because they are polarity reversed versions of each other) leaving just the M mic signal as the mono output.

MATRIXING LR STEREO TO MS

Any left/right stereo signal can be matrixed into its M and S components. Why do this? Mastering engineers frequently use this technique to widen or narrow the stereo image of recordings that are too narrow or wide. If the recorded image of a stereo mic array is too wide or too narrow, the same matrixing technique can also be used during mixing to adjust that image – but this should be a last resort – it is preferable to adjust the mic array to achieve a better image in the first place.

Without matrixing, a left/right stereo source can be made less wide by panning the two channels less extremely – but this may cause phase cancellation artifacts if the signal is not 100 percent mono compatible. Additionally, it is impossible to widen a stereo signal that is too narrow by using the pan pots – the knobs only turn so far!

After matrixing the left-right stereo signal to MS, the relative balances of the M (center) and S (width) components can be adjusted to widen or narrow the image width, and those MS signals matrixed back into stereo using the techniques described earlier.

To matrix LR stereo to MS in a DAW:

- You need to be able to polarity reverse either the L or R channel, so depending on your DAW you may need the stereo track split over separate L and R channels.
- Duplicate these L and R tracks, so there are two sets of them.
- Pan both channels of the first pair of tracks centrally, leaving both faders at unity. Route them both to an unused internal mono bus in the DAW – "Bus 1" for example. This is the common "M" signal. Do not route them to the main stereo output.
- Polarity reverse *one channel* of the second pair of tracks (it doesn't matter which channel). Pan both channels of this pair centrally, leaving both faders at unity. Route them both to a second unused internal mono bus in the DAW – "Bus 2" for example. This is the "S" (difference) signal. Do not route them to the main stereo output.
- If you have to use a plug-in to polarity reverse, make sure delay compensation is turned on in your DAW (if it is not automatic) to allow for any delay induced by that plug-in.
- You can now set up three input channels, M, S+, and S–, routed to the main stereo outs, and matrix the MS signal to stereo, changing the image width by manipulating the S level in this second set of channels. The input to the M channel should be "Bus 1," and the input to the S+ and S– channels "Bus 2." Don't forget to polarity reverse the S– channel, and to pan S+ and S– left and right.

Don't expect this technique to fix every image problem! If a recorded stereo image is far too wide, has a hole in the middle, or lots of out of phase content between the L and

R channels, there is little common M signal to be derived. Conversely, if a recorded stereo image is far too narrow and almost mono, there is little S difference signal to be derived. With a shortage of either component the technique is less effective. This technique is best used for subtle changes, not big "rescue" jobs!

MS Mic Arrays

Example 6.9: An MS array, matrixed to produce a good wide stereo image. (Compare this example with the stereo image of a spaced pair on an acoustic guitar in Example 11.14.)

Example 6.10: An MS array. This example starts with the S component turned all the way down in the matrix, leaving just the mono center. As the S component is turned up you can hear the image widen. By about 20 seconds there is too much S component and the image gets "phasey" with a "hole" in the middle.

6.7   THE DECCA TREE

The *Decca Tree* was originally developed by the Decca record label for orchestral recording and can be heard on countless records and film soundtracks. It is formed from three omnidirectional microphones, traditionally large diaphragm condensers, which are set up in a triangle as shown in **Figure 6.9**. The L mic is panned left, the R mic panned right, and the C mic panned to the center. The gains of the three mics should be set equally, although adjusting the C mic up or down can narrow or widen the perceived image.

Many variations of the Decca Tree are possible:

* Cardioid or wide-cardioid mics can be used instead of omnidirectional mics.

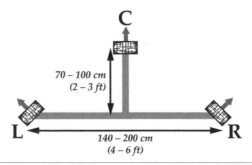

Figure 6.9   A Decca Tree.

- Combinations such as a cardioid mic for the C, and hyper-cardioid mics for the L and R can be used.
- The spacing of the C mic can be reduced, and the L and R mics spaced more or less widely in order to achieve the desired stereo image.

This array is famed for its expansive and immersive sound. It is not necessarily the most precise in terms of imaging accuracy – but its image characteristics are definitely pleasing. Neither is it the most mono compatible – with three spaced mics and the associated time arrival differences between them. Mono compatibility should definitely be checked prior to recording.

6.8 BINAURAL AND BAFFLE TECHNIQUES

Stereo loudspeaker systems create expansive and wide stereo images because of the inter-aural crosstalk and associated HRTF effects of the sound from each loudspeaker travelling to *both* of the listener's ears. The stereo microphone techniques discussed so far are designed primarily for loudspeaker system reproduction – and while they work fairly well on headphones, the perceived image is not the same as it would be on a loudspeaker system. Headphones, being binaural and not technically "stereo," produce a different image – lacking the inter-aural crosstalk and HRTF effects of a true stereo system.

Binaural microphone techniques capture characteristics similar to natural HRTF time delay and frequency filtering effects, at the time of recording. These pre-recorded HRTF effects (that would otherwise be missing when listening on headphones) are then reproduced by the headphones and interpreted as inter-aural crosstalk and HRTF effects by our brain. For this reason binaural mic techniques reproduce and image well on headphones, but not on stereo loudspeaker systems where an additional dose of HRTF effects are naturally and unavoidably imposed by the playback system and the listener's head.

Several manufacturers produce head-shaped or spherical baffles which have mic capsules permanently mounted in positions similar to our ears. Other flat baffle systems can also be purchased or easily home built to separate two standard omnidirectional mics. The presence of the baffle creates some acoustical separation between the two omnidirectional mics. The spacing between these baffled mics (and the size of the head-shaped or spherical baffle) approximates the separation of the ears on the average human head.

The *Jecklin Disc* is a baffle technique that can be easily constructed and is shown in **Figure 6.10**. A circular baffle, 25 to 35 cm (10 to 14 in) in diameter, with both sides covered with acoustically absorbent material is positioned between two omnidirectional mics that are 36 cm (14 in) apart. The mics are angled outwards at +20° and −20° from center, although this angle is variable.

Baffles can be added to any of the near-coincident techniques previously discussed to increase channel separation and image width, but accuracy when reproduced on stereo loudspeaker systems will be sacrificed.

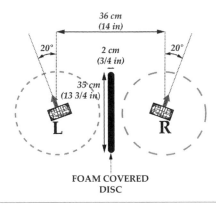

Figure 6.10   A Jecklin Disc separates two spaced omnidirectional mics, creating a binaural mic array.

PRACTICAL EXERCISE

Record a piano, acoustic guitar, drum set (or any other sound source that has width and takes up horizontal space) using a variety of the stereo mic techniques discussed in this chapter. Pan each channel hard left and hard right respectively, and listen carefully to the stereo images produced by each. Answer the following questions:

- When summed to mono how much does the image collapse and narrow? When put back into stereo how much does the image expand and widen?

- When summed to mono do you hear tonal changes or does the amplitude get significantly quieter? (These would indicate mono compatibility issues.)

- How does the overall sense of width and space compare between the techniques? Do some sound wider and more spacious than others? Do some sound smaller and more compact?

- How clear and accurate is the image between the speakers? Can you really pinpoint the precise location of a specific sound? A good test for this is to record some of the mic techniques over the hammers of a grand piano and listen to the transition of the notes from left to right. How much do you hear the notes moving across the soundstage? Do they move slowly and smoothly across and through the center of the soundstage, or do they hang in a certain loudspeaker before suddenly jumping to the other side?

- Tonally or timbrally, how does each technique compare? Are some darker, muddier, or more muffled sounding than others? Are some brighter, more open, and more transparent than others?

The Effect of Microphone Position

IN THIS CHAPTER:

7.1   ART AND SCIENCE

Small changes to a microphone's position can significantly affect the sound it picks up. There is no singular "correct" position when miking a particular sound source. The sound a mic picks up is dependent on many variables, including:

- The specific mic in use.
- Its distance and position relative to the sound source.
- The angle of pick-up relative to the sound source.
- The size and shape of the room.
- The mic's position relative to the room.
- The mic's position relative to any other sound sources in the room.

This short list should explain why in addition to being a little bit of a science, audio recording is an *art*!

7.2   DISTANCE AND TONAL QUALITIES

Proximity effect was discussed in **Chapter 3** (the boost of the low frequencies when a directional mic is used close to a sound source). The distance at which proximity effect becomes apparent varies significantly between different mic models – even between those of similar pick-up patterns. It certainly varies between mics with different pick-up patterns – the more directional the mic, the more pronounced the proximity effect.

Proximity effect can be exploited in beneficial ways. A thin sound might be warmed up and made thicker by positioning the mic relatively close to the sound source. Conversely, a sound that is quite boomy and full might be made less muddy by moving the mic further away. A few inches difference in mic distance can have a significant effect on the amount of proximity effect.

For most rock and pop type recording, particularly in smaller project and home studio rooms, directional mics are most commonly used. This means that a lot of proximity effect can build up on the tracks recorded. The muddying effect is cumulative and somewhat exponential – the more tracks it is apparent on, the bigger the problem. To reduce proximity effect problems, don't automatically position a mic super close to each sound source – consider whether it can be backed off a little to reduce low and low-mid frequency build-up. The increase in transparency and clarity will make mixing easier because less corrective EQ will be required.

Air naturally absorbs high frequencies over distance, so if a mic is positioned far away from a sound source the sound will be darker and less bright. This natural EQ is a powerful characteristic that our auditory system recognizes as distance information. The sound is moved back in the stereo image, particularly when combined with room reflections and reverberation. If you want a sound to naturally appear "back" in the mix, try recording it from more of a distance.

Figure 7.1 Correct and incorrect mic positions on a saxophone. 1: Put too close to the bell, the mic picks up a honky sound that favors the lowest few notes. 2: A mic positioned further away will pick up the sound of the entire instrument.

7.3   "ZOOM FACTOR"

We do not generally listen to sound sources from just a few inches away – we usually listen from several or many feet away. If we are listening to a piano we hear all the constituent elements of the piano blended together over the distance between the instrument and our ears:

- The impact of the hammers on the strings.
- The warm resonance of the strings and soundboard.
- In the case of the grand piano, the reflected sound coming from underneath the instrument, and bouncing off the open lid.

A directional microphone used up close is like a zoom lens on a camera. It focuses in on the sound coming from just a small area of a much larger sound source. For example, a microphone placed very close to a saxophone's bell, as in **Figure 7.1**, picks up the honky sound coming from the bell very well. The lowest notes will appear much louder than the others because the bell is where almost all of their sound comes from – most of the higher note sound comes from the open holes further up the instrument. A close mic does not pick up a complete or natural sonic picture.

THE LONGEST DIMENSION RULE

A good rule of thumb to pick up a natural sound of most acoustic instruments in the studio is to take the longest dimension of the instrument and position the mic that far away (or perhaps just a little closer if it's more than a couple of feet). This gives the component sounds radiating from all over the instrument distance to blend together and form the "whole" and natural acoustic sound we are used to hearing.

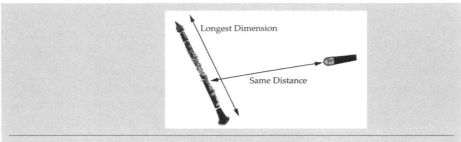

Figure 7.2 "Longest dimension" positioning on a clarinet allows the mic to pick up the blended "whole" instrument sound.

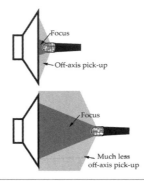

Figure 7.3 Positioning a mic further away allows it to pick up the sound of the entire cone, with less off-axis coloration.

A directional mic positioned right up against the grill of a guitar or bass amplifier cabinet will focus on the sound made by just a small portion of the loudspeaker cone, as shown in **Figure 7.3**. Backing the microphone off by a foot or so will not only make the sound less muddy and boomy, but also pick up the characteristics of the entire speaker cone. Instrument cabinet loudspeakers are very non-linear in their response, and exhibit complex distortion patterns over their entire surface – they are much less accurate than traditional loudspeaker drivers, but much more characterful. Often, a more desirable, detailed, less congested, and more mixable sound can be achieved by introducing a little distance between the speaker cone and the mic.

PRACTICAL EXCERCISE

Record an acoustic guitar with a single microphone. Keep the mic close, about 12 cm (5 in) away from the guitar.

- Position the mic directly in front of the sound hole. A thick, beefy, body sound should be picked up. The mic is close to, and on-axis with the sound hole, and that character dominates.

- Position the mic a few frets further up the fretboard from where it joins the body of the guitar. Zingy, stringy, sizzly details should be picked up from this mic position. The mic is close to, and on axis to the neck, and that character dominates.

Neither of these sounds accurately represents the acoustic guitar, because of the mic's "zoom factor" – but each is an important part of the instrument's complete sound character.

- If the mic is put in-between these two positions, perpendicular to the guitar, a blend of both can be picked up.
- Move the mic left or right by just a couple of inches to change the relative balance of these sound components, and listen to the balance of the characteristics picked up.
- Move the mic a few more times, by another inch or two, until you find an appropriate blend that sounds like the guitar's "whole" sound – a good balance of "body" and "string."

Increasing the mic's distance will reduce the "zoom factor," and allow a more natural sound to be picked up more easily.

- Position the mic about 30 cm (1 ft) from the guitar and find a more balanced, natural sounding sweet-spot for it by moving it a few inches at a time sideways, up or down.

7.4   OFF-AXIS RESPONSE

As discussed in **Chapter 3**, all microphones (even omnidirectional mics) become more directional at higher frequencies – so it is important that mics are always pointed in exactly the right direction.

- When recording physically small sound sources (point source images such as vocals or brass instruments, for example) the results of positioning the mic on-axis vs off-axis are relatively predictable – a mic sloppily or inaccurately positioned off-axis will have its sound colored by the characteristics of its off-axis response, and the sound will become muddy, muffled, dull, and confused.
- On larger sound sources such as drum sets, acoustic guitars, string basses, and large acoustic ensembles, sound from parts of the sound source the mic isn't specifically aimed at are in the off-axis part of the mic's pick-up pattern.

Consider the acoustic guitar being miked in the previous exercise:

- A mic positioned to get great pick-up of the bright, zingy string sound, is off-axis to the sound hole and most of the guitar's body – the sound of body and sound hole will be subject to the mic's off-axis coloration, and will possibly make the track too dull, congested, and muddy, compromising its usability.

- A mic positioned to get great pick-up of the big warm body sound is off-axis to the sound coming from towards the neck – the stringy, fret board sound is subject to the mic's off-axis coloration, and will not be as bright, zingy, or clear as it should, possibly compromising the track's usability.
- Angling the mic a little left or right will change the recording's characteristics by putting different components more on-axis or off-axis. If you want more string sound, but with a darker "zing," then try positioning the mic closer to the neck, angled towards the sound hole.
- An overly bright sound can be darkened by positioning the mic so the sound source is slightly off-axis – if the mic has good, smooth off-axis response characteristics.

The only way to find the best mic position is to experiment – listen while moving the mic a couple inches at a time, and/or changing its angle slightly to favor the desired characteristics.

INCREASING MIC DISTANCE

A very natural acoustic guitar sound can be achieved by using a single mic 45 cm (15 in) or more from the instrument. This extra distance results in:

- Less proximity effect, and a clearer sound.
- A natural balance of all of the instrument's component characteristics.
- Less potentially undesirable off-axis coloration because more of the instrument is on-axis to the mic.

The tradeoff of this approach is that the close perspective is lost and replaced with a more distant sound.

Using an omnidirectional mic instead of a cardioid mic will eliminate proximity effect and make the off-axis pick up sound better, so omnidirectional mics can be positioned a little closer than directional mics without sounding so isolated. But omnidirectional mics should only be used if the recording room characteristics are desirable – in most small home or project studio rooms this is not the case.

"Zoom Factor"

Example 7.1: A mic set up close to an acoustic guitar's sound hole primarily picks up the body of the sound colored by proximity effect.

Example 7.2: A mic set up close to an acoustic guitar's neck primarily picks up the lighter stringy quality of the sound colored by proximity effect.

Example 7.3: A mic placed 45 cm (18 in) away picks up a clearer, more accurate, blended picture of the guitar's natural sound, and is not colored by proximity effect.

7.5 DIRECT VS REFLECTED SOUND

Unlike in many diagrams explaining the travel and trajectory of sound waves in an environment, sound does not travel in straight line laser beam patterns from the sound source to the microphone. It's simpler to represent it that way, and yes, a lot of the sound does do that – but not all of it. Most acoustic instruments and sound sources radiate sound in all directions, but it's more complex than that – different frequency content is radiated in different directions, and not all of that frequency content remains audible over the same distance as other frequency content! This sound travels outwards to the floor, walls, and ceiling, which reflect it back into the room towards the mic, and the other boundaries, which reflect it again. An infinite number of reflection paths are quickly created, which give the room its character. See **Figure 7.4**.

The closer a mic is to a sound source, the greater the ratio of direct to reflected sound – the sound will be more dry, dead, in-your-face, and up-front.

As a mic is moved further away from a sound source, the level of direct sound decreases and the relative amount of reflected sound increases. This means that the sound of the room or environment is heard more. A more distant mic's sound can be anything from "a little less up close and personal" but "beneficially more live," to quite set back, unfocused, reverberant, and distant.

Most of the time we listen to musical instruments and singers in a room – a space with a floor, walls, and a ceiling. The reflections from those boundaries are an essential part of the natural sound we are accustomed to hearing. An uncomfortable sensation of "deadness" is experienced when walking into a recording studio's dry vocal booth for the first time because the reflections and room sound that we are used to hearing are missing.

Unnaturally dry sounds, lacking reflected content certainly have their place in contemporary music production styles alongside more natural or stylistically wet, reverberant sounds.

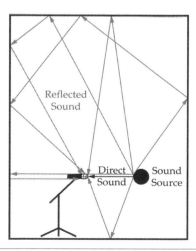

Figure 7.4 Direct and reflected sounds are picked up by a microphone, and complex "room signature" reflections are quickly generated.

7.6   FLOOR REFLECTIONS – THE GOOD, THE BAD, AND BOUNDARY MICS

When a sound source is close miked in a large room (even a fairly reverberant one), the amplitude of the reflections from the walls and ceiling are of a relatively low level compared to the dry, direct sound reaching the microphone. This is due to the fact that the reflected sound's amplitude drops as it travels a longer path to the walls and/ceiling, and then back to the mic. Still, these low level reflections can have a huge impact on some sound sources. The floor is much closer to both the sound source and microphone so the reflections from a hard floor are louder than the reflections from the walls and ceiling – and they have a fundamental impact on the record sound.

Floor reflections are not a long swishy reverb tail, but can be an extra sheen and dimension – more "oomph" and power, indistinguishable from the dry sound. They can add life and excitement to a sound, and we are used to hearing floor reflections as part of a natural listening experience.

- A mic very close to a sound source picks up mainly dry sound which overpowers and masks reflected content – and the result is a dry, dead, in-your-face sound.
- Moving the mic a few feet away allows floor reflections to become audible.
- Moving the mic many feet away decreases the dry, direct sound and increases the amount of wall and ceiling reflections (room sound or reverb) that the mic picks up.

Acoustically reflective floors can add beneficial floor reflections to a recording – but significant floor reflections can also cause phase problems and comb filtering due to the

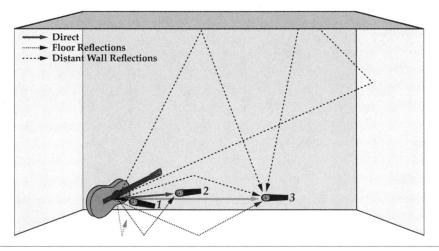

Figure 7.5   1: A close mic favors dry, direct sound. 2: A few feet away, floor reflections become part of the sound. 3: With a more distant mic position reflections from the entire room (reverb) are picked up by the mic.

distance and consequential time arrival differences between the direct and reflected sound at the microphone. It is important to really listen for any thinning or strangeness in the timbre of the recorded sound source, in all its pitch and frequency ranges, and at all dynamic levels to confirm that the sound is not being negatively impacted by excess reflections.

If the sound of comb filtering is identified, the mic position should be adjusted to minimize the problem. Moving the mic by just a few inches can change the phase relationships of the direct and reflected sound at the mic position and make things better, or worse! Do not position a mic and assume it is picking up the best possible sound. Try a few different positions – they may sound worse, but you'll have verified that the initial placement was best.

Thin, lightweight carpet and rugs can cause poor sounding floor reflections because they only absorb high frequencies, so the reflections from a carpeted floor are muddy and dull. Many instruments, such as acoustic guitars and drum sets, really benefit from the hype of bright floor reflections. Most studios have hardwood floors because the reflections sound great – and if necessary the room can be damped down with thick, heavy carpet or rugs.

Boundary mics positioned on the floor exploit floor reflections as part of their design, as discussed in **Chapter 3**. The boundary (the floor) is necessary for the mic to function well and have good low frequency response. Because the diaphragm is only a few millimeters above the floor boundary, the phase and comb filtering problems caused when the direct and reflected sound sum at the mic capsule are in such high frequencies that they are irrelevant. This does not mean that a boundary mic will always pick up good sound though! Many instruments radiate their high frequency content quite directionally, and not necessarily towards a mic positioned below the plane of the instrument. So while a boundary mic on the floor does not suffer from phase and comb filtering problems between the dry and floor reflected sound, it is often better to use a conventional mic, up and away from the floor, to capture the best blend of direct sound and floor reflections.

Floor Reflections

Example 7.4: An acoustic guitar recorded in a carpeted room.

Example 7.5: An acoustic guitar recorded in a room with a reflective wooden floor.

7.7   DISTANCE AND STEREO ARRAYS

The top diagram in **Figure 7.6** shows a near-coincident array positioned relatively close to a sound source. The sound source extends through most of the effective pick-up area of the array. Panned hard left and hard right during mixing this results in an expansive image that takes up the entire width between the loudspeakers.

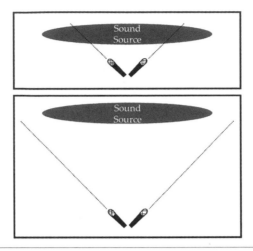

Figure 7.6 Top: A near-coincident mic array close to a sound source creates a wide image. Bottom: Moving the mic further away from the sound source results in a narrower stereo image.

In the bottom diagram, the same array is moved back from the sound source. The sound source is now more concentrated in the overlapping center pick-up of both mics. Even panned as wide as possible during mixing the image will be narrower than when the array was closer to the sound source.

But – image width is not all that changes as a stereo array is positioned at different distances from the sound source.

When the array is positioned closer to the sound source the amplitude of direct sound is increased and the relative amplitude of reflected room sound is decreased – the sound is drier and more up-front (just as it is with a single mic).

Moving the array further away from the sound source increases the relative amplitude of reflected sound and decreases the amplitude of the direct sound – the sound is more distant and reverberant (just as it would be with a single mic).

The positioning of stereo arrays is a balancing act between the desired image width and wet/dry balance:

- A stereo array up close = a wider, but drier image.
- A stereo array further away = a narrower, but more reverberant image.

You should not compromise desired image width for the sake of wet/dry balance or vice versa. As previously discussed, different stereo arrays produce different widths and imaging characteristics – you should experiment with different arrays and/or different microphones until the desired combination of image width and reverb is obtained.

CASE STUDY

PROBLEM: An acoustic guitar miked with an XY coincident pair is appropriately wet or dry, but the image is too narrow.

SOLUTION: Try a near-coincident pair in order to widen the image without changing the wet/dry balance too much.

PROBLEM: An acoustic guitar miked with a near-coincident pair is too reverberant or "roomy," but the image width is good.

SOLUTION: Try a spaced pair of cardioid mics a little closer.

Stereo Array Distance, Image Width, and Wet/Dry Balance

Example 7.6: A drum set recorded with a near-coincident pair, above and slightly in front of the drum set. The image of the drum set is wide, and relatively tight and dry.

Example 7.7: The same drum set, with the same stereo mic array positioned 20 feet in front of the drum set. The drum set appears narrower, taking up less of the image width, but an increased amount of reverb takes up the entire width of the image.

7.8   SPILL – ENEMY OR CREATIVE TOOL?

Whenever multiple microphones are positioned close to each other, each one will pick up sound that's not really intended for it. This spill is problematic if it does not sound good in itself, or if comb filtering and mono compatibility problems exist between multiple mics in the same room.

THE 3:1 RULE

In any multi-mic situation (including close drum mics, or recording multiple singers or a horn section with individual mics) the 3:1 rule should be used in order to reduce the level of spill relative to the desired sound in each mic. **Figure 7.7** shows that the distance between each mic should be three times the distance between each sound source and its mic. This will certainly not eliminate spill totally, but it will minimize its potentially negative effects.

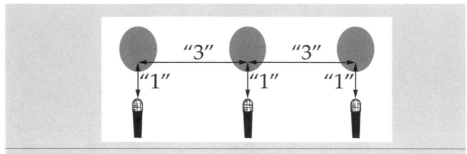

Figure 7.7   Applying the 3:1 rule when miking three singers.

Spill is not always the enemy though. It *can* sound good.

One way to improve the sound of spill is to use mics that have better off-axis response. Cheap mics may make sound sources on-axis to them sound good, but they usually compromise the sound of spill because of their poor sounding off-axis response.

When mixing rock and pop music, *gates* or *strip silence* features can be used to silence mic channels in-between drum hits. Gating out spill and removing the natural acoustical connection between the multiple instruments has a huge effect on the sound – it becomes ultra-clean and surgical. This may be stylistically and aesthetically desirable for some rock and pop projects because the drum set tends to be treated as a collection of individual, separate instruments. In jazz and some grungier pop styles though, the drum set is treated more as an organic whole and not as the sum of many individual parts – so a super clean, gated drum sound could be inappropriate and undesirable.

If gating is undesirable, less aggressive *expansion* can be used to reduce the level of the spill rather than eliminate it completely – however, ensuring good sounding spill is captured, or minimizing undesirable or bad sounding spill acoustically through mic technique and instrument location in a room is generally preferred to electronic solutions by most engineers working on acoustic music projects.

Good sounding spill is *not* the enemy. *Bad* sounding spill is. Strategies to "improve" the sound of spill include using mics with good sounding off-axis characteristics, directional polar patterns than put sources of spill in their null(s), and to record in a room with a good sound (because the sound of the room *will* be picked up by the mics). Spill can also be managed by exploring the position of the sound sources in the room – both the position of the sound sources relative to each other and their mics, and relative to the room itself. For example, a mic facing an instrument but pointing towards a reflective wall is going to pick up more reflected spill than a mic facing an instrument and pointing towards an absorptive wall surface. With the right mics and techniques, good spill can be a creative tool that shapes the sound and energy of the mix.

Spill

Example 7.8: A multi-miked drum set with all of the mics on all of the time. The spill gives the sound a natural "organic" character.

Example 7.9: A multi-miked drum set with the kick, snare, and tom tom mics gated to remove the significant spill in those mics. The sound is cleaner, tighter, and more focused. For some musical styles it might be considered too "bland."

7.9   WHY MINOR CHANGES IN MIC POSITION CHANGE THE SOUND SO MUCH

All of the topics discussed in this and previous chapters related to microphones and stereo arrays have a combined effect on the sound a mic picks up. For example:

- Moving a microphone closer or further away affects proximity effect, distance perspective, the direct vs reflected sound ratio, and the mic's phase relationship with any other mics which also pick up the same sound source.
- Moving a microphone left, right, up, or down, affects the on-axis sound picked up, the spill picked up, and the mic's phase relationship with other mics which also pick up the same sound source.
- Changing the angle of a mic affects not only the on-axis sound picked up, but also the off-axis spill picked up.

EQ cannot fix *any* phase related problems, such as the timbral shifts of comb filtering related to reflected sound or spill issues, so it is essential to listen critically to the sound produced by each mic, *and* the combination of all the mics set up in the same room before committing and proceeding with the recording session. EQ should be a last resort anyway. If the sound produced by any mic isn't right it should be corrected prior to tracking (through mic choice and placement) before relying on electronic "last resort" processes such as EQ.

7.10   EXPERIMENTATION AND EXPLORATION

Mic position *X* might have worked really well on guitar *A* in studio *B* when using mic *C*. But if any one of those variables are changed that mic position may not work as well, and time must be taken to experiment and explore until great sound *is* captured by the microphone(s). In addition to changing mic position, some other things to experiment with include:

- Changing the instrument: Two different instruments of the same type may sound different, and propagate sound differently, necessitating different mic positions. The new instrument may sound so different that an alternate mic is desirable.

- Changing the recording room or the instrument's position in a recording space will change how the instrument interacts with the room. Finding where the instrument naturally sounds best in the room may necessitate a change in mic position relative to the instrument, and/or a change in the microphone(s) used.
- Changing the mic will change both the on-axis direct sound and off-axis spill picked up, and a slightly different mic position may be necessary to get the best sound from the new mic and instrument combination.

It doesn't take long to try a few different mic positions or to set up a few different mics.

SHOULD I RECORD MANY MICS, WHEN I ONLY NEED ONE OR TWO IN THE MIX?

There are different schools of thought regarding how to choose the best microphone for the sound and the mix. With the high track counts of DAWs, gone are the days of having to experiment with mics and mic positions until you narrow the choice down to one mic and position and commit to it before pressing the record button.

MORE MICS!

One option is to set up multiple mics, maybe in different positions, audition them to make sure they are each producing potentially useful sound, and to record them all for selection at a later date. Just because you record them, does not mean you have to use them. As already discussed, simultaneous use of multiple mics, each a different distance from a sound source can result in phase and comb filtering problems.

I have found this approach confronts a novice engineer with a bewildering amount of options when mixing, and it is easy to fall into the trap of wanting to use every track. Rarely are more than two or three mics per sound source combined in a way that does not compromise the sound.

FEWER MICS!

An alternative option is to commit to just one or two mics. Set up many mics (possibly in many positions), audition them carefully, tweak their position, and select the best sounding/most appropriate one or two to record. Making these decisions prior to pressing the record button makes decision making during mixing easier – you are presented with a less daunting array of more considered options. The more mics you set up, the more physical objects and reflective surfaces are in the way of capturing the sound you're looking for – so do take down any mics you're not using before pressing the record button.

7.11 PRACTICAL TIPS TO HELP SET MIC POSITION

It is time consuming and clumsy for you, the engineer, working alone, to position a mic in the studio, run into the control room to listen to it, then repeatedly run back and forth to make further adjustments. A good way of making this process easier is to route the mic signal to a pair of isolating headphones in the studio. You can then wear these, and monitor the mic's sound as you move it around. Once the mic sounds good in the headphones, it should be double-checked through the monitors in the control room.

Unfortunately for your hearing, to really check the sound a mic is picking up, the performer needs to play at full performance volume. Closed-back isolating headphones used at a sensible level will protect you from hearing damage while you're crawling around a loud drum set or a guitar amp, and help you hear the mic's sound and minimize the natural sound in the room.

If multiple mics are used on a single sound source and the mics are not intended to be a stereo array, it is essential that they be checked for phase and comb filtering problems:

- With each mic panned to the same position, listen to each separately by muting them or soloing them alternately.
- Then, solo or unmute them all at the same time and listen for any hollowing, thinning, or other phasey negative shifts in tonality.

Do any tonal or timbral characteristics of the sound disappear when all the mics are on? If so, then the mics need repositioning relative to each other.

Mono compatibility should also be checked when setting up stereo arrays:

- Listen to the image with the channels panned hard left and right respectively.
- Then listen in mono (either push the mono button, or pan both channels centrally).

The image will collapse to a much narrower mono phantom center – that is expected. But are there are any significant shifts in the timbre of the sound? Do any characteristics of the sound disappear too much? Or does the sound take on any strange, thin characteristics? If so, there are mono compatibility problems that must be addressed by adjusting the mic array or using a different stereo array.

PRACTICAL EXERCISE

- Set up a single mic on an instrument, for example, an acoustic guitar, a saxophone, or a kick drum.
- Record a minute of sound.
- Move the mic a few inches forwards, backwards, up, down, or to the side, and record another example.

- Compare the two and identify the specific differences between them. Which one sounds "better," or truer to the original source being recorded?
- Move the mic again, and repeat the process.
- Try this exercise with different instruments.

The Recording Room

8.1   ROOM SOUND

A significant and often overlooked weak link in the recording chain is the room that the recording takes place in. A room's "sound" and character is created by the reflections the floor, walls, and ceiling produce:

- Different boundary materials reflect different amounts of sound.
- Different materials reflect and absorb varying amounts of high, mid, and low frequencies.
- Different distances between the boundaries change the character of the room sound.

A room's sound needs to be complementary to the source being recorded, and to the aesthetic goals of the project. Unfortunately, the small square and rectangular rooms commonly found in home and project studios are not ideal for recording or mixing – unless alterations are made to their acoustical properties.

Many consumers and gear-heads are excited to buy a new mic or pre-amp and expect it to radically improve their recordings – but the full value of that new equipment will not be fully realized until it is used in a good sounding room. If a recording room has acoustical problems, great performers with great instruments cannot be recorded well – even by the best mics and pre-amps. It isn't possible to turn a small square room into a perfect sounding room – but it is possible to fix some of its major acoustical problems. Ultimately, if you want your recording to sound like it was done in one of the world's best professionally designed and constructed studio rooms, then you have to go and record in one of the world's best professionally designed and constructed studio rooms!

8.2   LIVE ROOMS

A *live* room has *reflective* boundaries – the walls, floor, and ceiling are hard surfaces that reflect sound back into the room. Musicians and performers generally like bright reflective rooms because the reflections provide instant feedback about how they sound. Live rooms:

- Provide natural reflections and reverberant content, giving recordings life, vitality, and excitement.
- Provide a natural reverberant "glue" that gels multiple performers together.

A desirable large room characteristic is *isolation* within the room. This means that the sound from a sound source in one part of the room should not overpower or cause significant spill issues in the mics set up on another sound source elsewhere in the room. Simple square and rectangular rooms do not have good intra-room isolation. The carefully designed, "irregular" geometry of professional facilities contributes to better intra-room isolation characteristics.

Figure 8.1 A live room with hard, reflective surfaces that reflect the sound back into the room towards the mics and performers. (Kansas City Kansas Community College, Kansas City, KS).

8.3 DEAD ROOMS

A *dead* room is one in which the boundaries absorb sound rather than reflect it. Absorptive acoustical materials are strategically placed on walls and ceilings. An overly dead room, such as a voice over booth, is a very unnatural environment and can be uncomfortable to those not familiar with that acoustic. Musicians generally find dead rooms more challenging to perform in – the room does not naturally supply as much instant feedback, so some musicians have difficulty relaxing and performing confidently. A good engineer will have a little light reverb dialed into the headphone mix to help the performer and increase their comfort level in a dead space. It is not desirable or necessary to record this reverb, but it is an important part of the headphone mix.

Dead rooms:

- Mitigate some of the acoustical problems caused by less than ideal "live" room shapes, sizes, and dimensions.
- Give the engineer more control when adding artificial reverbs and acoustics, electronically.

Non-classical vocals are one of the few sources that record better in a dead room.

Figure 8.2   A dead room has absorptive surfaces that minimize reflections. (Sky Recording, Kansas City, MO).

8.4   ROOM SIZE

The size of a room is often an indication of its characteristics and best uses. Is the room small, medium, or large? Generally, the larger the room, the easier it is to control and to make acoustically suitable for recording. For different room sizes there are sought after *golden ratios* of length, width, and height – which are rarely attainable except in new constructions or big budget remodels.

Small live rooms tend to be the most problematic to record in. The reflected sound the mics pick up (even when close miking) tends to sound small and compact – because the reflections are temporally very close to the dry, direct sound. Loud sound sources can overload small rooms, resulting in confused and muddy recordings, which lack clarity and transparency.

Small rooms are generally treated with acoustical absorption to reduce problematic reflections, however in most cases the treatment needed to control these problems leaves the room too dull and lifeless – characteristics that then become prevalent in recordings made in the room. Absorption products become less effective at lower frequencies, so it's easy to end up with a room that sounds dull because too much high frequency content is absorbed, while boomy low frequency problems have not been addressed. On the other hand, a small, dead room works well for vocals and voice recording.

Larger live rooms have a more open sound – the reflections add desirable characteristics of depth and space. Depending on the size, geometry, and boundary materials, large live rooms can exhibit either big and bold, but relatively short and tight "room" sounds, *or* more extended swishy reverb tails. A well designed large live room can make instruments like drums sound huge and impressive as well as and acoustically glue sound sources together.

8.5   CUBIC AIRSPACE

Cubic airspace is important!

Too much sound is problematic in a small room because the sound does not have enough airspace in which to disperse and decay – the frequency balance of the sound is changed, and the reflections in the room become too prevalent in the recording. On the other hand, a room that is large and reflective is going to impose its longer reverberation characteristics on all the recorded sound sources in the room – even when close miking. Bad, inappropriate, or excess room character is impossible to remove from a recording – so it is important to record in rooms that suit the sound sources and the project aesthetic.

The more instruments or voices that are being recorded simultaneously, the larger the room needs to be – not only in terms of square footage, but also height. A room with low ceilings will always sound like a room with low ceilings – there will be a compact character to it, because the sound has nowhere to go, and it may be impossible to get mics as high as they really should go. Low ceilings are great for absorbent vocal or amplifier booths, but not for a choir or jazz big-band. Artificial reverb cannot remove the small room or low ceiling reflections already recorded – it can only add to them.

8.6   STANDING WAVES AND RESONANT FREQUENCIES

Parallel surfaces are particularly undesirable in recording rooms and control rooms! *Standing waves* occur when a sound wave reflects back over and interacts with itself.

Axial, one-dimensional standing waves are the simplest and easiest to predict. They occur between two reflective parallel surfaces, for example, the front and rear walls, or the side walls, or the floor and ceiling. Each of those dimensions is probably different and each generates a different set of potential problem frequencies. Standing waves will boom or ring noticeably after the actual sound source has silenced, or will seem weak, as if something that should be there has disappeared. This ringing, or *resonance*, is most prevalent in smaller rooms.

The lowest potential axial standing wave frequencies for a room's dimensions are calculated using the equation:

$$f = v / 2L$$

v is the speed of sound, and L the length, width, or height

If the length of a room is 3.6 m (12 ft), the lowest problem frequency is 47 Hz:

$$344 \ (m/s) \div 7.2 \ (m) = 47 \ Hz$$
$$1130 \ (ft/s) \div 24 \ (ft) = 47 \ Hz$$

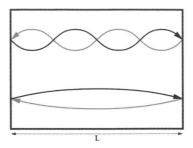

Figure 8.3 Two frequencies a sound source might generate are shown reflecting axially between two parallel walls in a room. The bottom plot represents the lowest frequency that can cause an axial standing wave – a half wavelength. The top plot represents a higher frequency at a multiple of the half wavelength frequency.

Other potential standing waves will occur at multiples of each dimension's fundamental frequency, so 94 Hz, 141 Hz, 188 Hz, 235 Hz, etc. for this dimension. Similar calculations should also be made for the width and height dimensions if the surfaces are parallel and at all reflective.

There will be places in the room where these frequencies either constructively reinforce (boost) or destructively cancel (attenuate) as they reflect over themselves. A microphone's position in the room will determine whether it is in an area of destructive or constructive interference for a particular frequency. An area of destructive interference for one particular frequency (or set of frequencies) may be an area of constructive interference for a different frequency (or set of frequencies).

Tangential standing waves occur when a sound wave bounces around a room in a two-dimensional pattern between four surfaces, and *oblique* standing waves occur in three dimensions between all six (or more) surfaces in a room.

Even though a sound source may be a point source (such as a loudspeaker or a singer's mouth), standing waves are generated throughout the room, because sound waves do not reflect like laser beams, but over a hemisphere of angles, rapidly creating an infinite number of complex reflection paths, some of which will create standing waves. The higher a standing wave frequency is, the less significant its effect is likely to be. The larger the room, the lower the potential standing wave frequencies are – in many cases approaching the lower limits of audibility.

Identical, or very similar dimensions between multiple rooms axes are particularly undesirable, square rooms being the worst because although there are fewer different standing wave frequencies, the problems at those frequencies are greatly increased. A room with non-identical dimensions may have more problem frequencies, but each problem is less pronounced. A very small cube-shaped room 8 ft (length) × 8 ft (width) × 8 ft (height) will be very difficult to record or mix great sound in even with extensive acoustical treatment!

8.7   FLUTTER ECHO

Flutter echo is produced when sound reflections between two parallel surfaces are perceived as individual events. A "ringy" or "pingy" character is imposed on all the sound in the room, affecting its frequency content and most noticeably producing an echo after percussive events. Flutter echo can be heard in rooms with dimensions as small as 4.5 m (15 ft) if there are parallel untreated reflective surfaces, *or* if the parallel surfaces at either end of this dimension are not as acoustically treated as the other surfaces in the room. A microphone placed close to a sound source at one end of a 6 m (20 ft) dimension will pick up a reflection approximately 40 ms later, and then at subsequent 40 ms intervals as the sound travels to the opposite wall and then back to the microphone repeatedly.

8.8   MICROPHONE DIRECTIONALITY AND ROOM CONSIDERATIONS

If a room is very reflective and live, cardioid and hyper-cardioid microphones used close to the sound source will minimize the room sound picked up. However, directional mics exhibit proximity effect when used close to a sound source and often have muddy sounding off-axis characteristics – so recordings can quickly gain excess low frequency build-up. Moving the same directional mics further away will reduce proximity effect, but increase the relative level of (potentially poor sounding) off-axis reflected sound picked up.

Omnidirectional mics have similar tonal characteristics whether used 6 inches or 6 feet from a sound source due to their lack of proximity effect. They can produce transparent and spacious recordings at a greater variety of distances than directional mics. They do pick up much more off-axis spill and room reflections than cardioid or hyper-cardioid mics though. The amount of reflected sound picked up can be decreased by positioning the mic closer to the sound source – but even with an omni mic the zoom factor of a close positioning can impair the sound. A recording that sounds bad because the mic was too close will only sound slightly better even if corrective EQ is possible.

If a room's sound is not desirable, or bad sounding spill is too prevalent, omnidirectional mics are not a good choice – it is impossible to remove spill and room sound during mixing. In a less than good sounding room, directional mics are usually preferable, even though you have to work harder to find the best mic position and probably end up using corrective EQ.

Bidirectional mics are a great solution when extreme side rejection is required, as long as there is not too much spill or reflected room sound coming from behind the mic, because of their sensitivity at 180°.

In order to be able to beneficially use the widest choice of microphones and mic techniques it is necessary to make the recording room suitable for its intended purpose.

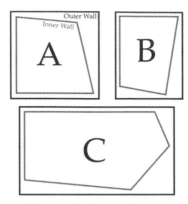

Figure 8.4 Some "room within room" shapes. Rooms A and B have no parallel inner walls, and only one set of perpendicular walls. With a little more engineering, pentagonal shapes can also be used, as shown in room C.

8.9   ROOM SHAPE

To avoid standing waves and flutter echoes, parallel walls and surfaces should be avoided. In new construction or an extensive renovation this is relatively easy to do. Even with a low budget it is possible to build additional drywall surfaces into a room to create non-parallel walls, and with the addition of some doors, any large spaces behind a new angled interior wall can be usefully repurposed as storage!

If room within room construction or renovation is not possible, various commercially available acoustical products can be applied to existing wall and ceiling surfaces to reduce standing waves, flutter echo, and excess liveness.

8.10   ABSORPTION

Standing waves, flutter echo, and excess reverberation can be controlled by applying *absorption* products to walls and ceilings to soak up some of the sound hitting those boundaries and reflect less sound back into the room, as shown previously in **Figure 8.2**. Absorption products are generally applied along parallel axes of a recording room in "equal but opposite" patterns. Twenty percent coverage using a good absorption product can have a significant effect. *It is not necessary to cover every square inch of the surfaces!* Over-treatment will produce a room that is too dead and dry for most recording purposes, and the recorded sound will be dull, lifeless, and probably muddy and boomy.

Absorption products have an *NRC* rating – *Noise Reduction Coefficient*. This is a measure of how much sound they absorb. Values between 0 and 1 (or more) are typical. The higher the NRC, the better the product is at absorbing sound. NRC is not a simple percentage and an NRC of 1 does not indicate complete absorption – values higher than 1 are possible.

Absorption products have an average NRC calculated for all frequencies and also individual NRCs for different octave bands. High frequencies are very easy to absorb and control, while lower frequencies are much more difficult. *All absorption products become less effective at lower frequencies.*

To control lower frequencies, the absorption product must be thicker, and be appropriately placed away from a boundary – ideally a quarter wavelength away, which is a realistically impossible distance from a wall for lower frequencies! Inexpensive one inch thick foam, with an overall NRC of about 0.5, is only good at absorbing mid and high frequencies (1 KHz and above) – it has little effect on the low-mid and low frequencies. Two inch thick foam is a commonly purchased broadband absorption product, and has an overall NRC of around 0.8 – but it is only effective above about 500 Hz. This means that a room treated exclusively with this product will still have low and low-mid frequency standing waves and a relative deficiency of high frequency liveness and brightness, causing the room to sound dull, muddy, and boomy.

The effective frequency range of absorption products can be significantly extended downwards by positioning them away from the wall (or ceiling) by a few inches using some kind of spacer. However, control of frequencies below 150 Hz is still difficult, because their wavelengths are so large relative to the 1 to 4 inch thick absorption products typically applied for broadband control. *Bass traps* are specific products designed to absorb the longer wavelengths of low frequency energy. They are much bigger and thicker products that are usually placed in corners or along axes where multiple boundaries intersect – locations where bass frequencies can be most efficiently absorbed.

If you intend to use acoustical foam, you should check building codes in your area. Some foams do not meet fire code regulations for construction materials and cannot be used. Mineral fiber or mineral wool products offer more effective absorption and better fire retardancy than foam.

8.11 DIFFUSION

An alternative to absorption is to scatter reflections so that they don't directly reflect directly back on themselves to create standing waves or flutter echoes. *Diffusion*, in the form of *diffusors*, randomly disperses reflections (rather than absorb them). Diffusion retains a room's sense of liveness and open space, and does not change the frequency content of the sound in the room – avoiding the dulling and muddying effects that too much absorption has. Commercial diffusion products are readily available, ranging from inexpensive styrofoam to expensive wooden devices, or they can be home built.

A mixture of absorption and diffusion is typically applied to many medium and large rooms, to absorb excess reflections while randomly scattering a controlled amount back into the room. In some studio designs, some walls are treated exclusively with diffusion and others with absorption. In other designs a mixture of absorption and diffusion is applied to each

Figure 8.5 A home built diffusive wall randomly scatters reflections, opening up the sound of the room, and keeping it relatively bright.

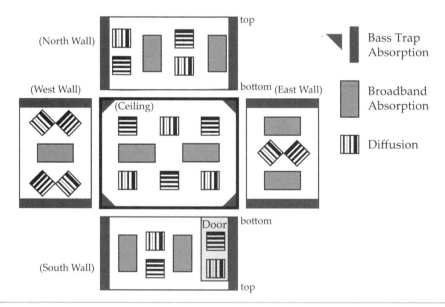

Figure 8.6 A generic treatment of a small- to medium-sized rectangular room. Standing waves and flutter echoes are reduced using a combination of absorption and diffusion products, and bass traps are used to tighten up the low frequency sound of the room.

surface. An acoustical consultant and some relatively superficial room-within-room construction are the best way to get great sounding recording rooms, and the materials for home-built custom treatment often cost less than buying commercial wall mounted treatments. But if an acoustician or simple construction are not realistic options, most reputable manufacturers of commercial acoustical treatment products offer consultation services to help the end user make informed purchasing and treatment decisions.

8.12 THE PURPOSE OF THE ROOM

The sound sources and the musical styles to be recorded dictate a room's desired acoustical characteristics. This is why some facilities feature only acoustically dead vocal booths, others feature semi-live large ensemble spaces, and others have a mixture of live reverberant drum rooms, semi-live, and dead rooms.

- Drums certainly benefit from being recorded in fairly live, medium to large rooms. Without the reflections of those sized rooms the recorded drum sounds can be dead and lifeless.
- Acoustic guitars and most other acoustic instruments really benefit from being recorded in at least a slightly reflective room – the life is sucked out of them if the room is too dead. Conversely, a recording made in a room that is too reverberant will have too much potentially inappropriate room sound, and lack clarity and intelligibility.
- Pop vocals and spoken word are usually best recorded in very dry rooms to maximize intelligibility and provide a clean, intimate, up close perspective. The engineer then has the ability to add artificial acoustics and effects during mixing. It *is* appropriate to cover a high percentage of the surface area of a vocal booth with absorption.
- Rooms can be too live, even though they do not have parallel surfaces and standing wave problems. Minimal absorption can be applied in order to tame the excess liveness. In medium to large rooms sometimes just one or two surfaces will be treated. In smaller rooms, partial but equal treatment of all surfaces usually produces better results.
- A room that is "too bright" generally has a frequency imbalance in its reflection characteristic. Thin boundaries reflect higher frequencies while letting lower frequencies pass through them and escape. Thinner absorptive treatments can be used to "darken" a room's sound because they are only effective at absorbing higher frequencies.
- A room that is "too dark" or "too dull" does not have enough high frequency reflection – probably due to too much absorptive treatment in the room. Diffusion can be added to brighten up a dull sounding room without adding standing wave or flutter echo potential.

Recording Room Acoustics

Example 8.1: A drum set recorded in a larger live room is exciting!

Example 8.2: The same drum set recorded in a smaller deader room is dull and lifeless.

Example 8.3: A pop vocal recorded in a smaller deader room is controllable, mixable, and in-your-face.

Example 8.4: The same vocal recorded in a larger live room cannot escape the reverb of the room. This "dry" track is less clear, and less punchy.

8.13 ACOUSTICAL "HOME REMEDIES"

Let's get a few myths out of the way!

- Egg boxes are not a good absorption product. They are effective over only a very narrow mid frequency range, above which they act as diffusion. Plus, they are not at all fire retardant!
- Curtains are relatively thin, providing only high frequency absorption and therefore muddying the sound of the room. They are an ineffective absorption solution. If you must use curtains in a recording or mixing room, get the thickest, heaviest ones you can. They will be more effective over a wider frequency range, although no curtains will effectively absorb low frequencies.
- Carpet, too, is relatively thin – so lining walls with it is inappropriate and will darken and muddy the room sound by absorbing only high frequency content.

So, what "on hand," cheaper, temporary home remedies can reduce some of the more significant and common acoustical problems found in smaller rooms?

- Egg crate-style foam mattress pad material can be fixed to walls as absorption – however, commercial absorption products look better, perform better, and reputable products are more fire retardant. It is possible to cut ugly pink or yellow mattress pads into smaller squares, and cover them with nice looking material – but this could make them less fire retardant, so it still isn't a solution for commercial use. Open-cell foam is preferred for acoustical absorption because of its more even absorption characteristics throughout its effective frequency range. Closed-cell foam should be avoided because its frequency abruption characteristics are uneven. It's definitely advisable to spend the extra money on a good quality, open-cell commercial absorption product, or make absorbers from wood framed mineral wool, wrapped with fire retardant material.
- Comforters and duvets are relatively thick and heavy, so they can be used as temporary absorption solutions. They can be hung over extended mic stands to form enclosures around instruments or a singer and their microphone. They can also be very effective when draped over an open grand piano lid to separate the piano sound from the other sources in the room – including a pianist/vocalist who wants to sing at the same time as playing the piano. They can be hung on walls as broadband absorption, reducing standing waves, flutter echoes, and live room sound – but cheap thin, lightweight products will not have much of an effect on low or low-mid frequencies. Low frequency absorption can be increased by spacing the comforter a few inches or more from the wall.
- A sofa or a couple of soft comfortable lounging chairs with thick heavy cushions positioned in the corners or around the edge of the room are effective bass traps.
- Bass traps can be relatively inexpensively made from commercial construction products – mineral fiber or rock wool panels and fiberglass insulation. One approach is to use 4"

thick mineral wool, framed around the edges to form 2 ft by 4 ft panels, with the mineral wool material kept in place with chicken wire. The whole thing is then wrapped in a material such as burlap in order to keep the mineral wool fibers from escaping and becoming an irritant or dust. Those panels can be placed (in order of preference):

1. At 45°, down the corners of the room.

2. Along the wall/ceiling intersections.

Another common design involves making cylinders of mineral wool, rock wool, or dense flexible fiberglass, which are covered with material. These bass traps are then placed in the corners of the room. A third design involves cutting 2 foot by 2 foot panels of mineral fiber diagonally in half to form triangles, lightly gluing these triangles together to form columns, covering them with material so they look nice, and stacking them floor to ceiling in the corners of the room. An internet search for "homemade bass traps" will provide lots of information.

- A *gobo*, or *sound barrier* can be easily constructed from some wooden plank frames and plywood, the plywood covered with absorption, and the whole thing wrapped in nice looking material. Put on casters, these moveable barriers can be placed between sound sources to either isolate them from each other or from the room. Treating one side of a gobo with thick absorption, and the other with diffusion provides various options of sound control.

- Commercial mic stand mounted absorption can be positioned behind microphones to reduce reflections of the sound source that can produce comb filtering after they bounce off an untreated wall or the control room window behind the mic.

Figure 8.7 The guitar speaker cabinet and its mic (in the right of the picture) can be placed inside the "cage" of homemade gobos (in the left of the picture) to isolate it from the room and reduce its spill into any mics set up on other sound sources in the room.

PRACTICAL EXERCISE

- Set up a vocal or instrument microphone in your usual recording room.
- Record examples of the same sound source using different acoustical treatments behind the sound source, behind the mic, and to the sides of the mic and sound source.
- In a fairly live or untreated room, try absorption products.
- In a well-treated or acoustically dry room, try diffusion products.
- If the room has a hardwood, tile, or stone floor, try recording with some carpet or a rug on the floor, and then with it removed.
- Listen and evaluate the room sound in these recordings. Listen for complex reverberation characteristics (or the lack of them), and phasey, thin sounds produced by flat reflective surfaces if the rear of the mic is close to a wall or window.

Recording Vocals

IN THIS CHAPTER:

9.1 IS IT *REALLY* ABOUT THE MIC?

In a book about microphones and mic techniques, I have to start this chapter by saying that the mics and recording technology are secondary to the performance, and that a good portion of this chapter will not focus on mics or mic techniques! A technically better vocal sound, captured on a super-expensive bling-sputtered large diaphragm condenser mic will not persuade the public to buy more records than a killer vocal performance recorded with a dynamic mic costing the same as two dinners! But as an audio professional it is important to aim for the highest technical standards.

The vocal is the most important element of many musical styles – particularly pop and commercial music. It is the vocal performance that most listeners identify as "the song," and is often the element you spend the most time getting right when tracking and mixing.

9.2 GETTING THE PERFORMANCE

Many bands and singers are used to doing live performances where any little mistake is over as soon as it's happened – to be corrected at the next performance. The recording studio can be an unfamiliar environment. Everything about their performance is put under a microscope. Little flaws are magnified (the sound, tone and timbre; inflections and phrasings; wrong notes, wrong words, etc.), and any blemishes recorded will exist for the life of the recording. This puts the performer under a great deal of pressure, and they have to be prepared to work to a level of precision and perfection that they may not be accustomed to, or initially comfortable with, sometimes for an extended time.

To have a good session and deliver "the" performance, a singer needs to be:

- 100 percent comfortable with the material they're recording. They must know the song top to bottom, inside out, and upside down!
- Feeling good, and in good health.
- Having a good day.
- In the mood to focus for an extended period.
- Able to respond to constructive criticism – leaving the ego at home!

To get a singer relaxed and comfortable, have on hand any supplies they might need – drinks, lozenges to suck on between takes, etc. Avoid sugary drinks – focus on lemon and herbal teas instead. After doing a few vocal sessions, any engineer, producer, or studio owner should have a list of items that should be provided for all subsequent vocal sessions.

The recording room also needs to create the right ambience and atmosphere. It should be clean and professional looking – generic, but warm and welcoming. Learn your performer's quirks, likes, and dislikes. If they like to be surrounded by candles and low lighting, make it happen. Anticipating and providing for a client's every need is your job. It makes you look good, assures you of future custom, and results in good word of mouth advertising from satisfied clients.

The engineer and producer's interactions with a performer can set them at ease and promote a great performance, or conversely, keep the singer from being able to deliver "the" performance. As an engineer and/or producer, you will be communicating with the artist via the talkback system in the studio. You must be able to:

- Communicate well, and speak the singer's vocabulary – musical and technical.
- Be clearly and easily understood.
- Be personable.
- Quickly develop a trusting professional relationship with the artist.

With the exception of legendary professionals who can deliver amazing performances regardless of the situation around them, most artists perform better if they feel comfortable with and trust the engineer and producer.

TALKBACK...

Be careful and aware of what is being transmitted through the talkback system – and what is not! You have a performer in the studio who is in an unnatural and uncomfortable place, where everything they do is put under the sonic microscope – it can make some people very insecure. If you are telling a joke to someone in the control room, make sure the performer hears it too, otherwise they may look into the control room, see people laughing, and assume that they are the joke.

You should be a coach – the most important use of the talkback system is for you to listen to what is being said and also what is not being said, and to respond appropriately to get the performer to deliver their best performance.

KNOW YOUR MUSIC THEORY!

It is essential that music engineers understand basic music theory, and the sound sources being recorded – otherwise it is impossible to communicate musically and coach the performers towards delivering a magical performance. Experienced performers have favorite engineers and producers because they have, over the years, developed a bond, trust, and musical understanding, and they work well together.

BE A PROFESSIONAL!

As a home or project studio owner/engineer, or an employee in a commercial studio, you should:

- Have a personality, demeanor, and be presented in a way that is likeable, polite, and positive.
- Be able to quickly establish professional trust and a close working relationship with the artist.
- Quickly establish what role the client wants you to fulfill. Are you simply the engineer, capturing their performance to the best technical standards? Or is the client receptive to feedback and coaching – *producing* – from you in order to get them to deliver the performance the song needs?
- Know the sound sources you are recording. How do they sound naturally? How does a good recording of that particular voice or instrument sound? What microphones and techniques can be used to obtain those goals?
- Be able to talk music, instruments, and gear. Know scales, chords, and rhythm values – it will help when discussing the musicality of parts and performances. Know how instruments and amplifiers work, so that if something doesn't sound right, or isn't working properly, you can offer helpful suggestions to remedy the problem.
- Be a psychologist! If things aren't going well, what can you say or do in order to improve the physical, psychological, or emotional state of the artists and help them deliver the performance of their life?
- Be positive! Ultimately, if something about the performance is not quite right, someone in the control room (the producer, engineer, or producer/engineer in most home and project studio environments) should be able to identify what's not right and encourage the performer to try something slightly different to make it right. A simple "It sounds great! But let's try the last phrase again, and I really want you to focus and push into the high note at the end" promotes a much better performance, vibe, and relationship between both sides of the soundproof glass than, "OK, let's try that again because you were flat and late on the last note."

9.3   VOCAL TRACKING METHODS

When using analog tape, the number of tracks is more limited than on modern DAWs. It used to be common practice to record three or four vocal tracks, either in their entirety or with a punch in or two, and then *comp* or compile a good vocal track from the best parts of each of those tracks to a spare tape track. When using a modern DAW, it's possible to use an approach similar to this, or to work on the vocal track more linearly, top to bottom, concentrating on getting each phrase right before moving on to the next, punching in and re-recording on the same track as many times as necessary.

Punching in on analog tape is a destructive process – there is no Command-Z to undo a punch that is too early and accidentally erased the end of the previous phrase! Tape stretches and wears out the more it is stopped, rewound, stopped, played, and cycled – so re-recording or punching in a particular phrase too many times is not good for the tape or its sound. This type of wear and tear is irrelevant when using modern DAWs, and most systems have an "undo" feature in case of an incorrect punch or edit.

Some pros and cons of recording a handful of complete vocal takes, and comping the best parts together to form the vocal performance include:

- Continuity is generally better – phrasing, performance intensity, and style are more consistent throughout the longer takes.
- The process is more comfortable for a performer who is used to singing the song top to bottom, and not jumping in somewhere in the middle.
- There may still be parts of the performance that are less than perfect, despite recording multiple versions.

Some pros and cons of building up a vocal performance on one track, and punching in, making as many edits as necessary include:

- A perfect performance is possible on one track. This means that only one set of processing plug-ins, or one mixer channel is necessary during mixing, and the mix process is more streamlined.
- Depending on the singer, there may be less continuity of phrasing, intensity, and performance style.
- There may be more timbre or tonal differences between different punches, created by inconsistencies in the distance between the singer and the mic.
- If the singer does not know the song intimately enough and cannot deliver convincing performances of isolated smaller phrases, punching may be a slow process.

One good approach for most home and project studio situations is a hybrid, somewhere in-between the two tracking methods described above:

- Record multiple takes, top to bottom, or in large sections.
- Identify which take has the best performance of each part of the song.
- Identify any sections or phrases that are still not ideal, and punch in to replace those on an additional track as necessary. Use plenty of pre-roll and post-roll, so that the singer is confident of their entry, and so that you can spot continuity differences, and fix them immediately.
- Comp the final performance together from these tracks.

Whichever method you use, have a copy of the lyrics on hand so you (or an assistant) can mark off which parts of each take are good, as you are recording. This way, you instantly know which sections you still have to work on. Even if you are building a track a small section at a time, having the singer warm up with a couple of beginning to end run throughs will help them feel comfortable.

IS IT REALLY ABOUT PERFECTION?

QUESTION: What's more important to the success of a song? A) the emotion, energy, and overall performance style? Or B) the fact that one note was a little off here or there?

ANSWER: A! The overall musicality, power, and emotion of a performance are more important than perfection. A minor blemish will go unnoticed by most listeners in the context of an otherwise amazing performance. As a last resort, minor mistakes may be correctable using pitch and time editing tools – but those tools leave telltale signs, and over-correction will remove the groove, style, and musicality from the performance.

9.4   MIKING INDIVIDUALS

Large diaphragm cardioid condenser microphones are the usual choice for vocal recording because of their big, hyped, detailed sound. They are often mounted upside down on a large boom stand – this way the mic and stand do not block sight lines to any music stand below the mic. Even though large diaphragm mics are more popular choices, small diaphragm mics, which are usually flatter and more transparent, may suit some singers.

A *pop filter* should always be used for voice recording when the mic is within a couple of feet of the singer. Make sure there are at least a few inches between the singer and the pop filter, *and* the pop filter and the mic – the pop filter needs this distance on both sides to work effectively and dissipate the plosive air currents that cause pops and booms.

If you have access to multiple vocal mics, you should experiment with them to decide which one suits the singer best and produces the most pleasing sound. Just because a certain mic is another engineer's favorite doesn't mean it will sound great on the singers you're recording. For example, a mic that has a presence peak where a singer's sibilance or nasal resonance lies, will rarely be flattering.

Think about mic distance and proximity effect:

- For an up-close and in-your-face sound, position the mic closer to the singer, 10 to 15 cm (4 to 6 in) away, with a pop filter between the mic and singer.
- For a more natural, transparent sound with more of a sense of depth, position the mic 20 to 30 cm or more (9 to 12 in) away from the singer.

The further away a directional mic is, the less proximity effect there will be, but the more room sound there will be – so listen for warmth and fullness vs clarity and diction in addition to direct sound vs room sound as you move the mic back and forth to find the ideal position.

Don't forget about the more open, honest, and transparent character of omnidirectional mics! Their lack of proximity effect allows the singer to get closer without muddy coloration – but make sure there is still enough distance to allow the pop filter to work. There will be more room sound picked up by an omnidirectional mic, particularly potentially problematic reflections from any window or wall directly in front of the singer – but if the singer is close to the mic, and the mic is at least a few feet away from any wall or window, reflections will be minimized relative to the direct sound.

Some vocal mic techniques to try include:

1. The most "in-your-face" and brightest sound is produced by close miking. The mic is typically placed directly in front of the performer, at a distance of 10 to 15 cm (4 to 6 in), with a pop filter midway between the vocalist and microphone.

2. A slightly less bright sound, less prone to the booms and pops of plosive air currents, is produced when the microphone is positioned just above the singer's mouth, facing directly forward. The mic is not directly on-axis to the mouth, hence the slightly less bright sound which may mellow some excess sibilance.

3. Positioning the mic at, or slightly above eye height, angled down towards the mouth keeps it out of plosive air blasts, but on-axis to the mouth. This technique restores some of the brightness lost in the previous technique. It also encourages the singer to face straight ahead and slightly upwards, possibly improving their sound and performance. It is also easy to set this mic over and out of the way of a music stand. Angling the mic towards the nose instead of the mouth will change the characteristics of the sound picked up – whether this is beneficial or not depends on the singer!

4. Positioning the mic below the mouth, angled up towards the mouth can sometimes benefit a singer who sounds thin and nasally, or overly sibilant. The sound will be fuller and warmer, but less punchy than other close placements. If a music stand is being used this technique can be difficult to set up though.

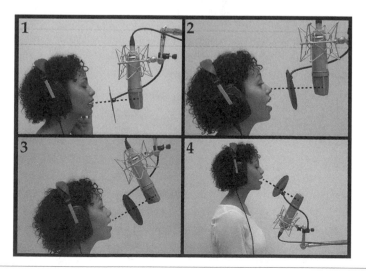

Figure 9.1   The different vocal mic positions described in the main text.

If the singer needs lyrics or music, use a music stand – otherwise you'll hear the rustling of hand held papers. The music stand should be positioned high enough that it does not encourage the singer to look down – if they do occasionally look down, their position relative to the microphone is changed and the timbre of the recorded voice will fluctuate. The music stand is also a hard reflective surface that causes reflections that the mic may pick up, coloring the vocal sound. Covering the stand with a piece of carpet can help minimize these reflections, as can angling the stand more horizontally so the reflections bounce behind the mic rather than into it.

Do encourage good mic technique! If a singer is getting much louder on some notes or phrases, have them lean back from the mic slightly. If there are very quiet passages they can lean into the mic a little. This will even out their recorded levels, making compression and mixing easier. Do watch out for excessive tonal changes related to proximity effect and reflected sound if the singer to mic distance changes – if there are any distracting timbral changes, have them maintain a more constant distance from the mic, adjust your recording levels accordingly, and be prepared to have compressors work a little harder during mixing.

Ultimately, it's all about the performance. So if the artist you're working with can only feel at home if they have a handheld mic so they can sing like they do on stage, give them a handheld mic. The handheld mic could be a prop, with a studio vocal mic set up just beyond it, or it may be the mic you record through.

Solo Vocal Recording

No EQ is used on these examples.

Example 9.1: A vocal recorded with a cardioid mic just a few inches away. This perspective may be considered too close.

Example 9.2: The same singer recorded with a cardioid mic about 9 inches away. The sound is close and powerful, but still fairly natural sounding.

Example 9.3: A vocal recorded with a cardioid mic, about 18 inches away. This sound may be too distant for some aesthetics, but favored for others because of its organic neutrality.

Example 9.4: A vocal recorded with an omnidirectional mic, just a few inches from the mic. Notice the lack of proximity effect compared to the close cardioid mic recording.

9.5   VOICE AND ACOUSTIC GUITAR

Some singer/guitarists need to sing and play at the same time – it is difficult or impossible for them to perform well when they try to record the guitar or vocals in isolation.

Figure 9.2 A singer/guitarist miked with cardioid mics. Each mic picks up significant off-axis (colored) spill.

Figure 9.3 Using bidirectional mics on-axis to their desired sound source reduces spill, but the nulls are not quite aligned with the respective sources of spill, so rejection is not maximized.

Figure 9.2 shows vocal and acoustic guitar being recorded simultaneously. Using a cardioid or hyper-cardioid mic on the voice, the guitar is off-axis, below the mic's main pickup. The guitar spill is subject to the mic's off-axis coloration, and doesn't usually sound good. A cardioid mic (or two) on the guitar, provides a good guitar sound, but vocal spill is colored by the guitar mic's off-axis characteristics.

Bidirectional mics can be exploited to minimize spill between the voice and guitar, as long as there are no sound sources or undesirable room reflections behind the mics. Because bidirectional mics reject sound directly above and below them, there will be less voice picked up by the guitar mic, and less guitar picked up by the vocal mic, as shown in **Figure 9.3**.

Aiming the mics by their null points (at 90° and 270°) will reduce spill even further. Listening carefully for proximity and perspective changes, front/back distance adjustments can also be made to really get the null points aimed at the sources of spill while keeping the desired sound sources on-axis. With a good mic, even if the voice or guitar do end up just a few degrees off-axis, the sound should still be great. In fact, if the vocals are over sibilant or the guitar is too bright, moving the mic slightly off-axis will gently roll off some high frequencies as a preferable alternative to EQ. A null point optimized set up is shown in **Figure 9.4**.

Figure 9.4 The angles and distances from the mics to their respective sound sources are changed to keep them more on axis with their desired sources while aiming their null points at the sources of spill.

THE HEADPHONE MIX

In the control room you have probably dialed in a rough mix that sounds good to you, and which may be a good starting point for the final mix. That mix may not give the singer (or other performer) what they need to hear in order to stay in time and in tune – so be prepared to provide them with an alternate mix. In a DAW this can be achieved using a stereo pair of auxiliary sends containing different amounts of each track than the control room mix.

Concentrate the singer's mix on the essentials that provide rhythm and pitch information:

- Drums.
- Bass.
- Rhythm guitars.
- Piano, and traditional keyboard sounds.

If the singer is having trouble with rhythm, increase the ratio of rhythmic sounds in their mix. If they are having trouble with pitch, increase the sound of pitched content, and possibly themselves. If you turn something up, try to turn some other elements down, so that the headphone volume doesn't creep up and get out of control. Ultimately you'll have to experiment to see what works best for each singer.

IS THE SINGER CONSTANTLY FLAT?

- Reduce their level in the headphones. This encourages them to sing louder – and in the process, open up and potentially sing a little sharper.
- Turn the entire headphone mix down. Quiet sounds are perceived as being slightly sharper than loud sounds, so this can make the singer think that they are even flatter and raise their pitch to compensate.

- A little vocal compression while recording (but not recorded) will allow the singer to "go for it" a little more, and possibly hit the notes more accurately without hearing too much of themselves during louder passages.

IS THE SINGER CONSTANTLY SHARP?

- Raise their level in the headphones. This can encourage them to back off a little, and possibly sing a little flatter.
- Turn up the entire headphone mix – keeping it within safe listening levels of course. Loud sounds are perceived as slightly flatter than quiet sounds, so this could make the singer think they are sharp and lower their pitch to compensate.

REVERB IN THE HEADPHONES?

Some singers like a dry mix, others like some reverb. A little generic reverb applied to the usual mix candidates will produce a more organically blended mix that the singer may prefer to sing to. Reverb on their own vocals, while recording, also gives the singer important feedback about their performance and pitch. Most singers and musicians prefer performing in reverberant spaces, so reverb does often help – but you don't want so much that it prevents the performer from hearing the details of their performance.

It is easily possible to control all of these elements independently from the control room mix using an aux send from a DAW or mixer.

9.6   SMALL VOCAL GROUPS

If you're recording a small group of singers (backing singers or a harmony vocal group for example) you have to decide whether to record each singer individually or the whole group simultaneously. Singers from performing groups are probably used to working together. They are used to being next to each other and hearing each other at the same time – so it makes sense to set them up in the same room simultaneously. Tracking each singer separately provides more isolation (which is possibly desirable), but it does not give the singers the ensemble sound they are used to, and it may be impossible for them to hear their harmonies correctly when isolated from the full ensemble – so they may struggle and lack confidence.

If you decide to record the whole group simultaneously, you have the choice of giving each singer their own microphone, or setting them up around a single mic or stereo pair. Individual miking will give the sound an up-close perspective, a pop music "in-your-faceness," and gives you more control during mixing. When individually miking multiple singers in the same room, do adhere to the 3:1 Rule. **Figure 9.5** shows how the more directional pick-up pattern

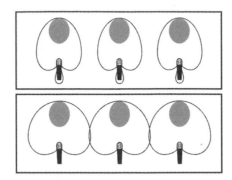

Figure 9.5 The increased directionality of hyper-cardioid mics (top) results in less spill from adjacent singers than if cardioid mics were used (bottom).

of hyper-cardioid mics can be used to usefully isolate each singer more than cardioid mics. Remember that hyper-cardioid mics are sensitive to their rear, so reflections from a glass window or wall might cause more coloration problems than if cardioid mics were used. Stand or wall mounted absorption products positioned behind the mics can reduce these reflections.

Positioning the singers around a single microphone or a stereo pair are also valid approaches, but they work only if the singers are naturally well balanced. The sound will be more unified – less individual, and more of a blended whole. This may require some extra time to physically move each singer closer to or further away from the mic until an appropriate balance and blend is achieved. Compression is trickier than on individual mics, so if a punchy, in-your-face, compressed sound is desired, individual mics should be used. Remember that if you mic a group of singers with a single mic, it will only provide a mono point source image, with no width to exploit the stereo soundstage.

9.7   LARGER CONTEMPORARY VOCAL GROUPS

Different miking options when recording choirs or large vocal groups for non-classical or "pop" projects include:

- Close, individual mics for each singer.
- A stereo pair covering the entire group.
- Multiple, spaced, zone mics.

(An approach to classical choir recording is discussed in **Chapter 15**.)

INDIVIDUAL MICS

Individual miking captures an isolated perspective of each singer, which then needs to be artificially blended into the group sound. Each voice can be processed and shaped and nuanced individually to form the mix. The engineer is in full control of the soundscape and perspective created. The benefits of individual miking include:

- Each voice can be EQ'd differently to create blend, tonal contrast, or clarity.
- Each voice can be compressed individually for maximum control and impact.
- A close-up perspective is recorded, and individual voices can be panned to create the most effective stereo image for the mix.

Individual, close miking can only be used if:

- There are enough mics!
- There are enough pre-amps and inputs.
- There are enough mixer/DAW channels and enough compressors or plug-in DSP available during mixing.
- There is enough space to set up the mics adhering to the 3:1 rule.

A STEREO PAIR

Figure 9.6 shows a single stereo pair set up for a group of singers. Any stereo array can be used – the arrays and their respective characteristics are discussed in **Chapter 6**. The stereo pair should be positioned far enough back so that its effective pick-up encompasses the entire group. It should be at head height, or slightly above pointing towards the singer's mouths, or slightly lower if floor reflections are desired.

Characteristics of stereo pair miking include:

- The natural acoustic blend of the singers is captured – they sound like a unified, cohesive group, bonded by the room characteristics.
- EQ can only be applied globally to the whole group. It is not possible to EQ one singer individually to make them blend with the group more without negatively affecting the sound of the other singers.
- Compression can only be applied globally to the entire group. It is not possible to individually compress one singer who is louder than the others. Similar to gentle mix bus compression this global compression can add some "glue" or "gel" to the sound – but it does not allow for the same amount of dynamic squash that is typical of pop and rock vocals.

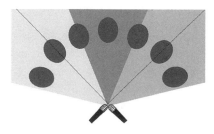

Figure 9.6   A group of singers set up around a stereo pair of mics.

- The stereo image cannot be manipulated much after recording. It must be adjusted by altering how the singers are set up and selecting an appropriate stereo array and positioning prior to recording.
- The balance between direct and reflected/reverberant content is adjusted by positioning the mic array closer to or further away from the singers. This not only affects the amount of reflected sound but also the perception of distance, front/back perspective, and stereo image width.

ZONE OR AREA MICS

For much larger groups of singers, bigger choirs for example, another option is to use multiple mics, each targeting a "zone" of the ensemble, as shown in **Figure 9.7**. The addition of more mics means that they can be positioned closer than a front array because each mic is only required to pick up a small part of the ensemble. This closer multi-miking produces an intimate perspective of a large choir that can be desirable in "pop" or non-classical projects, but is rarely desirable in traditional classical recording styles. The 3:1 rule should be adhered to – you don't want too many mics too close together. You do want the mics far enough away that each picks up a group of singers and doesn't zoom in on just the one or two voices immediately in front of it. The mics should be angled down from at least 30 cm (1 ft) above head height towards the singer's mouths.

Vocal Group Recording

Example 9.5: A vocal group recorded with individual mics.

Example 9.6: The same vocal group recorded around a stereo pair of mics.

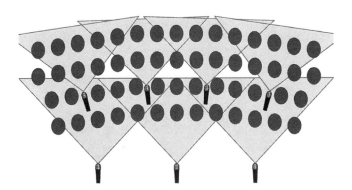

Figure 9.7 Multiple mics on a choir, each focusing on a "zone" or "area" of singers. (The pick-up areas drawn for each mic are just an approximation – it does not mean the mic doesn't pick up beyond those outlines.)

9.8 GANG VOCALS

Frequently used in contemporary pop music styles, gang vocals are different to a choir or chorus because of their unique musical intent. Gang vocals are usually unison, with lots of voices singing or yelling the same musical line to add impact and weight to certain parts of a song. They are not about being precisely in tune or robotically in time – the thickness and character of gang vocals come from tuning and timing imperfections.

The best way to record gang vocals is to get a group of people to perform together. To get a natural gang blend minimal miking should be employed. A stereo array or even a single mono mic can be used – just don't put the singers too far to the side of a directional mic, to avoid muddy off-axis sound. The illusion of even bigger gangs can be achieved by recording several takes and panning them throughout the stereo image. If multiple layers of gang vocals are desired, you can:

- Record each take in stereo, panning each one widely, on top of each other during mixing.
- Pan three mono takes, L, R, and C during mixing.
- Pan two mono takes, L and R during mixing, leaving the center of the image for the lead vocal.

Familiarity with different stereo images, panning techniques, and the gang vocal's context in the mix will help you decide what is best for the project.

TRACK STEREO AND MONO

If you have enough tracks, set up and record both a stereo array, and a single mono mic. Just because you track something, doesn't mean you have to use it! It's best to have something to discard rather than be wishing you had the extra material during mixing.

Just make sure you are disciplined enough to discard tracks if you do record multiple options and techniques. The mute button or delete feature are frequently responsible for making mixes and songs much better!

9.9 VOCAL PROCESSING TIPS

SPLIT LOUD AND QUIET SECTIONS OVER DIFFERENT TRACKS

A vocal performance with a wide dynamic range is a challenge to mix – not only because of the extensive fader movement and automation required to balance the vocals in the context of the mix, but also because it is impossible to effectively compress a track that ranges from

super-quiet to mega-loud! Vocals are compressed to make the sound more dynamically consistent, with less sudden volume dips and surges, and for the increased fullness, power, phatness,
and character that compression imparts on the sound.

- If a compressor is set to compress a loud section of vocals well, it will under-modulate
  the amplitude of quiet sections of vocal – the character and impact of the sound will be
  very different.
- If a compressor is set to compress a quiet section of vocal well, the compressor will
  over-modulate the amplitude when the singer gets very loud – squashing the sound too
  much, and sucking the life and detail out of it.

With plug-in automation in modern DAWs it is certainly possible to automate compressor
thresholds, or bypass plug-ins to switch between different compressors to fix these problems –
but an easier solution is to record the dynamically different sections of the song to different
tracks, each with its own EQ and compression, or split the relevant areas to different tracks,
after recording.

RIDE THE GAIN

With the low noise floor and large dynamic ranges of 24 and 32 bit recording systems, it's
tempting to set the vocal mic's gain based on the loudest moment of the singer's performance
and leave it there. While the quiet parts of the performance will definitely be using enough bit
resolution to sound good, it's difficult to mix and process a performance with wide dynamics
(as described above).

Engineers who work with the smaller dynamic range and limited track count of analog
tape are used to having to keep recording levels optimized and more consistent, so that quiet
sounds don't get too low and the tape hiss too present. By riding the gain to the recording
device while recording you can even out the recorded levels – you are being a manual, finger
operated compressor! You can do this regardless of whether you are recording to tape or a
DAW:

- If the singer gets quiet for a word, phrase, or section of the song, increase the gain to
  the recording device.
- As the singer builds up to a loud peak, reduce the gain to the recording device.

Have a copy of the lyrics next to you as you track. Get to know the song intimately and be
able to anticipate the singer's performance dynamics. During a practice run through or two,
mark when the singer is getting louder than average and when they are getting quieter than
average. During subsequent takes ride the signal level up during the quiet moments and down
during the louder moments. You should feel involved and connected to the singer and their
performance. You will end up with a much more even vocal track, and appropriate compression
will be easier to achieve throughout the mix, and less volume automation will be necessary.

If you're using a mixing console as the front-end into your recording system, it may be
possible to feed the recording device post-fader – in which case a fader can be used to push and

pull the recording levels. Non-stepped mic pre-amp gain controls can be used to do this, but they usually offer less precision and it's easy to over-adjust those very sensitive gain knobs.

Be careful though, particularly before you become an expert at using this technique – inappropriate gain adjustments are not easy to correct and compensate for after the fact. And a compressor or expander won't magically fix them for you!

COMPRESSION WHILE TRACKING

It used to be common for engineers to gently compress while tracking to analog tape, to avoid over-saturating the tape during loud moments and keep the levels from getting too low relative to the tape hiss during the quiet moments. The dynamic ranges offered by today's high resolution digital recording systems make this technically unnecessary most of the time, but a little gentle analog dynamic control while recording can produce a track that is easier to mix and is less likely to clip the A to D converters unexpectedly. Just a couple of dBs of gain reduction can also impart some of a desirable compressor's character (rather than perceived compression) onto the track.

If you do try this, make sure the sound of the compression *is* desirable and use just a little – it is *impossible* to undo bad sounding or inappropriate compression artifacts. Until you have thoroughly mastered compression it is advisable to track without it when using 24 bit or greater resolutions.

> By default, most DAWs do not record through their plug-ins. They just play back through them – so simply inserting a compressor plug-in on the track you're recording does not mean it's being recorded that way, and does not prevent A to D converter clipping.

COMPRESS INDIVIDUAL TRACKS, NOT GROUPS OF TRACKS

While sending 20 individual vocal tracks to a stereo group and putting a stereo compressor on the group might be more DSP efficient (or necessary if twenty hardware compressors are not available), it is usually impossible to effectively compress by more than just a few dB without undesirable amplitude modulations when doing so.

In an amateur choir there's often one singer who sings loud high notes much louder than the others – and way out of tune, but that's another issue…! Imagine this choir recorded with just one mic. If this single mic channel is compressed, the loud singer's amplitude will cause the compressor to turn the gain down – and it will turn down *all* of the other singers undesirably and inappropriately. If all of the singers have their own individual mics and each channel is compressed with its own compressor, the loud singer will be pulled down by their own compressor, while the others will not – blending the louder singer into the group.

The same situation arises if you sub-mix a group of channels or tracks to a compressor or stereo pair of compressors. A few dBs of "gel" or "glue" compression is all that is effectively possible even if all the performers are fairly consistent. More dramatic and better blends can be achieved by first compressing each track or channel individually.

DON'T OVER-EQ AS YOU RECORD

Fundamental frequency balance problems *should* be fixed as you record – particularly problems that reduce available headroom, such as an over-abundance of proximity effect on a close miked source. EQ is a last resort though, and the best solution is to adjust the mic position or mic choice in order to obtain a sound that does not need corrective EQ to sound great. But if all else fails and reducing proximity effect by moving the mic further away, or using a different mic is not an option, tweak the lows and low-mids down a little in order to get higher average levels to the recording medium. Do not be too creative at this stage – you do not yet know how the track will fit into the mix. You don't want to make EQ adjustments while tracking that end up inappropriate and require a second round of EQ to undo as you mix.

EDITING SOFTWARE VS PERFORMANCE

An engineer or producer should never settle for a substandard performance while recording. As previously discussed, "fix it in the mix" is a myth. Good luck with a singer who exclaims "you can just fix it later!" With the exception of very minor corrections (which *can* be invisible), pitch and timing editors leave behind audible artifacts as evidence of their processing when asked to do too much. After you become familiar with specific editors you'll be able to hear them working! The general public may not hear their telltale signs (with the exception of the super-clichéd Cher/T-Pain effect) – but you will! If pitch and rhythm correction software must be used, target the processing to the small segments that need correcting – do not leave the plug-ins running continuously because they can impart undesirable artifacts even when correction isn't needed.

Don't forget that a memorable song is a *musical performance*. A powerful and emotional performance is *not always about perfection*. In the context of a magical performance, a slight flaw will probably go unnoticed by most listeners. If a phrase is re-recorded in order to correct a slight problem, the emotion and power may just not be the same.

> Learning which mistakes can be fixed invisibly by editors and which ones will require re-recording will allow you to produce better vocal tracks:
>
> - If the singer can do another take and repeat the same great performance but be more in tune or better in time, recording another take should be the solution.
> - Only if the emotion and power of the performance is lost in subsequent takes, should editing software be used.

Extensive vocal editing takes time – so a "you can fix it later" artist is great for the engineer or studio billing by the hour! (But of course, more expensive for the client!) If the performer is able, it's usually much quicker to do another take! Being too attached to a performance can also lead to over-criticality – get a trusted third party set of ears in, someone who can listen with a fresh perspective and give you their opinion on what *really* needs editing or processing to fix. Even better – re-record it so it doesn't need the processing and is 100 percent natural!

9.10 VOCAL EQ FREQUENCIES

The fundamental pitch frequencies of vocals range from about 80 Hz (for the lowest notes a bass can sing) to just over 1 KHz (for the highest notes a soprano can sing). These are the frequencies that identify the pitch of the note. Harmonics above these frequencies produce the timbre of the voice, the sibilance of the "CH," "S," and "T" and "Z" sounds, and the breath and air of the sound. The following frequency information will help you focus on the correct frequency area when working on vocal tracks – but the specific frequencies and amount of boost or cut necessary will depend upon the singer, the mic, the room characteristics, and the mix context.

- *Bottom, weight.* Below 120 Hz. Usually unnecessary in the voice track, so it can be cut.
- *Boom, muddiness.* 150 to 300 Hz. Too much thickness in this range can be caused by proximity effect, in which case a low or low-mid attenuation will help vocal clarity. Conversely, some singers may need a little boost here to reduce perceived thinness or scratchiness.
- *Boxiness.* 400 to 600 Hz. This range can often be attenuated in order to give the vocal sound more clarity and intelligibility. This range includes some fundamental frequencies of higher pitched or female vocals, so attenuating too much can make the vocal sound unnaturally thin.
- *Honkiness.* 600 to 800 Hz. Attenuation here can remove a bull-horn, megaphone, AM radio-like character.
- *Definition, nasally.* 1 to 2.5 kHz. Our ears are most sensitive to this frequency range because it contains so much important speech intelligibility and diction information. It can be reduced to make a voice less *thin*, or boosted (when lacking) for more *clarity*.
- *Presence.* Around 5 kHz. Can be boosted to give the singer an edge and allow them to cut through the mix – but make sure it does not make sibilance too bright and sizzly.
- *Sibilance.* 5 to 10 kHz (different for each singer). If a singer's Ss and Ts stick out too much, use the boost-sweep-cut technique described in **Chapter 4** to find the center of their sibilance and apply a gentle attenuation.
- *Air.* A wide filter above 12 KHz. A boost of a few dBs can give a vocal a sultry, breathy intimacy. If the frequency is too low, it can boost too much sibilance, or undesirable, harsh characteristics below 8 KHz.

CHAPTER 10

Drum Miking

10.1 WHAT KIND OF SOUND DOES THE PROJECT CALL FOR?

In most pop and rock music, the drums are the second most important instrument – second only to the vocals. They provide the beat, the groove, and the foundation over which the other instruments play. Their sound can be natural, or heavily stylized and influenced by microphone, mixing, and recording techniques. Before deciding how to mic a drum set you need to be familiar with the band's sound, and all the instruments being recorded – if you don't know how specific instruments should sound, or how the musicians are trying to use them in the context of the band's sound, how can you appropriately record them? Preferably this should be done before the band comes into the studio. Listen to other recordings they've made, or check out a gig or rehearsal. If neither of those are possible, and even if they have already been done, you can't really decide what mics and mic techniques to use until you've carefully listened to the instruments in the studio. Every instrument is different, and the sonic goals of each project are different – "this is how I always mic it" doesn't guarantee the best results and is an inexcusably lazy approach to recording.

A drum set can be miked with anything from a single mono microphone, to 20 or more mics! Natural sounds tend to be preferred for jazz and folk styles, whereas huge, studio-crafted, power-house sounds provide the basis of rock music.

- Directional mics zoom into individual drums and instruments, producing a more focused sound.
- Omnidirectional mics produce a more transparent blended sound.
- As more mics are used to individually mic drums and cymbals, the closer and more discrete the recorded sound becomes.
- Using fewer mics promotes a more natural acoustic sound.
- Close miking will reveal and magnify rings and resonances our ears don't notice when listening from a distance.
- Gating can reduce close miking rings and resonances, or it can produce an ultra-clean, surgical sound.
- Compression can do anything from subtly even out varying dynamics in a performance, to totally reshaping the drum sounds into brighter snappier sounds or huge sustaining power-house sounds.

A modern rock/pop drum sound is a studio crafted sound, influenced by recording and mixing techniques so much that you must have a sonic goal in mind before starting the project.

DRUM MIKING PRACTICALITIES

- Make sure mic stands do not touch any part of the drum set.
- Make sure mic stands do not touch other mic stands.

- Make sure mic stands are set up properly – no center columns touching the floor, only the rubber feet or wheels touch the floor, clutches should be tightened but not over-tightened.
- Make sure mic cables are secured so they will not fall and touch things. Cables should always run horizontally along the floor or vertically up stands – no "loose" cables strung diagonally.
- Stress relieve cables so they do not pull on mics – you don't want to end up with hi-hat or overhead mics pointing at the ceiling half way through your session! Stand clips or gaff tape can be used for this.
- Coil slack neatly (over-under, or figure-8) near or under the mic stands. Mics and mic stands may move, so you need slack there, *not* at the snake box or mixer.
- Make sure the mics are positioned so that they are not in the way of the player. Your job is to capture a performance – the gear cannot interfere with that.

10.2 HOW MANY MICS DO YOU REALLY NEED?

On an average drum set you need at least five mics to get a contemporary drum sound and have the ability to adjust balances, EQ, compression, and effects:

- A stereo pair of condenser overheads – in front of and over the drummer's head, or directly above the drum set.
- A dynamic mic would be a traditional choice for the kick. (There are condenser mics made for kick drums, and some that have both dynamic and condenser elements.)
- A dynamic mic on the snare.
- A small diaphragm condenser on the hi-hat.

These five mics allow discrete processing of the most important and most used elements of the drum set – the kick, snare, and hi-hat.

In this situation, the overhead mics also function as tom tom mics – as well as for any other un-miked instruments. Remember that EQ applied to the overhead mics will change not only the cymbal sound, but also the tom toms. The overheads also pick up the snare and hi-hat – so the sound of those instruments is a combination of their dedicated mics *plus* the overheads – when EQ-ing, make sure you check how the close mics and overheads sound *together*.

Without their own mics the tom toms will appear more ambient and distant than the snare and kick – so if they are used frequently and more than five mics are available, give the tom toms and any other additional instruments their own mics.

Double miking the snare drum will give it more brightness. Double miking the tom toms can give them more body and resonance. (See **Double Miking** in **Section 10.4**.) Large drum sets may also benefit from having more than two overheads – an added center overhead mic, or individual mics positioned closer to specific cymbals. The ride cymbal is usually quieter than crash cymbals, so it can often benefit from its own dedicated mic.

The less a drum set is miked individually, the less it is possible to adjust the balance, EQ, or process individual instruments without negatively affecting the other instruments. When fewer mics are used it is more important that each instrument in the drum set sounds great and that the natural balance of the drum set is perfect.

FEWER THAN FIVE MICS?

If you have a limited number of mics or input channels, here are some options:

Only one mic? Mono is your only option! The mic must be carefully positioned to capture an appropriate recorded balance. Try these positions:

- A meter (3 ft) in front of and 60 cm (2 ft) above the drum set – the distance blends the individual sounds together.
- Above the drummer's head, angled towards the center of the drum set – the drummer listens from this position, and plays so the balance is good to them.

Two mics? Try a stereo pair of overheads in either of the above positions. Or try adding a kick drum mic to a single overhead – to add bottom, thump, and low frequency power to the sound. In a relatively live space you could also try two mics (ribbon mics work well for this) 1 m (3 ft) in front of the drum set, 1 m (3 ft) off the ground, spaced 45 cm (1.5 ft) from the center of the kick to form an equilateral triangle.

Three mics? Stereo overheads plus a kick drum mic would be preferred to record a stereo picture of the drum set with increased kick drum presence.

Four mics? Adding a snare mic will give you balance and perspective control and allows individual processing of the kick and snare (the two loudest and most important elements of a rock drum set). The snare mic will also pick up plenty of hi-hat spill – the relative balance of which can be adjusted by changing the polar pattern, distance, and angle of the snare mic to the hi-hat.

Every drum is different, every drummer plays differently, and different musical and song styles demand different drum sounds. It's important to really listen before tracking, and experiment in order to get the most desirable sound. There is no such thing as a universal "best mic position" for any type of drum – there are just too many variables!

Drums – Minimal Miking

Example 10.1: Drum set, single condenser mic, in front of and above the drum set.

Example 10.2: Drum set, single condenser mic, above the drummer's head.

Example 10.3: Drum set, stereo pair, above and in front of the drum set.

Example 10.4: Drum set, stereo pair above the set, plus a kick drum mic.

10.3 KICK DRUMS

A dynamic microphone is typically used on the kick drum because a kick drum is:

- Very loud.
- Does not contain any essential super-high frequency content.
- Can beneficially be made a little bigger and beefier by the transient compression characteristics of a dynamic mic.

Many general purpose instrument mics sound great on kick drums, but there are also low frequency instrument mics specifically designed for kick drums as discussed in **Chapter 3**. General purpose instrument mics may not sound as instantly big and powerful, but if the specific characteristics of a low frequency instrument mic don't suit the drum, a flat mic is a better choice – you don't want to have to EQ out the sound of an already heavily contoured mic as well as apply additional EQ to refine the sound.

Rock kick drums usually have a hole in the front to allow a mic to be positioned inside the drum, where it picks up a snappy, punchy sound. Generally:

- The closer the mic is positioned to the center of the beater side drum head, the more snap and click the sound will have.
- The further back from this position the mic is, the beefier and boomier the sound will be.

The mic does not have to be placed directly on axis with the center of the drumhead, but if it is off center it is usually angled so that it is aiming towards where the beater impacts the head. The mic can go anywhere from 6 or 10 cm (2 or 3 in) from the beater side head, to close to the resonant head (the head with the hole in it). Moving the mic an inch or two has a huge effect on the recorded sound.

Avoid positioning microphones right at the sound hole, and be careful positioning mics just outside it. A lot of air moves in and out of that small hole at high velocity, and that whoosh of air can produce plosive-like booms and pops in the mic.

Kick drums can also be multi-miked:

- A mic added to the outside of the front head will pick up a less clicky, boomier sound that can be blended with the mic inside.
- A more distant kick drum mic, a few feet in front of the drum, can be isolated from sources of spill by constructing a tunnel from the kick drum to behind the mic using heavy blankets, duvets, or comforters, draped over chairs, mic stands, or other supports.
- Reverse wired loudspeaker mics (either home built or commercial products) can be positioned in front of the drumhead. These "microphones" pick up a *very* boomy sound that in isolation is not desirable, but can really add weight to the kick sound when blended with a conventional mic inside the kick drum.
- A PZM boundary mic placed inside the drum can also produce a huge boomy sound, similar to a reverse wired loudspeaker mic, that can be blended with a conventional kick mic.

Figure 10.1 Top Left: Looking through the hole into a kick drum with a mic typically placed for single mic recording, several inches from the beater-side head. Top Right: A mic about 15 cm (6 in) outside the center of a jazz kick drum. Avoid miking at or close to the outside of a hole as small as the one in this drum – a very strong air current is forced through a hole this small. Bottom: A combination of a sub-kick mic, and a conventional mic inside the drum.

- A condenser mic, or even a ribbon mic can be used (carefully) outside the kick drum – and blended with a mic inside the drum. *Never position a ribbon mic on-axis or close to a kick drum though – the SPL and air currents can perforate the fragile ribbon. Angle it down at 45°, at least 45 cm (1.5 ft) away.*

Kick Drum Miking

Example 10.5: Kick drum, miked with a flat kick drum mic.

Example 10.6: Kick drum, miked with a reverse wired loudspeaker cone mic, alone.

Example 10.7: Kick drum, the flat mic, and loudspeaker cone mic combined.

Example 10.8: Kick drum, miked with a low frequency instrument mic.

Low frequency wavelengths are so long that the couple of feet distance between the inside and outside mics doesn't cause comb filtering problems in the beef and body of the sound. However, the click can suffer. To fix any phasing in the click sound you can either:

- Change the distance between the mics slightly until the problem is minimized.

Or:

- Measure the distance between the mics.
- Calculate the delay time it creates.
- Add that delay electronically to the mic inside the drum, or advance the track of the mic outside the drum. Listen carefully to see which solution interacts best with the overhead mics.

NO HOLE?

Jazz kick drums do not usually have a mic hole in the front. The role and sound of jazz kick drums are different – they are much warmer, more boomy, less clicky, and more of an accent marker than relentless rhythm maker. A kick drum with no hole will never sound like one with a hole in it, regardless of microphone technique and any processing applied!

For the brightest sound on a kick with no hole, a mic should be positioned on-axis, in the center of the drumhead. Positioned too close, the sound will be very muddy and boomy due to proximity effect – so avoid positioning the mic less than 10 cm (4 in) away. The mic distance can be increased to 30 cm (1 ft) or more for less proximity effect and a more natural sound – but increasing the distance will increase spill from the rest of the drum set and any other sound sources in the room.

If a drum is particularly dull and boomy sounding, and has no mic hole, a second mic can be positioned close to and pointing towards the beater impact point *on the beater side* of the kick drum, where it will pick up more click and snap. This mic should be polarity reversed during tracking, and the combined sound of both mics carefully auditioned prior to pressing the record button. (See **Section 10.4 Double Miking**.) Keep this mic and stand out of the drummer's way, and position the mic to minimize spill from the bottom of the snare drum. Listen for, and fix any drum pedal squeaks, rattles, and clunks before hitting the record button.

Condenser mics can also be used on kick drums, particularly for lighter styles such as jazz, folk, and other acoustic music. Some manufacturers make condenser mics designed specifically for this purpose. The SPL inside or close to a kick drum can be in excess of 140 dB, exceeding the capabilities of many regular condenser mics, so before using a condenser mic, check the maximum SPL listed on its spec sheet to see what it can and can't handle, and listen carefully for and avoid distortion of either the diaphragm or mic electronics.

PAD IT!

- The pad switch found on many mics can prevent the mic's electronics, and the preamp, from being overloaded and distorting at high SPLs.
- The pad button found on channel strips or a pre-amp may prevent the pre-amp from being overloaded and distorting at high SPLs.
- Pads will not prevent the diaphragm itself from over-excursion and distortion – only a lower SPL will.

A condenser kick drum mic will produce a much more detailed sound, with a brighter more transparent "snap" than a dynamic mic, but there will probably be more spill in the sound. For jazz music this spill may not be a problem (it can add to the organic quality of the drum set sound) but it may not be desirable in rock or pop projects.

10.4 SNARE DRUMS

Dynamic microphones are the go-to mics for snare drums because:

- A snare drum is very loud – especially at a distance of a few inches!
- The mic is directly in harm's way – near fast moving drumsticks which could easily damage or destroy a condenser mic capsule.
- There is little extreme high frequency content in the sound produced by the top head of a snare drum.
- The transient compression characteristics of a dynamic mic can increase the average level of the sound and make it a little bigger.

Make sure you position the mic and its mounting hardware so that it is unlikely to be accidentally struck by the drummer – this generally means that the mic is boomed in from behind the drum, away from the drummer, so it is pointing towards the drummer from the far side of the drum. The mic should be positioned with the capsule several centimeters (an inch or two) above the drum, either over the rim or just inside, angled down towards the center of the drum. The angle of inclination can be varied:

- A steeper angle, with the mic "looking down" towards the center of the bottom head, will pick up more tone and body for a potentially beefier sound.
- A less severe angle, the mic aimed towards where the stick hits the head, will potentially produce more attack.

In jazz, the snare drum is not played as loudly as in rock styles, so a directional condenser mic (with good off-axis pick-up characteristics) is also an option. In addition to the increased detail, the increased spill positions the drum "in the set" more, decreasing its sense of isolation and individuality – which is usually desirable in traditional jazz recording. When using a condenser mic it is even more important to have a great sounding drum and a mic which complements its sound. EQ will change not only the sound of the snare drum, but also the sound of all the instruments in the increased amount of spill. For example, you might make the snare sound great, but that same EQ might negatively affect the hi-hat sound when the EQ'd spill is combined with the hi-hat mic itself. You can also try adding a mic to the side of the drum, near or across from the tone hole, to capture a blend of the top and bottom sound.

DOUBLE MIKING

A single mic above a snare drum has a tendency to produce a dull, dark, boxy sound. The snares that produce the bright noise content of the drum are on the bottom, far from the mic. Double miking the snare drum by adding a second mic, 10 to 15 cm (4 to 6 in) underneath the drum, pointing towards the center of the snares, will add brightness to the sound.

- A dynamic mic with extended high frequency response, or a condenser mic are both suitable "snare bottom" mics.
- The kick drum is close to the bottom snare mic. By cutting the low frequencies from the bottom snare mic when mixing, the level of kick spill will become insignificant.
- Generally the bulk of the snare sound will come from the top mic (the body and weight of the sound), and a relatively small amount of the bottom mic will add brightness and snap.

Because the bottom mic is pointing in the opposite direction to the top mic, each mic's perspective of the drumhead movement is opposite – as the heads move downwards they cause the top mic's diaphragm to move outwards, but the bottom mic's diaphragm to move inwards. When the mics are summed together in the mixer or DAW, the body and beef of the sound (which is common to both mics) will cancel out significantly. During recording, the bottom mic should be polarity reversed using the Ø button on the pre-amp or console.

It is vitally important to check how the mics sum together before pushing record, so that you know you have the snare sound you want. You do not want to find out there is a phase problem during mixing, after the drummer has gone home and all the other musicians have already laid down their tracks to that drum recording!

Double miking can also add body, beef, and sustain to a tom tom – although the difference is less dramatic than the effect a bottom mic has on the snare drum. Adding a beater-side mic to a kick drum may add some snap to rescue a dull boomy kick (but there will also be a lot of snare spill added). The "opposite side" mic on any drum must be polarity reversed.

Figure 10.2 A double miked snare drum (dynamic mic on the top, small diaphragm condenser on the bottom) showing the different top mic angles described in the main text. (You would not normally use two identical mics at different angles simultaneously.) The mic stands are boomed in from behind the snare drum, in-between the tom tom and hi-hat. (The hi-hat is not shown in this picture because it would obscure the mics in the picture.)

10.5 HI-HATS

Small diaphragm condenser microphones are generally preferred for hi-hats because of their accuracy and better high frequency response. Brightness and sizzle (high frequency detail) are essential components of a hi-hat sound, and a few inches away, the SPL of a hi-hat is not in excess of a condenser mic's capabilities.

- The mic should be positioned above the top hi-hat cymbal in order to pick up the impact of the sticks on the instrument. The mic should be positioned at least 12 cm (5 in) above the cymbal, and can be up to about 20 cm (8 in) away. Make sure the area struck by the sticks is in the mic's pick-up. The mic can be pointed straight down; or angled in from slightly to the side of where the sticks hit the instrument; or positioned more out of harms way, towards the outside edge of the instrument, but still over the instrument, angled in towards where the sticks hit it.
- A mic positioned too close to the edge of the hi-hat will produce a brash crunchy sound.
- A mic positioned too near the bell in the center of the cymbal will produce a ringy clangy sound.

The hi-hat should *not* be miked with the mic to the side, pointing towards the edges of the hi-hat! As well as focusing on a brash brittle sound, the large rush of air as the cymbals close will cause plosive-like wind noise artifacts.

The close mics on snare drums and tom toms can magnify and reveal usually undesirable audible ringing frequencies caused by the drum's tuning. Gel and tape products can be purchased to dampen those resonances, but a cheaper and often more effective solution (if retuning the drum is not possible) is to gaff tape something similar to a credit card somewhere over the outer edge of the top head.

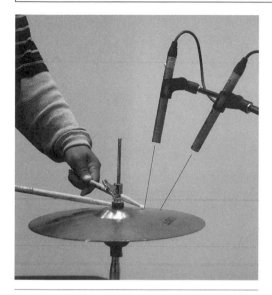

Figure 10.3 Some possible hi-hat mic positions.

Figure 10.4 A rack tom and floor tom miked from the top.

10.6 TOM TOMS

Tom toms can be approached similarly to snare drums, with a microphone 5 to 8 cm (2 to 3 in) above the rim of the top drum head (possibly slightly over the drum head), angled down into the drum. Generally, a steeper angle produces more tone and body, and a shallower angle increases attack. A condenser mic will pick up the drum's attack transients most accurately, but a good dynamic mic (with above average high frequency response) is also a good choice. Double miking can be applied to tom toms – the body and resonance of the sound can be increased by adding a bottom mic positioned 10 to 15 cm (4 to 6 in) below the bottom head, angled up towards the center of the bottom head.

Positioning a single mic in-between two tom toms is *not* recommended – both tom toms are off-axis to the mic, and subject to muddy off-axis coloration. Panning options are also reduced when one mic is used to pick up multiple drums. Also *not* recommended is positioning a bidirectional mic, aimed laterally, between the tom toms. This reverses the polarity of one tom tom and much of the drum set in that mic, causing phase problems when combined with the other drum mics.

Figure 10.5 *Not* recommended! This cardioid mic is off-axis to both drums! The sound will lack attack and punch, and the drums cannot be individually panned or processed.

10.7 CYMBALS AND OVERHEADS

Condenser mics are preferred as overheads because cymbals contain a lot of bright splashy high frequencies. Good quality ribbon mics are also a popular choice, because of their smooth high frequency characteristics. The "body" of cymbal sounds is surprisingly low though – down to around 250 Hz.

- Flat response small diaphragm mics are favored for their extended high frequency accuracy when a faithful recording is desired.
- Very small diaphragm mics are a great option too, producing an extra level of detail and transparency.
- Many large diaphragm mics also make good overhead mics – from flatter less sonically colorful models, to more characterful models which give the overheads some sonic hype, or mellow the brightness a little.

The function of cymbal or overhead mics varies depending on how the rest of the drum set is miked. If the tom toms (and any other instruments) are not miked, the overheads are also responsible for picking up those instruments:

- If the tom toms are frequently and dramatically used, there can be a distracting perspective shift from the closely miked kick, snare, and hi-hat, to the tom toms which are only picked up by the overhead mics.
- Without tom tom mics it may not be possible to get the tom toms loud or present enough without the cymbals becoming too loud.
- If the overheads are responsible for picking up more than the cymbals, any EQ that benefits the cymbals may negatively affect the tom toms and other instruments.

Any of the stereo arrays discussed in **Chapter 6** can be used as overheads, each with their unique imaging characteristics. Overheads can be positioned anywhere from 40 to 90 cm (1.5 to 3 ft) above the cymbals:

- The closer the mics are, the wider the stereo image – but the mics zoom in and over-emphasize the cymbals they are closest to.
- The further away the mics are, the more blended the picture of the whole set – but the narrower the stereo image, and the more room sound is picked up.

On wider drum sets, spaced pairs allow the microphones to be positioned so they evenly pick up all of the cymbals. AB spaced pairs can be set up as described in **Chapter 6**, with omnidirectional mics spaced 40 to 60 cm (15 to 24 in) apart. This doesn't usually put the mics in an ideal position though – they are too close together, not centered over the left and right banks of cymbals on either side of the drum set. A wider spacing is typical to center each mic over each bank of cymbals. This wider spacing can cause imaging problems in the form of a hole in the center, and "ghost" images to appear on opposite sides though – for example, a crash cymbal struck on the right is heard loudly on the right, but with a distinct, separated, blurry version appearing to the left of the stereo image.

Directional mics can be used instead of omnidirectional mics in spaced overhead arrays – this is particularly desirable in rooms that are not acoustically ideal, or if there are sources of spill in the room. Directional mics will increase the apparent width of the image, which can be good...or bad, if the left and right become too separated. Widely spaced overheads can be angled into the drum set to put more sound sources on-axis and reduce off-axis coloration. Be sure to check your overhead image, and push the mono button to check mono compatibility before pushing record!

Figure 10.6 A spaced array with a mic positioned over each bank of cymbals, at the first and third "quarter" divisions of the width of the set.

MEASURE IT!

The snare drum is one of the most used, and therefore most important instruments the overheads will pick up, whether the snare is individually miked or not – so it is important that its sound in the overhead mics is good, and will blend well with the individual snare mics. If the snare drum is not equidistant to both overhead mics its sound can be less precise and secure, and phasey comb filtering can be produced when a center panned dedicated snare mic is mixed with the overheads.

This is less of a problem when the snare drum is physically located in the center of the drum set, or is positioned wherever you want it panned. One way to tighten and solidify the snare sound is to measure the distance from the center of the snare drum to each overhead mic, and make them equidistant – although this is an impractical goal if the snare drum is not positioned centrally, and wider spaced pair overhead mics are used. If the overhead mics *are* spaced equidistantly from the snare drum, the snare sound arrives at both overhead mics at the same time, so is in phase in both – resulting in a more solid snare sound in the overhead mics that blends better with the individual mics, and is more mono compatible. A related approach, ideally suited to non-centrally located snare drums is described in the upcoming **Glyn Johns Technique** text box.

Coincident, near-coincident, and MS arrays positioned above the center of the drum set can produce stereo images with less of the undesirable ghost imaging spaced arrays can be prone to. The width of the image depends on:

- The array used.
- The angle between the mics.
- The polar pattern of the mics.
- The height of the array.

Figure 10.7 Near-coincident overheads.

In many cases these arrays will produce more cohesive, accurate images than a spaced array, but do not use them too close as they will focus on the cymbals nearest to them too much.

If all of the drums are individually miked, the overheads become dedicated cymbal mics. If this is the case:

- Directional mics can be positioned to focus on each cluster of cymbals to the left and right (and maybe in the center).
- Cymbals can even be miked individually, at least 22 cm (9 in) above the edge of each cymbal, aimed at a point about one-third of the radius from the back edge of the cymbal – where the sticks are not likely to hit the mic. Cymbals move a lot when hit hard, so make sure they won't hit the mics.
- Individual cymbal mics can be at a shallow angle positioned above and at the rear edge of the cymbal, or angled more steeply from directly over the cymbal – you have to experiment and see how the cymbals sound, whether the attack transient "tink tink" of the sticks hitting the cymbal is present enough, and how the spill sounds.
- Individual cymbal mics are not stereo arrays optimized for natural imaging accuracy – instead they should pick up the best individual cymbal sounds, which are then panned to create the stereo image artificially.

Positioning microphones underneath the cymbals is not recommended for recording, although it is seen in live concert sound. Although it reduces spill and isolates each cymbal sound, it also removes some of the percussive attack, and picks up off-axis, colored, tom tom and snare drum spill.

Drums – Full Set Miking

Example 10.9: Drum set, five mics: kick (dynamic), snare (dynamic), hi-hat (condenser), two overheads (condenser). The tom toms sound distant and ambient compared to the kick, snare, and hi-hat.

Example 10.10: Drum set, all instruments miked and mixed, and the snare drum double miked. Dynamic mics are added on the tom toms.

GLYN JOHNS TECHNIQUE

Glyn Johns is the recording engineer responsible for the huge drum sounds on many records by The Eagles, Led Zeppelin, The Rolling Stones, and The Who, to name but a few. The technique he developed uses only four mics! Because natural balances and the room are the majority of the sound, this technique does require great sounding drums, a good drummer, and a great sounding room to record in.

- A large diaphragm condenser overhead is positioned 90 to 120 cm (3 to 4 ft) directly above the snare. Listen for the whole drum set to be well balanced and adjust the mic position until you achieve that. If the cymbals are too brash, raise the mic. If the rack tom toms are too quiet, position or angle the mic more towards them.
- Measure the distance from the center of the top snare head to the overhead mic.
- Position an identical large diaphragm condenser mic 15 to 30 cm (6 to 12 in) above the floor tom, so that it is the same distance from the center of the snare drum head as the overhead mic you previously set up. Yes, this one is probably lower than the cymbals, and definitely out to the side of the floor tom!
- These two mics should be panned left and right.
- Add close kick and snare mics to fill in the bottom and weight of the kick drum, and body of the snare. The kick mic can be inside or outside the drum. These mics are not the foundation of the sound – the overheads should dominate. The close mics should supplement the sound of the overheads.

10.8 ROOM MICS

The sound of the room the drums are recorded in will even be present in the close mics used – it is impossible to remove the sound of a room from a recording. *Room mics* are dedicated to picking up the reflected sound in the room, so that it can be beneficially blended with the close mics. If the drums are being recorded in a good sounding, bright and live, medium to large room, the room character can add a layer of power and glue to the drum sound.

Because details and reach are important, quality condenser or ribbon mics should be used as room mics. Room mics can be:

- Any stereo array.
- Positioned 2 to 5 m (6 to 15 ft) in front of the drum set, at more-or-less any height, the array pointing towards the center of the drum set or towards the edges of the room for a more diffuse sound.
- Positioned more than 15 feet away in larger rooms with reverberant acoustics. Directional mics facing the outer edges of the room will focus on the reverberant sound.
- Often you do not need additional cymbal content in the room mics – but you do want more beef from the drums. To achieve this, try positioning a room mic (or pair) anywhere from 10 to 60 cm (4 to 24 in) above the floor, several feet in front of the drums.

Room mics pick up some similar content to the close mics, but the sound is delayed in the room mics due to the increased distance from the drum set. It is important to check for phase problems between the close and room mics. In a live room, the reflected sound in the room mics should be of much greater amplitude than any dry sound, so phase problems should be

Figure 10.8 A fully miked drum set, including room mics.

minimal. But if you notice a thinness or phasey sound as you turn up the room mics, reposition them to minimize this. Some engineers will time align the room mics by advancing them so that they are in phase with the snare mic. This is easy to do visually in a DAW, by moving the room mic tracks so an obvious kick or snare transient lines up in both the room mic tracks, and its respective close miked track. To bring out the sound of the room even more, some moderate to heavy compression can be applied to the room mics during mixing.

WHERE IN THE ROOM?

Where in a room do you set up a drum set (or any other sound source)? Typically, a central location works best for drums – no one wall is much closer or further away than the others, creating more evenly distributed early reflections, and the room and the resulting reflections are more symmetrical in the recorded image.

As well as trying different mics and mic techniques, do experiment with positioning the same instrument in different places in the room, because:

- The reflected sound the mic(s) pick up will change depending upon position.
- The spill picked up will change depending upon room position.
- The apparent low frequency output of the instrument will be increased by positioning it close to walls.
- Some rooms do exhibit more resonance problems in the center, so be prepared to move the drums if you hear room generated ringing frequencies (that are not the drums themselves ringing), particularly in the overhead mics.

Drums – Room Mics

Example 10.11: Drum set, room mics are added to the individually miked drum set in **Example 10.10**.

Example 10.12: A drum set miked with the Glyn Johns technique, in a large live room. No additional room mics are used.

10.9 ROCK DRUMS VS ACOUSTIC JAZZ DRUMS

In most pop and rock production styles, each drum is treated as a single unit, and those instruments are miked as individually as possible. Those discrete sounds are artificially given their own precise place in the mix and soundstage, and EQ, panning, gating, compression, reverb, and effects are applied differently to each. For example, to make a drum set bigger and more powerful than it is naturally:

- A short reflective room reverb can be applied globally to most of the mics. But why not do this naturally, with room mics?
- A short snappy snare, and small sounding tom toms can be turned into more powerful sounds by adding a longer, more obvious, stylized reverb to them. Do not apply the same processing to the kick, hi-hat, or cymbals – kick drums sound like they're in a tunnel, and high frequency sounds take on constant hissy characteristics when long reverbs are added to them.
- Compression can be added to the kick drum to bring out more snap, punch, and attack, or conversely to emphasize the tail and tone.
- Compression can be added to the snare to reduce the attack, and bring out and sustain the body of the sound, or conversely to emphasize the attack and crack of the sound.

In lighter acoustic styles such as jazz and folk, the drum set is treated as a more organic, blended, and unified whole. Each sound is less discrete, both sonically and functionally. There are different ways to achieve this goal:

- Use fewer mics. This means that the overheads are relied on to pick up a more complete picture of the drum set, and not just the cymbals. It is important to spend time positioning them so that the cymbal vs rest of the drum set balance is optimized – with fewer mics, balances are less adjustable during mixing.
- Use condenser mics instead of dynamic mics on the snare, tom toms, and even the kick drum. This will produce a brighter, more detailed recording, and more spill in each mic. *Embrace the spill!* It is not necessarily the enemy – good sounding spill can contribute to a less separated, more organic, blended sound. Good mics, with good off-axis pick-up characteristics are essential to capture good spill. With lighter styles of music, the SPLs produced by the drum set should be within the capabilities of most modern

condenser mics, and less aggressive drummers are (hopefully) less likely to inflict mic damage from an erroneously placed fast moving drum stick!

- Use omnidirectional mics to give the sound a more accurate, open, less muddy, more transparent character. Less EQ will be required because there is no proximity effect clouding up the sound. In addition, each drum sound is made less isolated because of the better sounding off-axis response and consequently increased pick-up of the sounds around the desired source. The picture painted by panning and balancing individual omnidirectional mics across the soundstage will be less precisely focused than one recorded using directional mics, but each sound will have a little more girth to it, and the picture of the entire drum set will be smoother and more organically blended.

Omnidirectional Condenser Drum Mics

Example 10.13: Drum set, the same drum set as the examples earlier in this chapter, but miked with omnidirectional kick, snare, hi-hat, tom tom, and overhead mics. Compare this with **Example 10.10**, which uses directional mics and some dynamic mics.

MIC POLAR PATTERNS AND NULL POINTS

A multi-miked drum set uses a lot of mics in a relatively small space. There are many sound sources all around each mic – the desired sound, and spill from other parts of the drum set. For maximum rejection of spill, select mic polar patterns carefully depending upon the specific physical drum setup:

- A cardioid mic has its null point directly behind it – making them ideal if there is another instrument directly behind the mic.
- If there is no sound source directly behind a mic, but there is one "not quite directly behind" the mic, a hyper-cardioid (with its null points at about 120° – 140°) may offer better rejection of that source of spill.
- If there is no sound source directly behind a mic, but there is to the sides, a bidirectional mic's extreme rejection at 90° can help isolate the desired source.

10.10 DRUM EQ FREQUENCIES

It is impossible to tell you what EQ to use! The examples below are fairly common, but the mic, instrument, performance, and mix context are all unknown variables that will change any EQ necessary. Where add or cut suggestions are given, don't be surprised if you end up having to do the exact opposite!

KICK DRUM

- Add *thump* – 60 to 80 Hz.
- Reduce low-mid *boxiness* – 200 to 600 Hz.
- Add *snap* and *punch* – 2.5 to 6 KHz.

Make sure the weight and body of the kick drum and the bass guitar do not mask each other because of too much similar low frequency content. Focus the low frequency energy of each on slightly different frequency ranges by using subtractive EQ on different frequencies for each instrument during mixing.

SNARE DRUM

- *Weight* – 100 to 250 Hz.
- Low-mid *boxiness* – 400 to 600 Hz.
- *Punch* – 1 to 2 KHz.
- Add *crispness* – 4 to 8 KHz.

A high pass filter can be used to roll off low frequency spill from the kick, toms, and bottom snare mic.

HI-HAT

- Cut low frequencies below about 300 Hz.
- Add *fizz* and *sizzle* above 6 KHz.

A high pass filter can be used to aggressively cut low frequency spill – but make sure the hi-hat doesn't sound too thin.

TOM TOMS

- Rack tom *body* – around 240 Hz.
- Floor tom body – 80 to 120 Hz.
- *Attack* – around 5 KHz.

The tom tom mics pick up a lot of spill, and the tom toms are usually infrequently played, making them a prime candidate for gating during mixing.

CYMBALS AND OVERHEADS

- Reduce the *low gong* sound below 500 Hz using a shelf or high pass filter – but make sure it doesn't get too shrill – there is desirable body down there!
- Reduce *clank* – 800 to 1 KHz.
- Add *fizz* and *brightness* above 7 KHz.

Guitars, Basses, and Keyboards

11.1 THE ROLE OF THE RHYTHM SECTION INSTRUMENTS

What type of music are you recording? To a certain extent this will suggest the relative importance of the rhythm section instruments. The bass and drums work together to lay down a foundation which the other instruments and vocals respond to. In most commercial styles the bass is
of equal importance, and should be of equal prominence as the drums. Guitars and keyboards
are musically less important in many rock, pop, and jazz styles (unless the instrument is taking
a solo, in which case it replaces the lead vocal in terms of focus and importance). They are,
to a certain extent, "fillers," providing harmonic information, and adding textural interest and
depth to the groove and foundation provided by the drums and bass. Most importantly, they
should never get in the way of, or negatively impact, the intelligibility of the vocals – which
they will certainly do if they are used too loudly in a mix, or with thin and piercing timbres that
over-emphasize the 2 to 4 KHz range. A common cause of vocal levels getting out of control
and needing to be turned up and up in order to be heard and *understood*, is that the harmonic
rhythm section instruments are too loud or have too much competing frequency content.

11.2 ELECTRIC GUITAR

An electric guitar is nothing without the amplifier and loudspeaker cabinet it is plugged into –
its sound is dependent upon them. Change either one, and the sound will be dramatically
different. Unlike good studio monitors, guitar cabinet loudspeaker cones and cabinets are
highly non-linear and have all kinds of frequency and amplitude quirks that make them so
characteristic and desirable!

When miking a guitar cabinet:

- Dynamic microphones are the usual go-to choice. There is little desirable frequency
  content above about 6 KHz in most electric guitar cabinet speakers, so the extended
  frequency response of a condenser mic is not essential.
- Condenser mics can be used for a brighter sound – but they are sometimes a little too
  bright and scratchy.
- Ribbon mics, with their smoother high frequency characteristics, can sound great!
  Remember that the front and back of many ribbon mics have slightly different
  characteristics – so do try them both out and decide which gives you the most pleasing
  sound.
- Radically different sounding microphones, for example, a dynamic mic and a condenser
  mic, will each accentuate different frequency components – so it can sometimes be
  beneficial to use multiple mic technologies, each chosen, positioned, and EQ'd to favor
  a specific timbre which can then be blended together.

A mic placed a few centimeters (an inch or two) from the loudspeaker cone will have
more proximity effect than one placed 15 cm (6 in) from the grille. Most dynamic mics start

Figure 11.1 A guitar cabinet loudspeaker miked on-axis for the brightest sound, and off-axis for a warmer sound.

sounding quite thin when they are more than 20 cm (9 in) from the sound source, so do adjust mic distance until you find the best sound. Because of the loudspeaker cone's unpredictable response and distortions, moving the mic an inch to the left, right, up, or down, can change the sound quite significantly, so do take the time to experiment and find the sweet-spot:

- For the brightest sound, position a mic on-axis in the center of the loudspeaker cone.
- For a warmer sound, position the mic off-center, towards the edge of the cone.

If a guitar cabinet has more than one loudspeaker cone, get your ears close, and listen to each in turn – *at a safe listening level!* Even better – try the mic on all of them, and see how each sounds from the mic's perspective. Decide which one sounds most suitable for the project, and record that one. Listen carefully for any buzzes or crackles indicative of a bad cone. Unless the loudspeaker cones sound radically different, there is little value to miking multiple cones unless mics with very different characteristics are used. Even then, the frequency content will be quite similar, and the performance identical – there will not be enough differences to produce a dramatic wide stereo image if the mics are panned left and right.

WHERE IS THE LOUDSPEAKER CONE?

Sometimes you can't actually see loudspeaker cones – they are hidden behind grilles. Shine some light on the situation – use a flashlight, or download an app for your phone so you can see through the grille and find the cone's exact position.

You want to record a sound that will work *in the mix*, and *not* necessarily the bright piercing sound the guitarist might usually dial in so they can be heard in the far reaches of a bar or club when doing a gig. Communicate with the guitarist, and have them come in and listen to what the mic is picking up. They are likely to know how to desirably change the sound once they hear what the mic is picking up.

For loud heavily distorted sounds, the interaction between the loudspeaker cabinet and the room is a big factor in the recorded sound. There is so much sonic energy bouncing around, and *lots* of this reflected content gets into the mics. Boomy, muddy guitar sounds are unfortunately typical when recording in a room that is generically treated with acoustical absorption products but not enough bass trapping – the high and mid-frequency reflections are attenuated by the treatment, but the bass still rolls around in the room.

The position of the loudspeaker cabinet in the room will affect the sound:

- Is the cabinet in the corner, or close to a wall? Or is it on the floor? In which case low frequencies will be boosted, and the sound made boomier. At the very least, try raising the cabinet off the floor for a clearer, brighter sound.
- Is the cabinet near reflective or absorptive surfaces? Reflective surfaces will make the sound brighter and more present, but there is a chance the sound picked up by the mics will be slightly comb filtered due to the reflections. Absorptive surfaces will deaden and darken the sound.
- Try the cabinet and mic setup in different places, and facing different directions in the room. The reflected content will change in each position, and will interact differently with the direct sound coming from the cabinet.

Do record a couple of takes of rhythm guitar tracks. Even if you don't vary the sound on each, the slight performance differences are enough to create wide, expansive stereo images when they are panned left and right. If only one guitar track is recorded, it often ends up a) panned centrally – which is boring, and it competes for physical space with many other sounds, or b) off to one side – which can cause asymmetry in the mix.

A close mic and a more distant mic (or even a room mic) will each pick up different characteristics, which can be blended together – however you need to listen carefully for phase and comb filtering problems caused because by the distance and resulting time delay between the mics. If a close and distant mic are panned left and right respectively, they may sound huge and expansive in stereo, but when panned together as a mono center, or summed to mono by a consumer playback system, there may be frequency cancellation. Do always mono check a multi-miked guitar sound to confirm the sound is still big and full in mono – it *will* get narrower, but is anything missing from the sound tonally when it is summed to mono? Changing the mics' distance relative to each other will change the comb filtering frequencies. There will probably always be some comb filtering, but it should be minimized. Small mic position adjustments produce dramatic changes.

A mic can be positioned behind the loudspeaker cone if a loudspeaker cabinet is an "open" design and you can see the rear of the loudspeaker cone. The signal picked up by this mic will be polarity reversed, so if combined with a front mic, there will definitely be cancellation. Before recording, the polarity reverse button on the rear mic's pre-amp, mixer, or DAW channel should be engaged, and the summed signal checked to ensure that there is no thinning, hollowing, or phasing.

DON'T DRAPE YOUR MIC!

Hanging a mic down the front of the loudspeaker grille is not recommended – unless the mic is a side-address mic designed for that purpose. Most dynamic mics are end-address, which means that a mic in this position is pointing at the floor, and the loudspeaker cone is off-axis. This results in a thick, muddy sound, full of comb filtering because of the reflections picked up from the floor.

A side-address mic in this position will be on-axis, and although not subject to off-axis coloration, the mic is *very* close to the loudspeaker cone – so proximity effect will be excessive, requiring corrective EQ. The recording will also have very little natural depth. As long as spill is not a problem, a more natural sound (requiring less corrective EQ) can usually be achieved by increasing the distance between the mic and loudspeaker cone. That said, sometimes mics are deliberately positioned very close to loudspeaker cabinets so proximity effect will increase the weight of a sound that is too light or thin, or for a very close perspective sound – try a close omnidirectional mic to avoid low frequency build-up if a super close sound is desired.

Figure 11.2 Do not drape end address mics down the front of the cabinet!

Huge, powerful amps and loudspeaker stacks are not the best choice for recording purposes. A medium-sized combo that exhibits colorful distortions at lower volumes is a good choice for recording. In many cases, the bigger and louder the amp/loudspeaker is, the noisier it is – and noticeable hiss, hum, and buzz can build up quite quickly when multiple tracks of guitars are recorded. A very small practice amp/loudspeaker combo will always sound very small, so is not a good choice for recording either.

Some guitar amps are notorious for only sounding "really good" when turned "up to 11"! Particularly tube amps. This high SPL is another reason that dynamic mics are commonly used on guitar cabinets. *Power-soaks* are devices that are put between the amplifier and the loudspeaker cone. They allow the amplifier to operate at high levels and impart its character on the sound, but cause the loudspeaker cone to output lower SPLs because they absorb some of the electrical power. They make recording safer for the mic, guitarist, any audience, and are essential if you're recording in a small room that is easily overloaded with sound. The only drawback is that causing the loudspeaker cone to work less hard may reduce its own distortion characteristics.

RE-AMPING

A guitar sound that is not "dirty" enough, or a clean DI'd bass sound, can be *re-amped* in order to add amplifier and loudspeaker character after the performer has gone home. A previously recorded (clean) sound is sent (via a mixer aux or DAW send) to a guitar or bass amp, with or without effect pedals. The cabinet is miked and recorded, capturing the *real* amp, cabinet, and loudspeaker cone distortions, which can be blended with or replace the clean tracks. It is always a good idea to have the sound of the cabinet recorded, even if you don't end up using it – the fact that you *may* want it later is reason enough to have it.

The output of a DAW, mixer, or multitrack recorder is the wrong level and impedance to connect to an amplifier or pedal directly, so a *re-amping box* is essential if you don't want to risk burning up your or the guitarist's equipment! Connect the output of the recorded track to the input of the re-amping box, and its output to the pedals or amplifier. You can even use a passive DI box, plugged in "backwards" to do this.

AMP SIMULATORS

Many hardware devices and plug-ins are available that simulate amp and loudspeaker characteristics – so a clean guitar or bass track (or any other track for that matter) can be dirtied up without an amp and cabinet while tracking, or in a DAW after it is recorded. Of course the result is not quite the same as using real amps, cabinets, and loudspeaker cones, and some simulators do sound cheap, thin, and "digital." A good amp simulator *can* save the day if all that is available otherwise is a bad amplifier and/or a bad room. Re-amping is usually a preferable alternative to amp simulation, and it provides many varied creative possibilities instead of you simply recalling a preset in a simulator – "everybody else" with the same simulator has that same preset, so it doesn't help you obtain your own unique and magical sound.

Miking Electric Guitars

> **Example 11.1**: Electric guitar cabinet, dynamic mic, center of the cone, just a few inches away.
>
> **Example 11.2**: Electric guitar cabinet, dynamic mic, near the edge of the cone, just a few inches away.
>
> **Example 11.3**: Electric guitar cabinet, condenser mic, close, center of the cone.
>
> **Example 11.4**: Electric guitar cabinet, condenser mic, two feet from the loudspeaker.

11.3 ELECTRIC BASS, AND DI BOXES

One way to achieve a good beefy recording of an electric bass is to mic the speaker cabinet. Doing this you include the characteristics of the amplifier, the cabinet design, and the loudspeaker cone.

- Regular dynamic mics or low frequency instrument dynamic mics are the go-to mics for bass cabinets.
- Condenser mics and ribbon mics can also be used, but they may pick up too much snap and high frequency content.
- In a good room, which is adequately bass trapped to be free of low frequency problems, and in which there are no sources of spill, an omnidirectional mic will produce a more neutral, less muddy sound, without the proximity effect of a directional mic.

The position of the loudspeaker cabinet in the room will have a huge impact on the recorded sound:

- If the cabinet is on the floor, or close to any walls, its perceived low frequency output will be boosted, and the sound may get too muddy and muffled. Conversely, this may help a small speaker cabinet sound bigger – but listen for low-mid frequency muddiness, and EQ it out on the amplifier if necessary.
- The cabinet and mic position in the room will change the recorded sound – so do experiment with positioning the cabinet in the center, a little off center, or more to the end or side of the room, and facing it in different directions. In a room with low frequency standing wave problems, the mic could be in a null point for the fundamental frequency or a significant harmonic of the key of the song, or it could be at a peak point where that frequency booms too loudly. If some notes seem louder or quieter than others (and it's not the player or instrument causing that!) try moving the mic and cabinet a few feet.

A good sounding reasonably large bass amp is necessary for a good bass sound. A small practice amp will always sound "small." You don't need a very loud amp/cabinet combination for a good recording, but you do need something that can produce weighty low frequency content. Twelve or 15 inch loudspeakers are ideal – 18 inch loudspeakers can lack focus and definition.

- A mic can be placed anywhere from a few centimeters (an inch or two) in front of the loudspeaker cone, making sure it is not touching the grill, to 60 cm (2 ft) or more away.
- The closer the mic, the greater the proximity effect, and the boomier and muddier the sound will be – but spill from adjacent sound sources will be reduced.
- Moving the mic 15 to 30 cm (6 to 12 in) away will produce a clearer sound with reduced low frequency build-up.
- Moving the mic a meter (3 ft) away will produce a sound more similar to the bass sound we hear when listening from a distance away – but it will also pick up more spill and room reflections.
- If the mic is positioned close to the loudspeaker, the brightest, crispest sound is picked up by a mic pointed directly at the center of the cone.
- A warmer, more rounded sound is produced when the mic is positioned towards the edge of the cone.

DESIGN THE BASS SOUND FOR THE MIC!

A close mic hears the bass amp very differently to how we hear it from a distance away. The mic then adds its own character. Adjust the sound of the bass amp so it sounds great through the mic and monitor loudspeakers in the control room before pressing the record button. Do not use the bass player's default settings and plan on "fixing it in the mix."

- If the bass sound is too boomy, turn down the lows on the bass amp, or move the mic further away.
- If it is too small and boxy, turn down the mids on the amp.
- If it is too twangy, turn down the highs on the amp.

Another approach to record a bass sound is to use a *DI* from the bass output or immediately following any effects pedals. A DI'd sound is crisper and snappier than a mic on the cabinet – but a cheap, poor quality DI by itself sounds small, compact, and lacking in real bottom and weight. Really good bass pre-amps can produce great results though – particularly characterful tube pre-amps! Using a good pre-amp instead of a cabinet and mic also removes a significant source of spill from the studio. The key to making a DI'd sound work is to experiment with the 120 to 350 Hz frequency range, as this is where the character of the sound is defined.

A DI'd (or pre-amp) signal can be blended with a cabinet mic – both should be panned identically, to the center:

- The mic provides the real lows, weight, and girth of the sound.
- The DI adds punch, clarity, and focus.

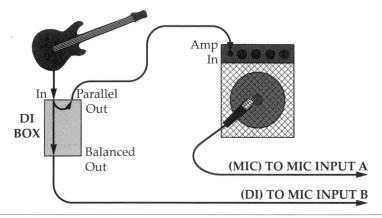

Figure 11.3 To record a bass mic and DI simultaneously, the DI box is inserted between the source and amplifier. The *thru* or *parallel* output is used to send the same signal to the amplifier – at the same level and impedance as the input signal. The balanced mic level XLR output is connected to the mixer or pre-amp.

The direct and mic signals should be recorded simultaneously, and *not* as two separate takes, which would have unavoidable performance differences. The set up for this is shown in **Figure 11.3**.

DIRECT BOXES

DI, or *Direct Injection* boxes take an unbalanced signal (usually line or instrument level, but sometimes even loudspeaker level) and convert it to a balanced mic level signal. *Passive* DI boxes do not require any power to operate. *Active* DI boxes require power – phantom power or sometimes batteries. Good active DI boxes generally have better frequency response, a more detailed and transparent sound, and higher output levels (requiring less pre-amp gain) than passive DI boxes. But a passive DI with a high quality transformer can certainly sound better than a poor quality active DI.

Any instrument or sound source with a line level or instrument level output can be DI'd, making it easy to plug the quarter-inch line level outputs on a synthesizer into the XLR mic inputs on a snake system.

Some guitar and bass amps have "direct outs" built in. These should be checked for noise and quality before use – a good studio DI might sound better. Do ensure that you are not plugging a post-amplifier loudspeaker level output into the DI box, unless the DI box is specifically designed to handle a loudspeaker level input, and all the necessary buttons to do so are pushed.

Some bass cabinets have multiple cones, sometimes of different sizes, and maybe even a tweeter. In this case, either:

• Position a mic far enough away so it picks up the blended sound of all of those transducers.

Or:

• Use multiple close mics – one on the woofer cone and one on the tweeter, for example.

For most bass sounds that are not slapped and popped, the tweeters are not necessary – if a cabinet has multiple 12 inch cones plus a tweeter, combining a mic on the best sounding 12 inch with a DI is usually sufficient.

Miking Electric Bass

Example 11.5: Bass cabinet, dynamic mic, center of the cone, about 6 inches away.

Example 11.6: Bass cabinet, DI only.

Example 11.7: Bass cabinet, the mic, and DI mixed together.

11.4 ACOUSTIC (UPRIGHT) BASS

The acoustic bass is a unique miking challenge because:

• The instrument is relatively quiet, which makes spill problematic unless the instrument is recorded in isolation.
• Sound dispersion is very uneven over the instrument – different parts of it radiate radically different frequency content in different directions.
• The instrument's desirable sound radiates over a very narrow focused angle directly in front of the instrument, but the sound is not a natural unified "whole" close to the instrument.

A single close mic is unlikely to capture a good bass sound. A combination of two (or more) of the following techniques will produce the best recording of the instrument:

1. Listen for the sweet-spot. Every instrument has a point in front of it where its constituent sonic components combine to form a great sound. With your ears close to the instrument, move around while listening for a sound that is big, warm, and full, with definition and some string attack, but not too bright, muffled, or cloudy. When you find the sweet-spot, put a mic in that position. Moving the mic a few inches – forwards, backwards, left, right, up, or down – will make a huge difference to the sound picked up. Experimentation is key, as no two basses are identical, and different player's styles coax different sounds out of the instrument.

   • A good starting point is anywhere from 30 cm to a meter (1 to 3 ft) away, with the mic angled down towards just above the bridge or top of the f-holes.

- The sounds to the left, center, or right of the instrument are each different, so be sure to try these different positions to see which sounds best.

- Sometimes a more distant mic like this can sound a little scratchy, and lack bottom end – so blending it with a closer mic is desirable.

2. A significant amount of sound comes from the f-hole.

   - A mic placed 9 to 15 cm (3 to 6 in) from an f-hole will pick this up.

   - Each f-hole sounds different – so be sure to try both.

   - F-holes do have a tendency to lack higher frequency details and sound muddy and undefined – a single mic on an f-hole rarely produces the best sound.

   F-holes can be used to provide "bottom end", mixed with an additional mic that provides definition and detail.

3. DI the pickup. For jazz and folk styles, contact pick-ups on the instrument's bridge are commonly used. If they are good pick-ups, correctly installed, they *can* sound quite good, and provide an in-your-face intensity that a mic doesn't have. Bad pick-ups sound truly awful though, and are unusable! Good pickups can be blended with an additional mic – a more distant mic, or an f-hole mic, or both. Like an electric bass DI, the pickups themselves do not portray the true weight and acoustic depth of the instrument.

4. Bridge miking. Some players have a small (omnidirectional) lavalier mic installed on the bridge instead of pick-ups. Again, these can either provide a beneficial layer of sound, or be unusable. Between the strings and the amplifying body of the instrument, this very close mic picks up an incomplete frequency picture of the instrument – so it is best used as one component of a multi-mic approach. Engineers have been known to take a studio condenser or dynamic mic, put them in a large foam windscreen, and wedge them into the hole in the bridge, pointing upwards or into the instrument – but a mic in this position produces a very boomy and inaccurate sound that needs combining with another mic which will fill in the detail and high frequencies that are missing.

Figure 11.4 Some of the acoustic bass mic positions described in the main text.

MULTI-MIC PANNING

Regardless of how many mics, DI boxes, and/or pick-ups are used simultaneously and blended to form a bass sound, they should always be panned identically. The bass is a narrow point source that needs to be horizontally compact, cohesive, and powerful in the mix. Panning elements of the sound differently will result in an unfocused, weak, smeared sound.

What mic should you use? Because basses are "bass instruments," dynamic mics are a common choice for close miking – "flat" general-purpose mics, or "low frequency instrument" mics. But, the acoustic bass is *not* loud, and *does* contain high frequency and low level details (string noise, finger and pluck noise, and the details of the bowed sound, etc.) so in addition to the right mic, a good, quiet, high gain pre-amp is also essential. Condenser and ribbon mics are excellent mic choices if a more detailed, transparent sound is desired.

Each mic used should make the sonic element it is providing sound great. For example:

- The body, definition, and stringy details should be accurately represented by a mic 30 to 60 cm (1 to 2 ft) away. That distant mic may sound a little lacking in low frequency weight, but that's okay – that's not the job of a more distant mic.
- A mic much closer to the f-hole or bridge is going to sound muffled, and lack the high frequency or "whole instrument" details – but what's important in that mic is that the low frequency weight of the sound is good.

Those two mics should then be complementary to each other when combined.

If a mic isn't getting the sound you want, try something quite different – crazy even! Surprising results can come from unlikely suspects!

LOW FREQUENCY ROOM PROBLEMS

Low frequencies are very difficult to control, and acoustically improper rooms can have very uneven low frequency characteristics – some frequencies will ring and resonate over-loudly, while others will be muted or almost disappear at certain places in the room. If a mic is picking up a relatively high ratio of reflected sound, these problems could be present in it – the bass will sound extra boomy on some notes, thin on others, or some notes will appear louder than others.

If the room is not professionally treated with permanent low frequency absorption and bass traps, commercial or homemade bass traps and gobos can be positioned around the instrument to absorb reflected low frequency content and reduce these problems.

Acoustic Bass

> **Example 11.8**: Acoustic bass, a condenser mic placed about a foot away, just above the bridge of the instrument.
>
> **Example 11.9**: Acoustic bass, a dynamic mic positioned a few inches away from an f-hole.
>
> **Example 11.10**: Acoustic bass, the two mics above are blended together for a more complete picture of the instrument's sound.

11.5 ACOUSTIC GUITAR

The acoustic guitar is a naturally wide source that can fill the stereo soundstage. But should you record it in stereo or mono?

- If there are multiple acoustic guitar players in a band, or multiple tracks of a single player are going to be recorded and panned to produce a wide image in a busy mix, mono guitar tracks are most useful. Multiple stereo acoustic guitar tracks tend to sound imprecise and confused when panned to different positions, due to their similar sounds.
- If just one single acoustic guitar track is being recorded, stereo miking is appropriate.

Condenser and ribbon microphones are ideal for recording acoustic guitar because of the high frequency content, low-level details, and transient information essential to its sound:

- Small diaphragm condenser mics are the go-to option for the most accurate and potentially brightest sound.
- Characterful large diaphragm condenser mics give the instrument a little extra power, hype, and smoothness.
- Cardioid mics are most typically used, but in a great sounding room, omnidirectional mics will produce a more open and transparent sound.

Remember that the closer the mic is, the more it will zoom in and focus on only a small part of the instrument's whole sound – so with close mics, you will probably need more than one, each positioned so that the component of the guitar's sound it is targeting sounds great. As mic distance increases, the sound becomes more natural and balanced which is usually desirable – but undesirable room acoustics or spill can make miking closer than ideal a necessity.

Some good single mic starting points are shown in **Figure 11.5**. These techniques can be used in isolation, or combined and blended:

1. A mic positioned 15 to 60 cm (6 to 24 in) away, in front of the guitar, pointing towards where the fingerboard and body of the guitar overlap, should produce a natural balanced sound.

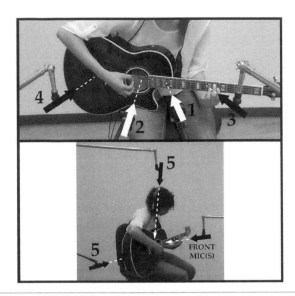

Figure 11.5   The acoustic guitar mic techniques described in the main text.

2. A mic positioned close to the sound hole will pick up a lot of boomy bass which needs rolling off or EQ'ing. This extra boom is in addition to any proximity effect. Even an omnidirectional mic positioned close to the sound hole will not pick up much definition or string detail.

3. A mic positioned further up the neck of the guitar will produce a thinner, weaker sound, with increased string, finger and fret noise, and less body and fullness. By itself this may not be appealing, but it can add zing and details to a body or sound hole mic.

4. A mic positioned beyond the bridge, down towards the larger end of the body will pick up a warm, full sound – less boomy than the sound hole, and with even less string, pick, and finger detail. This can be a good sound to blend with a mic accentuating the fingerboard components.

5. In front of the guitar isn't the only place to consider putting a microphone. A second mic positioned *behind* the larger end of the guitar body will pick up a different perspective. Another position that can produce great results when combined with closer mics, is above the player's shoulder, pointing down towards the instrument – this is near where the performer listens from, and evaluates their own sound.

Recording an acoustic guitar in stereo gives a single guitar track or a solo track width, depth, and space. Two spaced mics, one towards the fingerboard end of the guitar body, and the other just beyond the bridge, panned left and right will produce a large, wide, balanced stereo image, but any of the stereo arrays discussed earlier in this book can be used.

ACOUSTIC GUITAR PICKUPS

Acoustic guitar pick-ups tend to produce a flat, veiled, artificial "stringy" sound, which has no depth or transparency. They are rarely used by themselves. Pick-ups can, however, be blended at a low level with an additional mic or two, to add another character component to a mono or stereo guitar sound. Comb filtering can occur between the pick-ups and mics, so do listen carefully to the combined sound, and adjust mic distances to fix any problems.

A fairly reflective room will have lots of natural reflections that are picked up by close mics. As long as the room is not too small, the sound of those reflections can really suit some musical and production styles. A dry, less reflective room, with its more in-your-face sound will suit other styles. Regardless of the general room acoustic, floor reflections are incredibly beneficial to an acoustic guitar's recorded sound – they add a layer of sharpness, impact, and excitement, particularly in small, less reflective rooms – so do try removing any carpet or rugs if there is a hard reflective floor underneath, or put some plywood over installed carpet.

Acoustic Guitar Miking

Example 11.11: Acoustic guitar, a single mic positioned in the sweet-spot between the sound hole and neck of the instrument for a natural, balanced sound.

Example 11.12: Acoustic guitar, a single mic positioned closer to the sound hole.

Example 11.13: Acoustic guitar, a single mic positioned over the neck of the instrument.

Example 11.14: Acoustic guitar, two mics in similar positions to those in the previous two examples are combined and panned to produce a wide stereo guitar sound.

11.6 THE GRAND PIANO

ONLY A GREAT SOUNDING PIANO WILL SOUND GREAT!

Before even thinking about recording a real piano (grand or upright), *make sure it is well maintained and in tune!* Nothing can remove the out of tune honkey-tonk bar piano sound from a recording!

A piano is a physically large sound source that naturally takes up space. It lends itself to multi-mic techniques, which provide panning options that promote width and fill the soundstage. A mono piano track is usually very difficult to incorporate into a stereo mix effectively – it is either panned center, where it competes with many other fundamental sound sources, or panned off to one side, where it creates asymmetry unless balanced with another sound on the opposite side of the soundstage. Either way, an instrument that is naturally very large is made to sound small and compact.

Details, dynamics, and accuracy are paramount to the sound of a piano, and being a percussion instrument there are significant transients created by the hammers hitting the strings – so condenser or ribbon mics are recommended. Cardioid, wide-cardioid, and omnidirectional mics are all options. Omnidirectional mics will produce the most open and transparent sound, but if the lid is closed or partially open, or the room acoustics are not ideal, or there are other sound sources in the room, cardioid mics are preferred – so that reflections from the lid, the undesirable room sound, or spill are minimized.

OPEN OR CLOSED?

- For rock and pop music, it is usually preferable to record the grand piano with the lid open, or completely removed.
- It is best to isolate the piano in its own room, or overdub it separately, so that the piano mics do not pick up loud spill.
- Putting the lid in its short-stick position will only reduce the spill a little, and the sound picked up by the mics inside the instrument will not be as good as with the lid open.
- Keeping the lid closed decreases spill, but produces honky resonances that will be picked up by the mics inside the instrument.
- Short-sticks and closed lids are sometimes necessary in live sound reinforcement situations, but they are undesirable in the studio.
- If it is not possible to isolate or overdub the piano, drape comforters, duvets, or heavy blankets over the openings of the open lid, and use close mic techniques inside the piano, with the lid on short or full stick rather than recording with the lid closed. The sound will be less open, and more "dead" than without the isolating materials, but there will be less spill.

There are as many different piano mic techniques as there are recording engineers! The following suggestions, shown in **Figure 11.6**, should serve as starting points only:

1. A stereo array positioned 15 to 30 cm (6 to 12 in) above the hammers will produce the brightest, punchiest sound. A centered, near-coincident array produces a good stereo image, with individual notes localizing precisely throughout. The extreme high and low

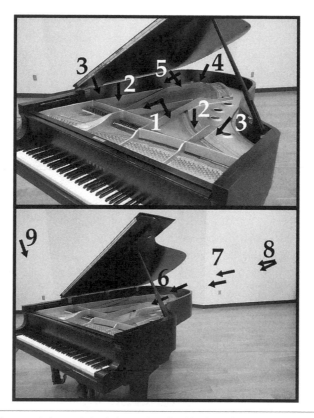

Figure 11.6 The grand piano mic techniques described in the main text.

notes may sound a little weak due to the distance between those strings/hammers and the mic array.

2. A spaced pair over the hammers will produce a wider image, with a more clear transition of low notes to high notes from one side to the other (if the mics are not too close). Divide the piano keyboard into quarters, and position a mic on the division between the first and second, and the third and fourth quarters. If the mics favor a particular range of notes too much, they are probably too close.

3. A widely spaced pair of *outriggers* can be added to a coincident or near-coincident pair centered over the hammers. This will give the extreme low and high notes the same perspective and proximity as the middle notes closer to the center array, and widen the stereo image.

4. A warmer, more resonant, but still punchy jazz sound with a wide stereo image can be achieved by adding a center panned mic over the low strings, towards the opposite end of the piano from the keyboard.

5. A crossed pair of "very-near-coincident" directional mics with just 10 to 15 cm (4 to 6 in) between the capsules, positioned mid-way down and about 30 cm (1 ft) above the strings, will pick up a full close sound with a good balance of punch and resonance. The stereo image will be wide, but individual notes will not clearly localize to discrete and precise positions throughout it.

6. If a slightly less close perspective is desired, try a pair of spaced mics positioned just inside the piano rim, 15 to 45 cm (6 to 18 in) above the strings – one towards the high strings, and one towards the low strings. This array picks up some punch in the high and mid notes, and the warmth of the mid and low notes. It produces an expansive, but imprecise stereo image – it is wide, but there is less accuracy in the localization of individual notes.

7. A very natural sound can be achieved by positioning a spaced pair of mics 30 to 60 cm (1 to 2 ft) outside the curved lid opening (with the lid attached, and on full stick), above the rim, angled down into the instrument. This image is still broad, but there is no precise note localization (which there isn't when we listen to the piano from a few feet away anyway).

8. For the most completely natural or "classical" type of sound, any stereo array can be positioned 4 feet to many feet away from the curved lid opening, angled down into the instrument – with the lid attached and on full stick. The mics should be high enough to "look down" into the instrument, meaning that the further from the piano they are, the higher they are positioned.

9. Mics can also be positioned near the pianist – above, or to either side of their head. The performer plays so the piano sounds good to their ears – so try some mics near their ears! Some mics spaced to the side of the pianist can even be used to pick up some key noise if that natural component of the piano sound is desirable. Closer mics are often blended with these more distant mics to add some detail and definition to the recorded sound.

PRACTICAL EXERCISE

Before setting up mics, explore the piano with your ears. With the lid open, get your ears inside the piano and listen. Move your head around, trying to anticipate the sound that will be picked up by mics in different positions and at different distances. Try the following:

- Listen from several feet in front of the curved opening. The sound should be a natural piano heard acoustically in the room. The different sounds coming from all over the instrument have been given distance over which to blend and combine into the "whole" piano sound.

||||➡

- Listen directly above the hammers. The sound should be typical of a modern pop sound – very bright, punchy, and percussive, and have the ability to cut through a busy mix.
- Listen from above the low strings at the opposite end of the piano. The sound should be warmer and more resonant, with an emphasis on the sustain.
- Listen from directly above one of the sound holes in the iron plate of the piano. A lot of sound comes from the sound holes, but it is an ugly honky sound – not somewhere to consider putting a mic.
- Listen for a more balanced sound – a blend between the punch, body, and resonance, but still with a close perspective. Try above the edge of the curved rim of the frame.
- Listen from under the piano – particularly if there is a hard reflective floor. There is a lot of aggressive sound down here, which is not usable by itself, but can be an excellent "grunt and power" component added to other mics.

Miking the Grand Piano

Example 11.15: Grand piano, a coincident stereo pair over the hammers.

Example 11.16: Grand piano, a near-coincident stereo pair over the hammers.

Example 11.17: Grand piano, a spaced pair over the hammers.

Example 11.18: Grand piano, a mic on the low strings is added to a spaced pair over the hammers.

Example 11.19: Grand piano, a crossed pair of directional mics positioned centrally, mid-way down the strings.

Example 11.20: Grand piano, a spaced pair over the rim of the piano.

Example 11.21: Grand piano, the natural piano sound captured by a near-coincident pair 6 feet in front of the open piano lid.

Different musical styles call for different recorded piano sounds:

- Pop, rock, electronica, etc. – bright and punchy.
- Classical – natural, more distant, a true acoustic piano sound.
- Jazz – a hybrid of those two extremes. Warmer and rounder than a pop piano, but still with a fairly close perspective.

Different songs on the same album, by the same artist, can be given different moods and textures by exploiting different piano sounds:

- Upbeat or beat-driven tracks might benefit from a brighter piano sound.
- Ballads generally suit a mellower sound.

Even think about giving different sections of *the same song* different piano sounds!

- During the verse, use mics that provide a darker, mellower sound.
- To give the chorus a lift, and an extra dimension, add or switch to mics that produce a brighter sound.

Subtle balance adjustments are all that is needed – not night and day differences! Making sure you check mono compatibility, don't limit yourself to two mics! It's easy to end up using seven or more!

11.7 THE UPRIGHT PIANO

The upright piano is a *very* different instrument to the grand piano. An upright will *never* sound like a grand – no matter how good it is, or what mic technique is used. Uprights always sound smaller and have less transparency, clarity, and resonance. The instrument is more difficult to mic because the strings and hammers are not as accessible as on a grand piano. Some possible mic techniques, shown in **Figure 11.7**, include:

1. With the top door of the piano removed, position a spaced pair of mics 15 to 30 cm (6 to 12 in) in front of the low and high strings respectively. This will produce the brightest, punchiest sound.

2. For a slightly less big and punchy, but still bright sound, remove the top lid of the piano (preferably also remove the front top door) and place a spaced pair 10 to 30 cm

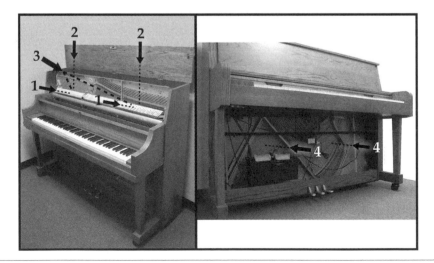

Figure 11.7 The upright piano mic techniques described main text. The black box in the piano in this picture is a humidity regulation system, which should be turned off while recording.

(4 to 12 in) over the opening. This technique will have a less clear stereo image than the mics in front of the hammers.

3. A more natural but distant sound can be achieved by removing the top lid and front door, and placing a coincident or near-coincident pair above the player's head, angled down towards the hammers inside the piano.

4. A warmer sound can be captured with the bottom door of the piano removed, and the lower portions of the strings miked each side of the performer.

Great results are rarely achieved by miking the backside of the piano – which is the amplifying soundboard. The sound is usually muddy and honky, and lacks attack, punch, and detail.

11.8 ELECTRIC KEYBOARDS AND SYNTHESIZERS

Unless a keyboard or synthesizer is played through a specific amplifier/loudspeaker combo for a specific amplified sound, electric keyboards and synthesizers are best DI'd – they will be cleaner. Some classic vintage synthesizers and modern "retro" models aren't really stereo – they just use a simple delay to widen the stereo image. If this is the case, studio effects units or plug-ins may be a better solution to make the sound wider if necessary. If the synthesizer or keyboard is really stereo, *always* record it in stereo – you will have more creative and interesting mixing options, and the sounds can exploit less congested non-central spaces in the stereo image, leaving the congested center for the kick, snare, vocal, and solo sounds that are typically panned there.

11.9 LESLIE SPEAKERS AND THE HAMMOND ORGAN

Leslie speakers have a rotating horn that reproduces high frequencies, and either a stationary sideways (or downwards) firing woofer, or a rotating horn for lower frequencies. It is necessary to mic both of these. The player controls the horns – they can be stationary, or rotate at various speeds, producing effects ranging from subtle tremolo to thick chorus-like grunge.

Because speakers can be very loud, and the horn's rotation causes strong air currents, dynamic mics are the "safe" close miking option. Condenser mics will produce a more open, detailed sound, but they may pick up too much mechanical noise, and are susceptible to distortion and popping because of the air currents created by the horn's movement. To minimize this noise potential, position dynamic mics at least 10 cm (3 in) away from the horns, and condenser mics at least 6 inches away, and *always use foam windscreens or a pop filter*. It's a good idea to feel for where the air currents are at a minimum and try to position the mics in those positions.

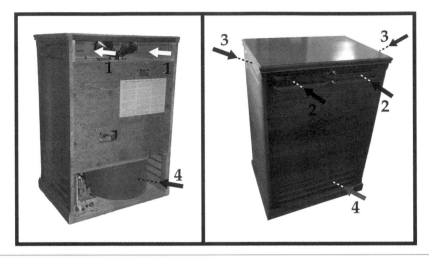

Figure 11.8   The Leslie speaker mic techniques described in the main text.

Some Leslie horn enclosures are open on both sides, others only on one side. The following mic techniques are shown in **Figure 11.8**.

1. For the clearest and widest swirl, try miking the rotating high frequency horns in stereo from the open side of the cabinet.

2. For a fuller, phatter, juicier sound, but a less precise, yet more immersive width, try miking the wider baffled side in stereo.

3. For a less obvious swirl, but differently dramatic and expansive stereo image, put mics on opposite short sides of the cabinet.

4. A side firing rotating low frequency driver can be miked with the baffle left in place, or removed. There is less of a need to mic a rotating low frequency driver in stereo because swirling low frequencies can be too distracting.

If the Leslie cabinet has a downwards firing low frequency loudspeaker, the mic should be positioned with its capsule underneath the cabinet, angled up towards the loudspeaker.

11.10 ACCORDIONS

Accordions come in different shapes and sizes. Some have a piano style keyboard and a buttonboard, and some have only buttonboards. In either case, sound comes from both ends of the instrument. A detailed recording of the accordion is usually desirable, so condenser or ribbon mics are preferable for studio recording as long as spill is not significant:

1. A single microphone can be placed about 60 cm (2 ft) in front of the accordion, at a height in the upper half of the instrument, aimed down towards the center of the

Figure 11.9   The accordion mic techniques described in the main text.

instrument. Positioning the mic directly in front, slightly over the keyboard, or slightly over the bellows will produce subtly different sounds.

2. For a stereo recording, use a spaced pair of mics, each placed about 15 cm (6 in) in front of, and 15 to 25 cm (6 to 10 in) wider than, the reed vents on each end of the instrument with the bellows extended, aimed towards the vents. Panning the mics hard left and right is usually inappropriate, and an exaggeration of the instrument's width, so pan them appropriately to form the instrument's place in the context of the mix you're working on.

3. If there are other sound sources in the room, a dynamic mic can be placed 10 to 15 cm (4 to 6 in) in front of the front reeds, above the keyboard, approximately one-third of the way down from the "low keys" end of the instrument.

11.11 EQ FREQUENCIES

It is impossible to tell you what EQ will be necessary! The examples below will help you start to identify frequency ranges and their characteristics. Where add or cut suggestions are given, they are fairly commonly required with close placement of directional mics, but don't be surprised if you do end up having to do the exact opposite!

ELECTRIC BASS

- *Weight* and *phatness* – 60 to 100 Hz.
- *Body* – around 400 Hz.
- *Definition* – 600 Hz to 1 KHz.
- *Snap* and *pop* – 2.5 to 5 KHz.

ACOUSTIC BASS

Similar to the electric bass, with the *slap* of the strings above 4 KHz.

ELECTRIC GUITAR

- Reduce *boominess* – below 250 Hz.
- *Body* or *boxiness* – 400 to 800 Hz.
- *Bite* – 2 to 6 KHz.

Try separating two similar guitar tracks by accentuating different *bite* frequencies in each using *subtractive* EQ – attenuate different frequency ranges adjacent to the *bite*, and most importantly, make sure the guitars don't mask the vocals.

ACOUSTIC GUITAR

- *Bottom* and *weight* – around 120 Hz.
- *Body* and *thickness* – around 240 Hz.
- *Harshness* – 1 to 3 KHz.
- *Brightness* – 5 to 8 KHz.
- *Shimmer* – above 8 KHz.

ACOUSTIC PIANO

- *Weight* – 80 to 120 Hz.
- *Body* – around 200 Hz.
- Reduce *muddiness* – 300 to 800 Hz.
- Reduce *honkey-tonk* – 1 to 2 KHz.
- *Presence* – 2.5 to 6 KHz.
- *Crispness* – above 5 KHz.

HAMMOND ORGAN

- *Weight* – below 120 Hz.
- *Body* – around 250 Hz.
- *Presence* – around 2.5 KHz.

ACCORDION

- *Body* – around 200 Hz.
- *Reedyness* – 700 Hz to 1.4 Khz.
- *Bite* – around 2 KHz.
- *Shimmer* – 4 to 9 KHz.

Strings, Winds, Brass, and Percussion

12.1 ORCHESTRAL STRING INSTRUMENTS

VIOLIN AND VIOLA

Reflections are essential to the sound of a string instrument. It is difficult to make an orchestral string instrument sound natural if it is recorded in a room that is too small or too dead. In a room that is too small the mic placement will be too close in order to eliminate the small room's undesirable sound, and there is no way to convincingly make it sound less closely miked during mixing. A room that is too dead is an alien acoustic to most musicians, so their performance suffers, and the few artificial reverbs that can take a very dry sound and convincingly make it sound like it was naturally recorded in a larger, more live, space are certainly not stock DAW plug-ins!

Flat condenser mics are the best choice to pick up the most detailed, natural, and uncolored sound of violins and violas – the presence peaks of highly characterful microphones can over-emphasize unflattering frequency ranges. The closer a mic is placed, the scratchier and more abrasive the sound is – but in order to minimize spill from adjacent instruments, sometimes closer than ideal miking plus corrective EQ is necessary. Some suggested mic positions include:

1. A mic positioned 45 to 60 cm (18 to 24 in) above a solo instrument (or an instrument in a section) angled towards the bridge, strings, and f-hole area will pick up a natural but fairly close perspective.

2. Frequencies below about 500 Hz propagate fairly evenly around violins and violas, but frequencies above this are focused in a narrow 30° cone, upwards from the top soundboard. Being directly in this beam can often sound too brittle, so to ensure you're getting the best frequency balance it is important to experiment with mic positions above the instrument.

3. An overhead mic can be placed above the performer's shoulder and head, pointing down towards the center of the instrument. This produces a slightly fuller, less edgy sound.

4. In a good sounding room, a warm and natural acoustic sound can be achieved by positioning a mic about 60 cm (2 ft) above and about 1 to 2 m (3 to 6 ft) in front of the instrument. The sound will be bright but less resonant, and there will be increased room sound compared to the closer techniques.

Blues, jazz, and rock players may have pick-ups on their instruments. These do not have the same sense of detail, transparency, or space that a well-miked instrument has, but they do have a unique sound that may be stylistically appropriate. Pick-ups can be DI'd and blended with a mic – the technique is similar to the bass mic plus DI technique discussed in **Chapter 11**. However, due to the smaller wavelengths of the higher frequencies of the violin and viola, phase cancellation and comb filtering between the DI and mic is more significant and needs to be minimized with careful mic positioning.

Figure 12.1 The violin and viola mic techniques described in the main text.

WHICH POLAR PATTERNS TO USE

Wide-cardioid and omnidirectional mics will pick up the most natural instrument sound. Their wider pick-up and reduced proximity effect allow closer mic positions to capture a more natural sound than a cardioid or hyper-cardioid mic. They also beneficially pick up good room sound. If the room is too small or too reflective, cardioid mics may be necessary to reduce the room sound – but more directional mics need to be positioned further away in order to pick up a natural sound, and in doing so will end up picking up more colored, off-axis room sound. Closer than ideal directional mic placement is necessary if there is too much spill or bad room sound, but the instrument's sound will be compromised and require more corrective EQ.

CELLO

Much of a cello's characteristic sound comes from its interaction with the floor – or the wooden sound box that cellos (and basses) are sometimes played on. The wooden floor or sound box amplifies the sound waves transmitted through the metal spike at the base of the instrument, to produce a full bodied, resonant sound. Positioning a mic closer than about 60 cm (2 ft) away doesn't pick up this passively radiated and reflected content. The further away the microphone, the more natural the sound will be, so a mic positioned up to 2 m (6 ft) away would be entirely appropriate if spill from adjacent sound sources is not problematic. The beauty of a cello's sound is in the subtleties and details – so flat response condenser microphones are a reliable choice.

1. Positioning a microphone too close, directly in front of a cello often produces a boxy, nasal, or scratchy sound.

2. A close mic positioned on the high string side of the instrument, slightly off-center to about 40° to the side, picks up a smoother, more balanced sound.

3. A mic positioned up to 2 m (6 ft) away, about 60 cm to 1 m (2 to 3 ft) high, angled below the bridge can pick up a combination of instrument and reflected sound. Different timbres can be picked up – body and floor reflections can be increased by aiming the mic further down the instrument, and the string and definition can be increased by aiming the mic further up the instrument. If the sound directly in front of the instrument is too thin, try moving the mic to the side in 15 cm (6 in) increments – and compare both sides to see which side sounds best.

4. A mic fairly high above the instrument, a little in front of it, pointing down will capture a sound a little more similar to the sound the player is hearing.

5. A cello is a relatively wide baritone source, and can also be usefully spot or solo miked in stereo – using an array 60 to 90 cm (2 to 3 ft) in front of, and about 75 to 90 cm (2 ½ to 3 ft) high, aimed down into the instrument. Coincident, near-coincident, spaced AB, or MS techniques can be used. A spaced pair gives you some creative control over the image width, which is important, because you do not want the instrument to take up the entire width of the soundstage – rather than spacing omnidirectional AB mics widely and panning them narrowly (which is prone to phase problems), space them about 15 cm (6 in), and pan them almost or hard left and right for an appropriate width.

For isolation and spill control purposes, it is sometimes unfortunately necessary to mic closer than 60 cm (2 ft) away. If this is necessary, be sure to keep the mic out of the performer and bow's way – and experiment with mic position to obtain a sound that requires the least amount of corrective EQ.

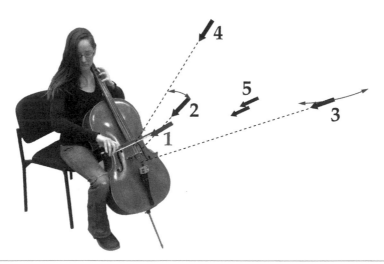

Figure 12.2 The cello mic techniques described in the main text.

STRING BASS

Close miking techniques for string bass are discussed in more detail in **Chapter 11**.

For an acoustic, orchestral bass sound which has a fairly close perspective, a blend of the first two techniques discussed in **Chapter 11** can be used:

- Find a natural sounding sweet-spot about a meter (3 ft) away.
- Add some bottom and roundness with a closer mic on the best sounding f-hole.

For a less close miked sound:

- A mic can be positioned up to 1.5 to 2 meters (4 to 6 ft) away, 1 to 1.5 m (3 to 4 ft) from the floor, angled towards the body below the bridge of the instrument, so that it picks up a blend of the direct instrument sound and floor reflections. Experiment with moving the mic to the sides about a foot at a time, to find the sweet-spot that produces a warm and defined sound.
- Adding a f-hole mic 30 to 60 cm (1 to 2 ft) away can add some low frequency grunt that might be missing from a more distant mic.

THE GOOD AND BAD OF CLOSE MICS

Good: For non-classical projects, the intimacy, "bow on string," plucking details, and reduced spill of close miking can be desirable – but you should experiment, moving the microphone a few inches at a time, to find a sweet-spot where the sound requires the least corrective EQ.

Bad: Close mics will also pick up more undesirable performer noises – fingers on the fingerboard, breathing, clothes rubbing, etc.

12.2 HORN SECTION INSTRUMENTS

TRUMPET AND TROMBONE

Trumpets and trombones are loud instruments – a trumpet can produce over 130 dB SPL close to the instrument's bell! Trumpets and trombones radiate a lot of their high frequency content very directionally, so positioning the microphone slightly off-axis will keep it out of the loudest SPLs, and mellow an otherwise overly bright or harsh sound. Position a trombone mic to the player's left to keep it out of the way of the instrument's slide. Use a small diaphragm condenser mic with high SPL capabilities for the most accurate recording, a large diaphragm condenser mic for more warmth and character, or a ribbon mic for a smoother, less harsh sound. Many condenser mics feature −10, −15 or −20 dB pads that can be engaged to prevent mic and/or pre-amp overloads at these high SPLs.

Figure 12.3   The trumpet mic techniques described in the main text.

1. For a bright sound, position a mic at least 30 cm (1 ft) away, up to 35° off-axis, angled into the bell.

2. For a more balanced, but still contemporary in-your-face sound, position a mic slightly off-axis, at a distance of about 1 m (3 ft).

3. In a good sounding room, without adjacent sources of spill, increase the mic distance to 2 to 3 m (6 to 9 ft) to de-emphasize brightness, and add warmth and body to the sound.

CLOSE MICS ON BRASS

Dynamic and condenser mics (with high SPL capabilities) can be positioned on-axis, less than 30 cm (1 ft) from trumpet and trombone bells. The sound will be:

- Brighter than we usually hear acoustically.
- Contain little buzzy details and breath and spit noises that we don't hear from a distance.
- Have increased amplitude spikes compared to more distant mics.

Like a close miked lead vocal, a track recorded this way will need more compression, EQ and automation during mixing – but spill or room sound will be minimized, and the sound will be more "in-your-face."

ACCURACY OR WARMTH?

Trumpets and trombones have huge dynamic ranges and contain large waveform peaks relative to their average level. Tube microphones or pre-amps, or for pop and rock, high quality flat response dynamic mics, will "eat" some of these peaks, smooth the waveform, reduce crispy brightness, and produce warmer, fatter, but less detailed sound.

SAXOPHONE

Saxophones come in different shapes and sizes, the most common being the soprano, alto, tenor, and baritone saxes. Even though the instruments have a shiny bell similar to brass instruments, sound does in fact come from the holes *all over* the instrument, depending on which holes are open or closed as the instrument is played. Large diaphragm condenser mics are a great choice for detail, power, and character. Ribbon mics can also sound great. Remember that the closer the mic, the more it will zoom in on just part of the instrument's sound, and accentuate breathing, performer noise, key clicks, and other instrument noises.

1. One place a mic should *not* be pointed is directly into the bell – the sound is thin, honky, and inappropriately loud when the lowest few notes are played.

2. For a close miked perspective of a curved instrument, a mic can be placed from 15 to 30 cm (6 to 12 in) in front of, and slightly to 30 cm (up to 8 in) above the bell, pointing back *past* the top of the bell towards the keys on the instrument – imagine the mic's pick-up pattern sweeping across a good portion of the horn, and not just into the bell. The higher the mic, the more it should be angled down towards just above the top/ back of the bell. Higher mic positions can favor the "left hand notes" of the instrument, while lower mic positions can get more "honky" on the low notes.

3. For an even more natural perspective suited to acoustic jazz and classical recording, take the longest dimension of the instrument, and position the mic about that far away (possibly just a little closer) and anywhere from a little above the bell to not much higher than the left hand thumb key on the back of the instrument. The higher the mic, the more it should be angled down towards just above the top/back of the bell.

4. Straight instruments really require two mics for close miking. One should be positioned about 30 cm (1 ft) in front the instrument, angled towards a point 1/4 to 1/3 up from

Figure 12.4   The saxophone mic techniques described in the main text.

the bell of the instrument – this will pick up warmth and body but lack brightness and the lowest notes. The second mic should be placed about 15 to 30 cm (6 to 12 in) directly below the bell, pointed up into it. This mic will pick up a very thin, nasally, buzzy sound that is nasty by itself, but blends well with the other mic, and gives the lowest notes balance.

5. If only one mic is available for a straight saxophone, it should be angled towards a point 1/4 to 1/3 up from the bell, 18 to 24 inches away (45 to 60 cm) to allow some floor reflections from the bell to bounce into the mic to brighten the sound and fill in the lowest notes.

LIVE SOUND VS RECORDING

In live concert sound mics are frequently placed closer than described in this book. This is to maximize the amount of amplification possible before feedback by getting as much sound into the mic as possible, and minimize the amount of spill from other sound sources on the stage. The sound when miking so close is compromised, and is not the best sounding or most natural. Extensive corrective EQ is required. This is a necessary trade-off in order to get the show loud enough, and have individual control of each instrument's sound and level. The recording studio is a much more controlled environment in which the goal is to capture *the best* sound, not just *the most* sound.

FLUTE

A flute's sound comes from all over the instrument, depending on the note that is being played. A good quality condenser mic will best pick up the subtle details of a breathy flute sound.

1. For a natural, classical sound, a mic 1 to 2 m (3 to 6 ft) in front of, and slightly above the performer's head, angled down towards the center of the instrument is a good starting point.

2. The flute can also be miked from slightly behind the performer, at head height, to pick up something similar to the sound the performer hears.

3. For a closer jazz or pop perspective, a mic can be placed about 30 cm (1 ft) in front of, and slightly above the instrument, mid-way between the mouthpiece and left hand keys – avoiding the wind currents and breath noise produced when the player blows across the mouthpiece. Omnidirectional mics are less troubled by wind currents and pops, so are a good choice for this position.

4. For a stereotypical rock or jazz flute sound, a mic (dynamic or condenser) *with a windscreen* can be positioned within a few inches of the mouthpiece, just below the strong wind current coming from the player's mouth.

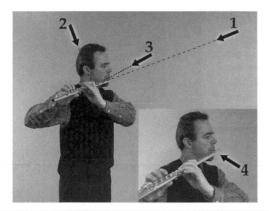

Figure 12.5 The flute mic techniques described in the main text.

Stereo miking is also an option. A coincident or near-coincident array can be positioned similarly to the third option above, but halfway down the instrument.

12.3 OTHER WIND AND STRING INSTRUMENTS

BANJO

1. A close miked perspective of a banjo can be achieved by positioning a mic 10 to 30 cm (4 to 12 in) in front of where the neck and body of the instrument meet – move the mic around and listen for the sweet-spot where there is a good blend of body, resonance, stringiness, and fingerboard sound.

2. Positioning a mic further up the neck produces a thinner, more metallic, buzzy sound.

3. A mic behind the bridge will produce a thicker, fuller, more resonant sound, with a dark "pluck."

4. An XY stereo array can also be positioned in the sweet-spot.

5. A pair of spaced omnidirectional mics about 30 cm (1 ft) from the instrument are also a good stereo option – when transparency is desired, and the room sound is good.

6. Raising the mic above (and in front of) the instrument, and angling it down towards the body will increase the floor (and possibly room) reflections picked up – producing a more vibrant, exciting sound.

MANDOLIN AND UKULELE

Mandolins and ukuleles are small quiet instruments, so miking options are a little more limited than for guitars and banjos. To accentuate the body of their light sound, angle the mic towards

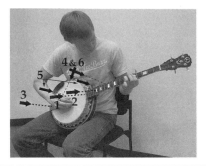

Figure 12.6   The banjo mic techniques described in the main text.

Figure 12.7   Angle a ukulele (or mandolin) mic towards the sound hole regardless of where it is positioned.

the sound hole regardless of where it is positioned. A good starting point is 10 to 15 cm (4 to 6 in) in front where the neck and body meet.

DOBRO (RESONATOR GUITAR)

The dobro is frequently played like a slide guitar, flat on its back on the player's knees. Try positioning a mic about 30 cm (1 ft) above and to the left or right of the metal resonator, angled into the resonator. There will be more body and "pluck" from the bridge side, and more bright stringiness from the neck side. If the dobro is isolated, and the room has good characteristics, pulling the mic a little further away will give the sound a more transparent natural proximity and tonality.

BASSOON

As with most other woodwind instruments, much of a bassoon's sound comes from the lowest open hole, and not the bell. Like baritone saxophones and bass clarinets, bassoons are physically large instruments, and different sounds come from all over the entire instrument. Miking too close presents some challenges.

Figure 12.8   Angle a dobro mic towards the resonator. Different sounds can be achieved from each side of the resonator. Keep the mic on the neck side out of the player's breath currents by positioning it slightly in front of the instrument.

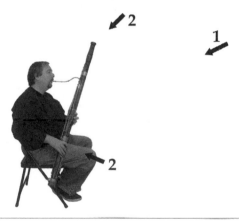

Figure 12.9   The bassoon mic techniques described in the main text.

1. A more distant, natural sounding approach is to use a condenser mic with a wide pick-up pattern, positioned 1 to 2 m (3 to 6 ft) away, at about the player's eye level, angled slightly down so the pick-up pattern sweeps across the entire instrument.

2. For a closer perspective, a mic can be positioned about 30 cm (1 ft) away, slightly to the outside of the instrument, a quarter to a third from the bottom of the instrument, blended with a second mic above and slightly in front of the bell, angled down so that it picks up the bell and lower notes.

Omnidirectional mics will pick up the beef and resonance of the lowest frequencies created by bassoons and contra-bassoons best – as long as the room reflections sound good, and spill from adjacent sound sources is not problematic.

CLARINET

The approach to miking a clarinet is similar to miking a straight soprano sax, ideally with two microphones. The first mic should be positioned about one-third of the instrument's length from the bell, about 30 cm (1 ft) away, angled towards the finger holes on the bottom half of the instrument. If only one mic is available, this is a good position to start with, but the mic distance should be increased to allow more floor and room reflections to be picked up. The second mic should be positioned about a foot below the bell of the instrument, and blended with the other mic to add brightness.

OBOE AND ENGLISH HORN (COR ANGLAIS)

For a natural perspective, take the longest dimension of the instrument and position the mic that far away, pointed one-third of the length from the bell. A closer perspective can be achieved with less mic distance – but no less than 15 to 20 cm (6 to 8 in) – pointed at the same finger holes. If the sound is a little dull and unexciting, add a second mic under the bell, similar to that described for the clarinet and soprano sax.

FRENCH HORN

The French horn is unique in that its bell faces backwards. In orchestral settings the rear reflective wall of the performance space or stage reflects the instrument's sound back towards the audience. Unlike other brass instruments, the player's hand is typically placed inside the bell, which can either gently mute the sound, or give it a piercing nasal quality. The high frequency radiation pattern from the bell is naturally quite narrow, but is diffused by the hand in the bell.

A mic positioned 30 to 60 cm (1 to 2 ft) behind the player, slightly off-axis to the bell will accurately capture the sound. If there is a reflective wall behind the instrument, a bidirectional or omnidirectional mic will pick up a blend of direct and reflected content.

HARMONICA

1. The classic blues harmonica mic is the Shure "Green Bullet," cradled by the player's hands. If the player does not have his or her own mic of this or a similar type, a decent dynamic vocal mic (because of its built in windscreen) can be used to get a similar hand cradled sound.

2. A stand mounted mic can be positioned immediately in front of the player's hands, which are then free to be opened and closed to create timbral effects.

3. For a lighter, more transparent sound, with a less close perspective, a condenser mic with a pop filter or windscreen can be positioned about 10 cm (4 in) in front of the harmonica.

Figure 12.10 Miking a French horn.

Figure 12.11 The harmonica miking techniques described in the main text.

HARP

The harp needs to be recorded in a good large room, and the mics need to pick up some room reflections. In small rooms the harp becomes too bassy – it is an orchestral instrument, and really designed for orchestral performance spaces!

1. For a natural perspective, a mic (or stereo array) can be placed about 2 m (6 ft) away, directly in front of to 45° to the side opposite the player, 90 to 120 cm (3 to 4 ft) high, angled into the soundboard of the instrument.

Closer mics can be added – or used alone if more isolation is necessary:

1. Brightness and presence will be present in a mic positioned at least 30 cm (1 ft) to the side of the top of the pillar (opposite the player), angled down towards the soundboard.

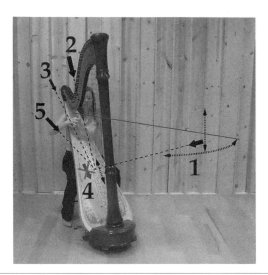

Figure 12.12   The harp mic techniques described in the main text.

Figure 12.13   Miking a tuba.

2. A fuller sound can be achieved by positioning a mic level with the top of, but at the rear of the instrument, on the opposite side of the harp to the player's head, angled down and forwards into the strings and soundboard.

3. Avoid placing a mic too close, directly in front of the soundboard – it will be too muddy and bassy.

4. Instead, for a closer beefier sound, position a mic at least 45 cm (1.5 ft) to the side and 45 cm (1.5 ft) above the soundboard, pointing towards the base of the strings in the center of the soundboard, on the opposite side of the instrument to the player.

TUBA AND SOUSAPHONE

In terms of range and musical function, the tuba and sousaphone are similar, but a tuba's bell points upward, and a sousaphone's bell points forwards.

1. For a natural tuba sound, a mic can be positioned about 60 cm (2 ft) above the bell. On a sousaphone the mic should be positioned in front of the bell.

2. A slightly off-axis position produces a less buzzy, warmer sound.

These are not close mic techniques, so condenser or ribbon mics are preferable to dynamic mics. An omnidirectional mic will pick up the very low fundamental frequencies these instruments can produce better than a directional mic.

12.4 PERCUSSION INSTRUMENTS

MALLET PERCUSSION INSTRUMENTS

The marimba and vibraphone are both large horizontally wide instruments. Their sound can effectively use the width of the stereo soundstage. A common approach is a pair of condenser mics spaced about 60 to 75 cm (2 to 2.5 ft) apart (or dividing the instrument into thirds), about 60 cm (2 ft) above the instruments bars. Other stereo arrays can be used, each with the imaging and phase characteristics discussed in **Chapter 6** – but a spaced array generally provides more even coverage of these wide instruments.

A xylophone is a little smaller, so coincident and near-coincident pairs are also practical options. If a spaced pair is used, the mics should be spaced a little over 30 cm (1 ft) wide, and 20 to 30 cm (8 to 12 in) above the instrument.

HAND PERCUSSION INSTRUMENTS

Shakers, claves, tambourines, triangles, and other small instruments can generally be miked with a single small diaphragm condenser mic (for the best detail and high frequency definition) positioned 15 to 45 cm (6 to 18 in) away, maybe slightly above the instrument, angled into it. Sometimes, close miking these instruments makes them hard to fit "back" in a mix. Increasing the mic distance to several feet (or more) records them at a perspective they might naturally want to sit in the mix at, rather than having to push a close miked sound back electronically and artificially using EQ and effects.

Larger membranophone instruments, including conga and bongo drums can be approached similarly to snare drums and tom toms for a close-up perspective, as discussed in **Chapter 10**. For a less close perspective that automatically mixes itself further back in the stereo soundstage (where these drums can be very effective), use a coincident or near-coincident stereo array 30 to 100 cm (1 to 3 ft) away and slightly above the instrument.

Figure 12.14 Stereo microphone techniques directly above a vibraphone's bars. You would only use one of these techniques at a time. 1) A spaced pair. 2) A near-coincident pair (or a coincident pair). 3) A slightly wider spaced pair, angled in towards the center of the instrument will produce a wider image – but listen carefully for a hole in the middle of the image.

12.5 EQ FREQUENCIES

It is impossible to tell you what EQ will be necessary, so the center frequency examples below are just suggestions to help you identify the frequency ranges of different characteristics. The specific mic, mic technique, room, instrument, and the way it is played are all unknown variables that will alter what EQ might be necessary.

- 50 Hz: *Woof.* Adds fullness to low frequency instruments. Reduces excess boom on low frequency instruments.
- 100 Hz: The *boom-box fake-bass* range. *Boomy.* Adds fullness and warmth to some lower instruments. Attenuate to reduce boom and muddiness in others.
- 200 Hz: Low-mid *mud.* Adds fullness to some instruments. Attenuate to reduce muddiness (therefore increase definition) in others.
- 400 Hz: *Hollow* sound. Reduces *boxiness.*
- 800 Hz: Reduces *honk.*
- 1 KHz: *Megaphone, bullhorn,* or *AM radio* character. *Nasal* thinness.
- 2 KHz: Just plain *nasty.* The *ear fatigue* range. Increases *diction* and *intelligibility* of a sound when boosted. Decreases *clarity* and *bite* when attenuated. Increases or decreases *attack, snap,* and *punch.* The lowest of the *presence* frequencies.
- 3 to 4 KHz: *Trashy, ugly, not-quite-high-frequencies.* Increase or decrease *definition, cut, snap,* and *presence.*
- 5 KHz: *Attack, punch, harshness, presence.*
- 7 to 8 KHz: *Brightness, sibilance, sizzle, shimmer. Scratchy* or *harsh* in some sounds.
- 10 KHz and above: *Air, breath, float, lightness.*

Beyond the Basics

13.1 "EAR CANDY"

A recording should be more than a "demo tape," and more than just the musicians presenting the song as they might in a live gig. There are no related visuals to accompany an audio recording – so the music and production aesthetics alone have to sustain the listener's attention. This chapter discusses some techniques and principles that can be employed to make better use of timbres and the stereo soundstage, and to craft a piece of sonic art that draws the listener in, and is compelling to listen to. The goal is to encourage the listener to want to play the track again because it was sonically and musically interesting, and because they wonder if there's any other cool "ear-candy" they might have missed the previous time.

13.2 FIXING DULL OR SMALL SOUNDING TRACKS

MYTH: COMPRESSION CURES ALL

A common mistake made by novice engineers is the addition of over-zealous compression as a cure for small, dull, or lifeless tracks, with the expectation that some magical hardware unit or plug-in will bring that track to life.

RESULT: What usually happens is that too much fast attack compression is applied and the sound gets smaller and less punchy, but because the output gain is turned up, it "sort of seems louder." But it's not *better*. It's just *different*. It's easy to convince yourself something sounds "better" just because you spent a lot of time working on it, or its average is a little louder.

SOLUTION: Compression, correctly applied and controlled by a skilled engineer who has a thorough understanding of the concepts and controls, can indeed make things bigger and punchier. Good, artistic applications of compression include:

- The "sound" of a classic compressor.
- Dynamic control.
- Deliberate creative effect.

Trying to rescue a track that sounds poor because of bad instruments, a bad performer, or bad recording technique, should be a last resort. It's much better to fix an imperfect sound at the source, and make sure it sounds great during the recording stage. As the saying goes, "garbage in, garbage out…"

Compression   @

Example 13.1: A vocal, with no compression.

Example 13.2: The same vocal compressed fairly heavily to even out the short-term irregularities in the performance.

Compression *(continued)*

Example 13.3: The same vocal, processed gently with a classic tube limiter known for its phatness and warmth.

Example 13.4: A snare drum, with no compression.

Example 13.5: The same snare drum, squashed with too much fast attack compression. The life is sucked out of the sound.

Example 13.6: The same snare drum, with about 6 dB of slow attack/medium release compression to bring out the initial attack of the sound.

Example 13.7: The same snare drum, with about 6 dB of fast attack/fast release compression to exaggerate the body and sustain of the sound.

MICROPHONE DISTANCE

PROBLEM: Directional microphones are the most commonly used type in small rooms, or larger rooms if there is significant spill from other sound sources. Remember that directional mics exhibit proximity effect, and the see-saw effect of EQ means that an overabundance of low frequencies has a similar effect to turning down the higher frequencies, making the sound dull, dark, and boomy.

SOLUTION: Reduce proximity effect by moving mics further away. This will instantly increase transparency and definition, and produce a brighter, more vibrant track. The trade-off is that there will be more spill from adjacent sound sources, and more room sound – but the better direct sound may outweigh those drawbacks. Isolation can be increased by using sound barriers and gobos (which will be discussed in **Chapter 14**).

Microphone Distance

Example 13.8: A miked electric guitar cabinet. Miked too close, it sounds dull and lifeless.

Example 13.9: Moving the mic back about 30 cm (1 ft) produces a more vibrant sound.

MICROPHONE FOCUS

The natural, acoustic sound of an instrument is the sum of all the sounds radiated from its entirety. The closer a mic is to a sound source, the more it zooms in on the sound coming from where it is pointed, and the less it picks up all the constituent components of the sound. While corrective EQ may be able to somewhat correct frequency imbalances, it cannot put back components that are either not there, or severely misrepresented. You must understand the instrument or sound source you are recording, and how it radiates its different sonic components. With this knowledge mics can be better placed.

Moving the mic further away de-focuses it, allowing it to capture more of the sound of the whole instrument. As discussed in previous chapters, some instruments radiate certain frequency ranges very narrowly – so correct placement is critical, and small changes have a radical effect on the sound the mic picks up.

DON'T FORGET TO LISTEN...

The most important tools you have are your ears – *not your mics*. Before setting up a mic, listen closely to the instrument or sound source from different positions. Move your head (and ears) around the instrument as it is played, and listen to how the sound changes. From where does it sound most accurate or best for the project? Put a mic there. Because a mic is more subjective in what it picks up than your ears, it will not sound the same, but it should be a good starting point.

Then experiment with the microphone, making further adjustments around that position, and anywhere else you feel like trying! If you are working with an assistant, have them carefully move a mic around the instrument while you listen in the control room. If you are working alone, send the mic's sound back into a pair of isolating headphones in the recording room – you can get an idea of the sound the mic is picking up as you move it around the instrument yourself.

Anything recorded by Tom Dowd would be a great example of using your ears to first listen to the sound, and then positioning a mic to capture what you heard.

Microphone Focus

Example 13.10: An acoustic guitar. Miked too close at the sound hole, the mic focuses on only part of the sound – the boom of the sound hole.

Example 13.11: Moving the mic back about 45 cm (1.5 ft) produces a more balanced sound incorporating the body and brightness coming from different parts of the instrument.

USING THE ROOM AND EARLY REFLECTIONS

Another cause of dead, dull, and unexciting tracks (particularly drum and guitar tracks) can be a lack of room reflections – the sound is simply too dry. We are used to hearing certain sounds in natural acoustics of some kind, and they become unnatural, bland, and lifeless when they are too dry.

A room treated with too much absorption is a common cause of dull sound. Many cheaper absorption products (for example, thin acoustical foam, carpet, curtains, and drapery) only absorb higher frequencies – so a room treated with these materials will have an overabundance of lower frequencies bouncing around the room to be picked up by the mics, and the room and recording will sound dark and boomy. Drum rooms are designed to be reflective but controlled, have a balanced frequency response, and no standing waves. Live rooms like this add excitement and punch to the sounds recorded in them – they make things sound huge!

A potential benefit of increasing the distance between the sound source and microphone is the increased pick up of important and beneficial room reflections. Positioning mics so that floor reflections are picked up can make some sounds instantly bigger, punchier, and more exciting. If your recording room has reflective floors (hardwood, tile, or concrete for example), remove any rugs that may be present. If your room has a carpeted floor, try putting sheets of plywood over it – the difference is night and day, particularly on acoustic guitars and drums.

THE ROOM MATTERS – EVEN WHEN CLOSE MIKING!

While it's true that the closer a mic is to a sound source, the less reflected sound it picks up, the presence of those reflections has a drastic effect on the recorded sound, *even when close miking.*

In larger rooms, choices have to be made regarding where to set up instruments and mics. The reflections produced by a sound source in the middle of a room will be different to those if it were set up at one end, or to the side of the room:

- Drums generally (but not always) sound best located somewhat centrally in a room. Other instruments are then set up around them.
- Other acoustic instruments can sound better set up non-centrally, with the mics positioned more centrally in the room.

Room reflections can be exaggerated by setting up room mics at the opposite end of the room to the sound source – listening carefully for, and correcting any phasing and comb filtering by adjusting the distances between the close mics and room mics.

As a last resort, reflections can be added artificially using an effects unit or plug-in. A reverb program that is predominantly early reflections, or a very short room, can work wonders on small, dull, compact, lifeless tracks – but of course if you have a room with good sounding reflection characteristics it's best to capture that natural acoustic.

Floor Reflections

Example 13.12: The same acoustic guitar as in **Example 13.11**, recorded with a reflective floor (no carpet or rug). The reflected content makes the sound brighter and more powerful.

BOUNDARY LOADING

A *boundary* is a wall, floor, or ceiling. The low frequency output of a sound source *or microphone* will be boosted by approximately 3 dB by each boundary that it is positioned close to. A bass or guitar speaker cabinet put on the floor in the corner of a room will have its low frequency output boosted by up to 9 dB! If a mic is positioned close to that source, it is also effectively boundary loaded, so there will be another 9 dB boost, *plus* any proximity effect – making the sound dull, dark, congested, and confused.

EQ is only partially effective at fixing phase-related anomalies, so all extensive EQ can do is make the sound less bad – fixing it at source by repositioning the sound source and microphone is the best solution.

- Avoid setting equipment up in the corners of rooms – unless the sound needs a significant bass boost.
- Try raising speaker cabinets off the floor with either commercial cabinet stands, sturdy chairs, or small tables.
- Due to the longer wavelengths of lower frequencies, a bass cabinet needs to be positioned further from boundaries than a guitar cabinet in order to minimize the effects of boundary loading.

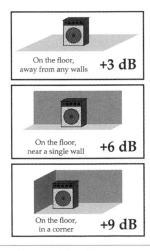

Figure 13.1   Speaker cabinet positions and the effects of boundary loading.

Boundary loading *could help* a small, thin sounding guitar or bass cabinet by giving it some added weight – but remember, a small speaker cabinet is always going to sound like a small speaker cabinet!

13.3 MULTI-MIKING = CLOSER MIKING

Move your ears (or a microphone) closely around a large instrument listening for where different components of the sound are best. Positioning multiple microphones, each picking up a different component of the larger instrument's sound, gives you the ability to blend those constituent elements into the "whole" sound during mixing. Blending multiple mics like this will allow you to position the mics closer than if you were using a single mic, which would have to be positioned more distantly to pick up the entire instrument's sound. In addition to having a closer perspective, spill and room sound will be reduced in these closer mics.

Multiple mics, each with a very different character, positioned adjacently, can also provide different sonorities that can be blended together. For example, a dynamic mic can be combined with a condenser mic on a guitar cabinet – the dynamic mic provides a smoother, darker sound, and the condenser a more airy, edgy sound.

SINGLE INSTRUMENT MULTI-MIC PANNING

- Most of the time, when acoustic instruments are miked with multiple mics in different places to pick up different component sounds (i.e. *not* a stereo array), the mics should be panned to the same position to form the synthesized point source sound. Panned widely these mics will produce an image that is smeared across the stereo soundstage, lacks focus, and has less impact and solidity.
- Two different mics placed next to each other and panned wide, will produce a slightly diffuse sound that is centered and has little width – the difference in sound between the two mics is relatively small, so it's not an effective way of spreading or creating a wide image. Panned identically two radically different mics can be effectively blended though.
- Multiple different sounding mics, on different guitar cabinet loudspeaker cones, also suffer similar imaging limitations. Different "identical" loudspeaker cones only usually sound subtly different, and the sonic differences between different mics is also relatively subtle – so the difference between the left and right channels when the mics are panned to opposite speakers is relatively small, producing a centered but smeared image with a limited sense of width. Recording multiple "identical" (or slightly different) performances and panning them across the stereo image is a much more effective image widening technique, discussed later in this chapter.

13.4 DISTANCE MICS – GUITAR AND BASS CABINETS

As discussed elsewhere in this book, the "zoom factor" of a close microphone can be beneficial to some sounds – including guitar and bass cabinet loudspeakers. It allows the specific timbres that radiate from different parts of the speaker cone to be selected creatively. However, this close perspective does not represent the natural sound of the cabinet. Many cabinets have more than one loudspeaker, so the "whole" sound is a blend of all of those loudspeakers – and the phase anomalies between them. A single mic, close to one loudspeaker cone, does not pick up these characteristics – the sound may be "in-your-face" and have some good grunt, but it can also be a little flat and one-dimensional.

A mic 20 to 60 cm (8 in to 2 ft) in front of a single speaker cabinet will pick up the sound of the entire speaker cone. A mic 1 to 2 m (3 to 6 ft) away is a true distance mic (and is only a sensible option if the instrument is recorded in isolation). Distance miking is particularly useful on a cabinet with multiple loudspeakers, as the increased distance allows the mic to pick up the blended sound of all the loudspeakers. The increased distance also increases the reflected content picked up:

- The sound of a more distant mic will be less boomy and muddy, and more open and transparent than a close mic. But the sound may get too "roomy" in some situations.
- Floor reflections picked up by a more distant mic may cause phasing and comb filtering. The distance between the cabinet and mic, and height of the mic and/or cabinet, should be adjusted to minimize this. The closer the mic and/or cabinet are to the floor, the higher the frequencies that are affected (maybe pushing them out of a problematic range), but the more boundary loading bass boost there is.

Depending upon the specific room acoustic, a distance mic can sound great by itself. A distance mic can also be particularly effective blended with a close mic:

- The close mic provides the weight and grunt of the sound.
- The distance mic adds power and penetration.

Regardless of whether distance mics are used in isolation or combined with closer mics, the effects of phasing and comb filtering need to be listened for and the setup corrected before pressing the record button.

13.5 COMB FILTERING – PROBLEMS

Comb filtering can give electric guitar sounds a strange unnatural timbre – something seems to be missing, and the sound is not quite as full as it should be. Comb filtering can be produced when a microphone is positioned more than about 15 cm (6 in) from a loudspeaker cone, as shown in **Figure 13.2**. The direct path to the microphone and the path reflected off the floor are different lengths, so the two wavefronts arrive at the microphone at different times and

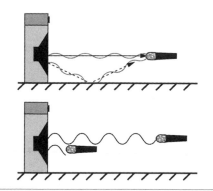

Figure 13.2 Causes of comb filtering. Top: A single mic more than 15 cm (6 in) from the loudspeaker cone. The two wavefronts arrive at different times, and at different points in their cycle. Bottom: Between multiple mics, different distances from the cone. The wavefront arrives at each mic at a different time and at different points in its cycle.

Figure 13.3 Raising the cabinet reduces the amplitude of the floor reflections picked up by the microphone.

points in their cycle. They interact constructively and destructively at different frequencies simultaneously, causing comb filtering. Large loudspeaker cones even produce comb filtering and phase artifacts because of the slightly different distances between different parts of the cone and a microphone (or your ears).

Raising a cabinet off the floor can decrease the amplitude of floor reflections – many of the reflections then bounce behind the microphone, in addition to their amplitude decreasing because of a greater distance to the mic, as shown in **Figure 13.3**.

High frequency comb filtering can be reduced by putting carpet, blankets, or acoustical absorption products on the floor between the cabinet and mic – but this may also deaden the sound, making it duller and less exciting. Remember that even 2 inch acoustical foam has little effect below 500 Hz, so the unattenuated lower frequencies still present affect the frequency balance picked up by the mic, making the sound more boomy and muddy.

BUT IT SOUNDS AMAZING WHEN I PAN IT!

A close mic and distance mic on a guitar cabinet may sound impressively wide when panned hard left and right – but when summed to mono, phase problems and comb filtering may be produced. You cannot ignore mono compatibility, and need ensure the sound sums to mono to play back well on mono systems.

Comb filtering should be minimized in both single mic plus reflections, and close mic plus distance mic situations:

- If you have an assistant, you can have them move the distance mic while you listen to it. Blend the close mic in and out with the distance mic in different positions. Listen for timbral shifts each time the distance is changed, and pick a spot where the sound is fullest when they are combined together.
- If you are working alone, put a pair of isolating headphones on in the recording room, and listen to the blend of both mics as you move the more distant mic around.
- Another method to try is to polarity reverse one of the mics, and listen to them both, panned identically and at equal amplitudes (trim them so the metered levels are equal, and put both faders at unity). As you move the distance mic, listen for where the combined signal is lowest – they will never cancel completely, hence listen for the least amount of this difference signal. This position is where the mics are picking up the most identical, or least different frequency content. Once this mic position has been found, return the mic's polarity to normal.

MORE THAN ONE DISTANCE MIC?

There is little advantage to setting up more than one distance mic. Adding another mic at another distance creates two more sets of time arrival differences, and the phase and comb filtering problems that come with them.

2 + 1

It's common to use a dynamic mic and a condenser mic as close mics on a guitar or bass loudspeaker, each producing different but equally useful characteristics. Because they are both positioned the same distance from the loudspeaker, their phase relationships are identical, and there is no comb filtering between them. Adding a third, drastically different mic, at a distance of at least 30 cm (1 ft) creates a trio of faders, and each can be adjusted independently to produce different characters and EQ effects.

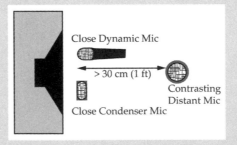

Figure 13.4 A top view of a trio of mics on a guitar cabinet.

When positioning mics at identical distances, make sure you know the position of the actual diaphragm inside each mic you use, and make sure the diaphragms line up (and not necessarily the front grille of each mic). The very front of each mic is not where the diaphragm usually is.

In a DAW it is easy to delay a close mic to a distant mic, or advance a distant mic to a close mic. This can resolve some direct sound phase issues, but create reflected sound issues, so *it is always best to resolve phase problems acoustically, by changing mic positions.*

Comb Filtering – Problems

Example 13.13: An electric guitar cabinet. A close mic and distance mic are combined together. The strange phasey thinning of comb filtering can be heard. It is usually desirable to minimize this type of artifact by adjusting the position of the distance mic.

13.6 COMB FILTERING – CREATIVE TOOL

Comb filtering *can* also be a creative tool!

Deliberately used, comb filtering can create wonderfully strange and unnatural effects.

- By blending two microphones, each a different distance from the cabinet, together as an identically panned mono point source image the overall EQ or frequency balance of a sound can be changed.
- The distance between the mics dictates the specific frequency bands affected, and the amplitude of each mic changes the amount of the effect.
- Engaging the polarity reverse button on one of the channels will produce the difference between the mics – this is an even more drastic effect.

These types of effects are probably *not* suitable for a standard rhythm guitar track, but they can be used on creative solo flourishes or as sporadic effects to turn a "demo tape" into an interesting recorded production.

For creative comb filtering it is usually best that the mics used are as different as possible – different technologies, different frequency responses, and different off-axis pick up characteristics. This makes the interactions between them more random, and you're more likely to get them to work together beneficially.

Always make sure that creative phase and comb filtering artifacts are:

- Controlled and deliberate.
- Appropriate.
- Mono compatible.

13.7 DOUBLE TRACKING

Double tracking involves recording multiple takes of the same material. Double tracking the rhythm guitar of a rock band is a classic tried and true technique:

- Record two takes of the rhythm guitar part, with or without *slight* performance and tonal variations between them.
- Pan one left, and the other right.

Even with the same mic on the same speaker and the guitarist trying to play the same material, there are enough subtle pitch and timing differences in the performance to create a huge, expansively wide stereo image of the guitar when the tracks are oppositely panned. A third take could even be added to the center (at a low level) to fill in that space if appropriate. Using a different mic and/or placement, adjusting the guitar or amplifier tone controls, or even varying the performance slightly can create complementary doubled tracks.

Although a little clichéed, this type of double tracking is a quick and effective way to get a more interesting rhythm guitar image exploiting the extremes of the stereo image that would otherwise be underutilized, and free up the center of the image to increase the clarity of the more important center panned sounds.

WHAT ABOUT PHASE PROBLEMS BETWEEN DOUBLE-TRACKED GUITARS?

When recording multiple tracks of the same rhythm guitar performance for creative panning purposes, the performance differences are usually enough that comb filtering is not a problem. However, you should always check the tracks summed to mono – so that no unanticipated mono compatibility problems are a surprise after the performer has left the studio!

Vocals are another candidate for double tracking:

- Entire vocal lines can be double (or more) tracked to make the vocal sound thicker.
- Double tracking the choruses, but not the verses, will give the chorus emphasis.
- In rap and hip hop, selective double tracking emphasizes single words or short phrases.

For double tracking to be successful, all the layers need to be rhythmically together, and close in pitch. But:

- If they are too different in rhythm and pitch, the result is a sloppy mess!
- If they are completely identical in rhythm and pitch, they blend together and the drama and effect is reduced.

In modern DAWs there are many ways to edit and align performances to follow a lead track – but it's more natural sounding if the performer can get them in time and in tune as they record. Even if the performer thinks they are repeating their performance exactly, there will be natural subtle differences between each take. If vocals are double, triple (or more) tracked, in unison or harmony, various stereo imaging options are available:

- Panning all the vocal takes center produces the most powerful sound.
- Panning them extensively across the stereo soundstage produces an expansively wide and interesting image – but it's not quite as hard or powerful as the center panned image.
- Panning them around the center, but not too wide, creates an image that retains some power and keeps the vocal image more center focused.

The context of the vocals in the mix, and potentially the meaning of the words, should dictate what works best.

Double Tracking

Example 13.14: An electric guitar, one take, two speaker cones miked individually and panned hard left and hard right. This produces a very narrow, smeared stereo image. It is not effective or an exploitative use of the soundstage.

Example 13.15: An electric guitar, two takes, double-tracked and panned wide left and right. This produces a huge, dramatic, interesting image.

Example 13.16: Multi-tracked vocals all panned center produce a powerful solid sound.

Example 13.17: Multi-tracked vocals panned widely produce a less powerful but more expansive stereo image.

13.8 ROOM MICS

Why use room mics? As discussed earlier throughout this book, a project recorded exclusively with close mics can:

- Lack depth and perspective.
- Sound clinical, flat, and bland.

Room reflections can:

- Add a layer of excitement and power to a sound.
- Act as glue that bonds the elements of a close multi-miked source (such as a drum set) together.
- Turn small, flat, compact sounds into bigger, more exciting, powerful sounds.

In a large (reflective) room, distance mics positioned more than about 5 m (15 ft) from the sound source become room mics – they pick up more reflections than direct sound. This is good, because with a delay of approximately 1 ms for every foot of distance between the room mics and the close mics, if the pick-ups of the close and distance mics were too similar there would be significant phasing and comb filtering problems. Room mics in a true live room can either be pointed towards the sound source, or towards the reflective walls and ceiling.

Any kind of stereo array can be used for room mics. However, in smaller spaces, spaced techniques are common because of the exaggerated sense of width and space they produce. In larger spaces, other mic arrays can be effectively used.

Room mics can be placed at ear height, close to the floor, or high in the air – facing forwards, backwards, sideways, upwards, and even downwards. Every room is different! Recording drums in a large live room, try a widely spaced pair of omnidirectional or cardioid condenser mics, high in the air, at least 5 m (15 ft) in front of the drum set. Try them pointing in towards the room, and also pointing out towards the edges of the room. Listen for the most dramatic (or most suitable) effect, and make sure the addition of the room sound has no adverse effects on the close miked drum sounds. Room mics can also be added to a guitar amp for solo lines, or a single room mic recorded as part of a rhythm guitar's sound.

SQUASH THE ROOM MICS!

Aggressively compressing the room mic tracks will make their sound even bigger and more powerful. This is particularly effective for drum sounds, because it raises the amplitude of the ambient reflections heard in-between the drum hits – producing a stereotypically huge rock drum sound.

Even a mono room mic can be effective and really solidify the center panned elements of a drum set. Try a condenser or ribbon mic at least 2 m (6 ft) in front of the drum set, 60 to 90 cm (2 to 3 ft) above the floor, pointing at the drum set. Compress it aggressively, by at least 12 dB, with a fast attack and fast release. This will reduce any content that might cause mic distance related phase problems, and bring out a solid and powerful sustaining room tone between the drum hits.

Room Mics

Example 13.18: A drum set recording, only the close mics, no room mics.

Example 13.19: The close and room mics mixed together.

Example 13.20: The close and room mics mixed together. The room mics are heavily compressed in this example. The room sound is wide and expansive.

Example 13.21: The close mics are blended with a heavily compressed, single, less distant room mic, 3 m (9 ft) from the drums, 75 cm (2.5 ft) high, pointing at the drums. The room sound is tight and focused in the drum set.

PRACTICAL EXERCISE

Learn to identify the sound of comb filtering:

- Copy and paste identical solo instrument material to two tracks in your DAW.
- Pan both to the center.
- Use a delay plug-in to delay one of them by 1 to 20 ms.
- Listen to the timbre changes as you change the delay time by a millisecond at a time.
- Each time, bypass or solo one of the tracks so you are just listening to one of them. Listen for how the sound gets fuller and more natural sounding without the effect of comb filtering.
- Try this with recordings of different instruments.

Setting Up the Studio

IN THIS CHAPTER:

14.1 THE THREE OR SEVEN PS

Pre-Production Planning. Or more assertively – **Proper Prior Planning Prevents Piss Poor Performance!**

Before a recording session, you need to research the band or musicians you are recording:

- What is their musical style?
- How many musicians are there?
- What instruments do they each play?
- What is their "sound"?
- How do their previous recordings sound? How do they want this one to sound?

Another very important question to consider is:

- Does the band have studio quality instruments?

The recording process will put their performance and equipment under a microscope and magnify any problems with an instrument or amp cabinet's sound. Some studios carry drum and amp inventory, so if there are any band equipment problems they can arrange to use those (if they haven't sourced alternatives prior to the session). Many studios have rental arrangements with local companies. If the client, or you as the engineer or producer, decides it is necessary to rent gear, make sure it is adequately provided for in the project budget.

HOW GOOD ARE YOU AS AN ENGINEER?

The saying goes:

> *"You're only as good as your last project…"*

But that's not true. Every project you do is advertising for future business, and part of your demo reel. You never know which of your (older) projects clients or prospective clients will hear, or when and where they will hear them! The saying should be:

> *"You're only as good as every project of yours that somebody might hear."*

Questions you need to ask include:

- How will the session be set up, and how will it be run?
- Does the available equipment inventory (mics, stands, pre-amps, inputs, etc.) support the ideal approach?
- Do the physical facilities and limitations of the studio support or impact the setup and approach?
- Will any compromises be needed? If so, ensure they will not negatively impact the recording process or end result.

Having answered those questions, you can decide how many mics, which mics, and what specific mic techniques you will use. You should create an "ideal" *input list* and *room plot*. You can't make any final decisions until you hear the instruments in the studio, but having a strategy enables you to efficiently get to work, and appear relaxed and professional. This sets the tone for the session and puts your clients at ease. The input list and room setup will no doubt change, and that is perfectly normal – just be sure to keep good notes and document all the changes. Weeks or months from the session, you want to be able to remember what you did, what worked well, and what could have been better so you don't do it again! Extensive notes, including exact positioning of mic stands and the height and angle of the mics, are essential in case it is necessary to re-record identical sounds at a later date. Take pictures of the exact setups with a digital camera and store the files with the rest of the session documents – this will help substantially if the need for recall arises. This is a good job for an assistant, intern, or a knowledgeable and reliable "extra" at the session!

INPUT LIST

PROJECT: _____
DATE: _____
ENGINEER: _____
PRODUCER: _____

INSTRUMENT	MIC	PREAMP	INPUT No.	PROCESSING	NOTES
Kick	D6	API 1	1		Short Round Base
Snare Top	SM 57	NEVE 1	2	2:1 Comp	Medium Boom
Snare Bottom	Beta 57	NEVE 2	3	2:1 Comp	Medium Boom
Hi-Hat	M44	NEVE 3	4	2:1 Comp	Tall Boom
Rack Tom 1	M88	NEVE 4	5	2:1 Comp	Tall Boom
Rack Tom 2	M88	NEVE 5	6	2:1 Comp	Tall Boom
Floor Tom	MD421	NEVE 6	7	2:1 Comp	Medium Boom
Overhead L	414 XLS	NEVE 7	8	2:1 Comp	Large Atlas
Overhead R	414 XLR	NEVE 8	9	2:1 Comp	Large Atlas
Bass Mic	MD421	API 2	10		Short Round Base. Gobo Around Amp.
Bass DI	Hot Box	API 3	11		
Guitar	R 121	SSL 1	12		Medium Boom. Gobo around Amp.
Synth L	Hot Box	SSL 2	13		
Synth R	Hot Box	SSL 3	14		
Sax	U87	GRACE 1	15		Large Atlas
Scratch Vocal	SM58	API 4	16		Tall Boom
Vocal	U87	API 1	1		Large Atlas
Vocal Doubles	U87	API 1	1		Large Atlas

recording and sound reinforcement

Figure 14.1   An input list for a recording session.

14.2 BANDS – SMALL ROOM RECORDING

In a recording studio with a smaller recording space, there is probably not enough room to set the entire band up at once. Even in a medium-sized room the setup may be cramped, uncomfortable, and not conducive to a great performance. If it's too cramped, mics will end up too close together, resulting in too much spill and less than ideal tracks. Better results in a small room studio are usually produced by overdubbing each instrument (or voice) individually, in isolation.

The benefits of this layer-by-layer approach include:

- Better isolation between the instruments produces a cleaner mix. Balance, EQ, and stereo image accuracy can all be more precisely controlled, and predictable results can be more easily obtained.
- If recorded in a room that is relatively dead, artificial reverbs and effects can be carefully controlled during mixing – the recording room itself does not impose significant acoustics of its own on all the tracks.
- Not all of the musicians need to be in the studio simultaneously. This may be helpful when scheduling busy musicians.
- As the engineer, you only have to set up a small number of mics at any one time. For a novice engineer this can make a session more manageable and approachable.

CHECK EVERYTHING!

It is imperative that each microphone is picking up good sound – and there are no problems such as distortion, crackly cables, or too much spill, etc. The more mics there are in use at any one time, the easier it is for an issue to go unnoticed until after the musicians have left the studio – by which time it is a major problem. Use the solo buttons on the console or DAW to check each mic sounds good, and watch the pre-amp *and* recording levels continuously.

The drawbacks of this small room approach include:

- The musicians have to play in smaller units or separately – not together. This can be difficult if they're not used to doing so, or do not know the songs well enough. Some bands need to play together in order to groove properly – so the musicality of the recording could be impaired.
- If the only room available is relatively dead, some instruments will lack the life and punch provided by a more acoustically live environment.
- Distance and room mic creativity is limited in smaller rooms.
- The performers rely entirely on the headphone mix in order to perform, so it is important that you can provide the mix they need, and make adjustments quickly and correctly.

The usual approach when using this recording method is to start with the rhythm section:

- Create a click track if necessary, and make sure the drummer plays to it. Most DAWs can do this as a real-time plug-in, or alternatively you can record the output of a metronome or other sound source the band provides to a spare track. A loop from a drum machine or a drum loop sample can also be used, but make sure the loop isn't changing the feel of the recording – if the band is not comfortable with it, get rid of it! Also, make sure you mute any click track as soon as the drums are recorded and it's no longer necessary for musical time keeping. It's easy to get used to it being there, becoming part of the song – and then you miss it and the song sounds empty when it's turned off!

- Record the drums. (A *guide,* or *scratch* track or two will be necessary for the drummer to play to. These other scratch tracks could be a hand held vocal mic, and a guitar or bass DI, performed in the control room. Scratch tracks are just there so the musician being recorded knows where in the song they are, and can deliver their part confidently and correctly. The scratch tracks will be replaced with better quality recordings later on.)

- Record the bass while monitoring the previously recorded drums and scratch tracks. It's usually better to mute any scratch version of the same track being recorded – it will make it more difficult for the musician to hear their actual performance, and mask musical and technical problems in the track.

- Record the guitars, keyboards, and other rhythm section instruments – in whatever order makes most sense for the musicians.

- Record the vocals.

- Record any horn and solo parts. (These last two steps may be reversed.)

Another approach to small room recording is to DI everything it is possible to DI, using amp simulators if necessary, and to have the piano player play an electronic keyboard or synthesizer. This allows more of the band to be in the recording room with the drum set (if the room is big enough) or in the control room, playing live together, and gelling and grooving better. Although these DI tracks may be compromised in sound, they can be used for the final mix, or some (or all) of them can be treated as scratch tracks and replaced with properly miked tracks in a similar process to the one described above. The difference is that having recorded the whole band in the first place, any overdubbed musician has the "band as a whole" scratch tracks to play along with, so will probably be more comfortable and perform better.

TALK MICS

In both small and large room sessions, give each performer a "talk" mic if they don't already have a vocal mic. Drums, speaker cabinets, and horns are loud sound sources, requiring their mic's gains to be relatively low – so they will not pick up quiet talking well. Any kind of vocal dynamic mic can function as a talk mic – plugged into an unused mixer channel, or a temporary DAW track (either an aux track or an audio track set to "input monitor"). The mic will not be recorded, but it will give the performer(s) the ability to talk to the control room, and to each other's headphones.

14.3 BANDS – LARGE ROOM RECORDING

Bands usually play better when they perform together and can hear all the parts they are used to hearing – the musicians can gel and groove, instantaneously feeding off each other's energy and musicality. A whole band session can be daunting. It's a lot of simultaneous inputs! Make sure you take the time to check the sound and input levels of each mic. In addition to checking channels individually, also confirm that multi-miked instruments sound good when all their mics are combined.

The benefits of recording the bulk of the band at the same time include:

- The band locks together more tightly, and the feel of the performance is usually much more organic and natural.
- It takes less time to record, because more instruments are recorded at the same time. This can be advantageous in terms of scheduling and budget.
- The spill (if properly controlled to sound as good as possible, and/or minimized) can glue the sounds together, producing a more organic sound, less separated than if each instrument was recorded in isolation.

The drawbacks of this approach include:

- Spill and isolation are harder to manage.
- It takes more time to set up the recording equipment and sound check the entire band, and more experimentation is necessary to get mic positioning optimized for their sound sources and spill.
- There are a lot more channels happening simultaneously, so a lot more things to continuously check for problems.
- Distance and room mics are impractical because they become "everything" mics.
- The producer has to pay attention to more musical parts and events simultaneously, ensuring the performances are correct and as good as possible. With so many things happening at once it's easier for mistakes to slip through the cracks, only to be noticed later.
- Headphone mixes can be more of a challenge because each performer may need different things in their headphones – "a one mix fits all" approach usually never works. Multiple headphone mixes can be set up on the mixer or in the DAW using auxes, or if a dedicated headphone monitoring system is being used, the performers can dial in their own mixes.

LEAVE ENOUGH HEADROOM

You don't want a great performance ruined by clipping and distortion because your recording levels were really high, and a performer got unexpectedly louder. With 24 or 32 bit recording systems there is no need to have the meters peaking as high as possible all the time. With the gain set so the meters regularly peak a little above -12 dBFS, there is plenty of headroom left for unanticipated amplitude increases.

A bad room, or poor positioning of a sound source in a room, can impair the sound of the recording. Instruments can spring to life in a good position in a great sounding room. One approach to setting up in a large room is to:

- Find the optimum place for the drums.
- Set up the other instruments around the drums.

Drums generally sound best located somewhat centrally in a room, but trial and error is really the only way to optimize their position. One technique to streamline the process is to set up only the snare drum or kick drum. Position it in different places in the room, and listen to it from the performer's perspective. Where in the room does it sound best/biggest/liveliest, etc.? Once this has been decided, put a mic on it and verify the sound is what you want. Then set up and mic the rest of the drums. Be sure to listen for room resonances, from potential overhead and room mic positions while doing this, and move the setup to avoid them.

It's often not practical to put the drums exactly in the center of the room, and it's necessary to move them back slightly towards one wall in order to fit the other musicians into the room comfortably. If this is necessary, try to position the drums closer to a longer wall and keep them centered between the farthest spaced walls.

Have mics for the other musicians on stands, and cables ready to go – but don't try to anticipate where the other musicians will want to set up unless this has been discussed during pre-production meetings or conversations. The band should set up how *they* are most comfortable. Try to angle sound sources and their respective mics in order to minimize off-axis pickup and spill – and choose mics with polar patterns that best do this. Really think about positioning other sound sources and mics by aiming the mic's null points, as described in **Chapter 9**.

For most rock and pop sessions the vocals are usually the focal point, and *must* be 100 percent right – so it's best to overdub them after the rest of the music has been recorded. Using a good vocal mic, it is difficult to get an isolated vocal sound when there are other loud sources also playing in the same room at the same time. Using a less sensitive mic, and having the singer "eat" the mic is not a preferred option – because the technical quality of the recording will be compromised. Overdubbing vocals also means that the rest of the band do not have to be present after their parts have been recorded. It *is* usually necessary to record a scratch vocal while the instrumental parts are being tracked though. This can be done in the control room (using a dynamic mic to avoid feedback and spill from the monitors), or in an isolation booth if one is available, or even in the main room with the rest of the band if the singer is not so loud that their sound will spill into other mics in the room (which will create a ghostly doubling effect when the "keeper" vocals are tracked later).

ABOUT CABLES

- Cheap cables and cheap connectors are a false economy. They will quickly become unreliable. There is signal degradation over long cable runs (including interference and high frequency loss), and the lower the quality of the cable, the worse it sounds.
- You don't need the ultra-over-priced-super-luxury brands, just good quality cables with rugged connectors on them. A good retailer/dealer will be able to advise you.
- Use the shortest cables possible. The shorter the cable, the less signal loss there is down the cable. There's also less of a coil lying somewhere for somebody to stand or trip on.
- Use good quality sub-snakes to get to mics clustered around the same instrument. Ten mic cables running from the wall to a drum set are an inconvenience to set up, and a trip hazard once set up. A single sub-snake running to the drum set, with ten much shorter mic cables connected to it not only looks better, but is also safer.
- Don't use cheap low quality snakes! There's no point in having great mic cables, and then plugging them into a cheap snake. If all that is available are cheap, discount or off-brand snakes, running multiple mic cables *would be* preferable.

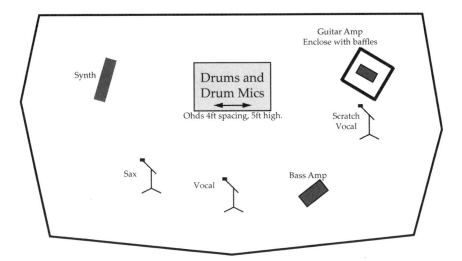

Figure 14.2   A band set up in a large room. This room plot shows the locations of the instruments from the input list shown in **Figure 14.1**.

14.4 ISO-ROOMS AND MULTI-ROOM STUDIOS

Quieter sound sources such as vocals, acoustic guitar, acoustic piano, and other acoustic instruments (horns, brass, strings, etc.) are difficult to record well if there are also much louder sound sources in the same room. These relatively quiet sources should be recorded in separate isolated rooms to decrease the bleed of the other sound sources into their mics:

- If a band has only one or two quieter sources, then it is best to isolate the quieter sources in separate rooms, or a single separate room if it is large enough.
- If a band is an acoustic ensemble, with just drums as a louder sound source, it may be easier to isolate the drums in their own room, leaving the majority of the performers together in the large room.

Smaller *iso-rooms* or *iso-booths*, built or treated to be acoustically dead and dry, work well for vocals (and some instrumental solos) because they produce a very intimate, close up sound, and allow different reverbs to be added during mixing. If small rooms are not treated with absorption they sound like unflattering small rooms. Broadband absorbtion is easy to apply, and will cheaply reduce the "room sound," but unless large bass traps are used, low frequencies will remain problematic. Because of this, basses and guitars do not sound their best in small rooms. Super dead rooms do not work well for other acoustic instruments either – they suck too much life and excitement out of the sound, and many performers find the unfamiliar and artificial acoustic difficult to perform in.

A HOME MULTI-ROOM SETUP

In a multi-room or home studio, it may be possible to record a band all at the same time and maintain isolation between the different instruments by putting them in different rooms. Some of the acoustical home remedies discussed in **Chapter 8** can temporarily transform other rooms into workable recording spaces. You don't need too many different rooms:

- Electric keyboards and synthesizers can be DI'd from the control room.
- A scratch vocal can be performed in the control room, and then it and any solos overdubbed later.
- Drums can be recorded in a more live room.
- Guitars can be recorded in a live or dead room, depending on the desired sound. In a live room, the sound will be more "open," and perhaps a little lighter and with more of a sense of depth. In a dead room the sound will be drier and more intimate, but possibly more boomy due to the lack of effective low frequency control in most domestic small rooms.
- Horns can be recorded in the less live rooms.
- Vocals and basses should be recorded in the most dead rooms.

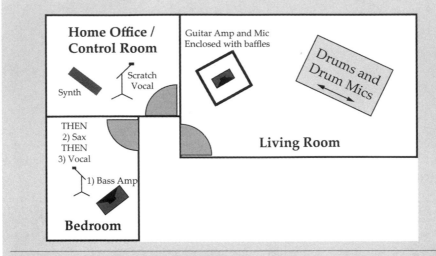

Figure 14.3 A possible setup for multi-room home recording.

It is also possible to DI and use amp simulators on guitars and bass, and have them play from the control room – but remember, the sound will not be the same as miking real cabinets.

14.5 GOBOS AND SOUND BARRIERS

Gobos are large acoustically absorbent barriers. They can be purchased commercially or easily home built from acoustic foam product or mineral wool, wood, and casters. They come in a variety of sizes, from 1 m to over 2 m high (4 to 8 ft), 90 to 120 cm wide (3 to 4 ft), and some even have windows in them to maintain sight lines between performers. Smaller stand mounted screens and acoustical deadeners are also commercially available.

- Gobos placed in front of, or around a particular instrument, can tighten the recorded sound, making it less influenced by room reflections.
- Gobos placed in-between instruments can reduce the spill of the sound sources into each other's mics.
- Gobos placed near walls can reduce reflections from sources close to that wall – deadening the recorded sound, and potentially reducing phasing and comb filtering problems at the mic.

If there are multiple instruments in a room and you need to reduce spill, remember that gobos will change the sound of the instrument they are positioned around. For example, if drums and piano are in the same room and there is too much drum spill in the piano mics, one solution would be to build a cage of gobos around the drums to reduce the drum sound

Figure 14.4   Gobos set up around drums isolate the close drum mics from the room, reducing the room sound in those mics. This can be good or bad depending upon the drum sound desired – if the drums sounded amazing without the gobos, why would you compromise that sound?

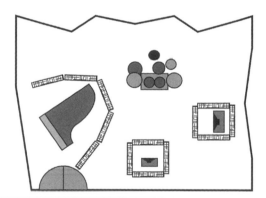

Figure 14.5   Gobos positioned around the piano, guitar, and bass cabinets isolate those instruments' mics from spill without changing the drum sound. The room sound is a less essential component of those instruments' sounds. A gobo "lid" or "roof" can also be placed over gobo "walls" to maximize isolation.

getting to the piano mics. But if the drums sound amazing, positioning gobos too close to them will remove too much of the room sound that makes them amazing, so it would be better to position the gobos closer to the piano to isolate it from the drum spill.

Applying diffusion products to one side of a gobo turns it into a mobile diffusor that can be used to break up reflections rather than absorb them, keeping the sound more live. In a large room, portable diffusors can be positioned around a sound source to reduce the natural room reflections, but create and add smaller space reflections from the closer boundaries they form. A few gobos with absorption on one side and diffusion on the other can be very useful!

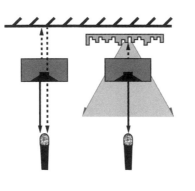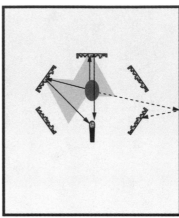

Figure 14.6   Left: A portable diffusor behind a speaker cabinet scatters reflections that could otherwise cause comb filtering at the microphone. Right: Diffusion gobos around an instrumentalist reduce natural large room reflections but keep the sound live by adding a smaller, more intimate environment to the sound picked up by the mic.

14.6 DRUM ROOMS

A bad sounding or dead room will suck the life out of a recorded drum sound! The best drum rooms are medium to large reflective rooms. They produce a lot of early reflections and a short, bright reverb tail. The room sound is clearly present in the close mics and gives the drums excitement and power, as well as acting like glue to blend the individual drum and cymbal sounds together.

The smaller the drum room, the more reflective it needs to be in order to give the sound similar life and punch to a larger room, but the sound will be smaller and more "roomy." Diffusion applied to the walls and ceilings of a slightly less than ideal room will break up and scatter reflections randomly, creating the illusion of a larger space. But anything bedroom sized or smaller, or rooms with less than 12 ft ceilings, is going to generate too many "small room" early reflections that need absorbing rather than diffusing – and even then the drums will sound like they are in a small space.

Ultimately, big, powerful, punchy drum sounds will always be more easily recorded in larger drum rooms which have high ceilings.

• In a studio with one large room and a smaller room or two, it is usually best to record the drums in the larger room, possibly with some other instruments also in there if drum spill can be managed so it is tolerable in other instrument mics.

• If a drum isolation room is necessary, then make sure it is also a live room, with a high ceiling, and not a dead vocal room!

14.7 STRING SECTIONS

Live string sections (in a rock or pop setting) are best recorded separately from the rest of the band. They are much quieter than rhythm section instruments and they themselves take up a lot of space in the room. If a separate room is not available, overdub them later.

1. Close mics, as discussed in **Chapter 12,** will produce the most individualized "Hollywood" sound, with a lot of definition and grunt.
2. A more blended, less individual, yet still close and contemporary "section" sound can be obtained by positioning a mic above each desk (pair) of violin or viola players, either from behind or in front, at a height of 60 to 100 cm (2 to 3 ft) above the instruments. A mic just under the music stand of each desk of cello or bass players will give them a similar perspective.
3. Area mics can be positioned higher, in front of blocks of string players, for more of a blended section sound.
4. A more distant front stereo array can also be used to capture the natural "in the room" ensemble sound.

Close (or desk), area, and distant techniques can be used simultaneously on the same instruments, and blended together to produce various perspectives – not only between different songs or recording projects, but even within songs.

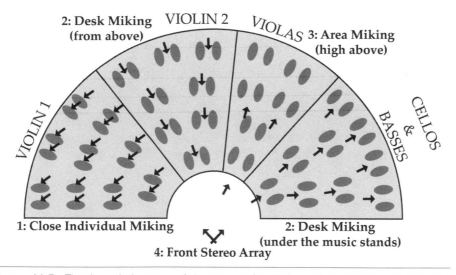

Figure 14.7 The close, desk, area, and stereo array mic techniques described in the main text are illustrated on different instruments of a string section. (This is just an illustration – the techniques used would usually be more uniform and not so different between the instruments).

14.8 HORN SECTIONS

The saxes, trumpets, and trombones found in commercial horn sections are best miked individually so that their relative balances, and the stereo image, can be created and optimized during mixing. Horn sections, like multi-tracked vocal images, can be all panned centrally (or quite narrowly) for the most powerful and assertive sound, or panned into a wide stereo image for a more interesting and expansive, but less aggressive sound.

CHAPTER 15

Miking Large Ensembles

15.1 ORCHESTRAS AND LARGE INSTRUMENTAL ENSEMBLES

It's the lucky few who record professional large ensembles on a regular basis, and while large ensemble recording may not be a goal of many people setting up home studios or just starting out in audio engineering, you never know when you might get a call from a local orchestra or choir, or a friend or relative's school, because they have a concert they would like to get a good recording of. This chapter is not meant to be exhaustive, but just to give you enough information to know how to approach large ensembles in a concert situation, and get good predictable results the first time you do.

LISTEN, LISTEN, LISTEN!

You cannot record, mix, or balance any recording project if you are not familiar with the type of ensemble or musical genre. For large ensemble projects it is essential that you are familiar with how an orchestra, choir, or jazz big band sounds – both as a live acoustic experience, and in a recorded format. Make sure you go to experience live performances and analyze respected commercial recordings.

Condenser mics are the obvious choice for this type of recording. Quality is essential, as is reach, because the sound sources are distant from the microphones. Small diaphragm condenser mics usually produce the most transparent sound, with the most natural frequency balance and best transient and high frequency details. Large diaphragm condenser mics can be used when a bigger, more characterful sound is desired. Flat mics, or those with smooth, wide, gentle presence peaks are generally preferred over those with more aggressive presence peaks (which can emphasize unflattering string instrument characteristics). In a live recording, if there is an audience present, or the event is being filmed, microphone choices may be a little more limited – the audience and cameras need their view to be as unobstructed as possible, so small diaphragm condenser mics are usually used. Pre-amps also have to be carefully chosen. Some engineers prefer flat, neutral pre-amps that emphasize accuracy, while others prefer pre-amps with more strident characteristics.

ENSEMBLE ARRANGEMENT AND THE STEREO IMAGE

Orchestras and choirs can be set up in different ways. There are many ways the string section of an orchestra or a choir might be set up, including those below:

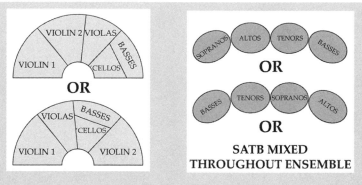

Different physical arrangements produce different recorded stereo images. The second of both of these examples spreads pitch content over the entire stereo image more evenly. Choirs can even set up with the different parts more randomly scattered.

Performer positioning should be optimized specifically for the recording. Physical arrangement should be changed from piece to piece – to produce the most appropriate, balanced, and interesting stereo image for each work.

15.2 MAIN ARRAYS

In a good acoustic, a great recording of a small to medium-sized ensemble is possible with just a single stereo microphone array. The skill and artistry of this minimalist technique is matching the choice of stereo array to the ensemble and the venue's characteristics, and the placement of the array. Any stereo array can be used in front of a large ensemble. **Figure 15.3** shows some common large ensemble mic techniques.

Main array options include:

1. Coincident pairs produce very mono-compatible, but the narrowest, and least expansive and enveloping stereo images. *Do try them though – they can sound great on the right ensemble in the right venue!*
2. Near-coincident pairs produce wider, less muddy images than coincident pairs – but they are a little less mono-compatible.
3. Spaced pairs, benefitting from the better low frequency response of omnidirectional mics, produce a bigger, beefier low end – which results in big resonant string bass, timpani, and bass drum sounds. The stereo image can be incredibly expansive, and instantly impressive and immersive – but this is at the expense of imaging accuracy and precision.
4. Three spaced omnis – a center mic, plus two additional matching mics set up symmetrically about half to two-thirds of the distance from the center mic to the edges of the ensemble. Although not the most accurate or precise image, this technique does

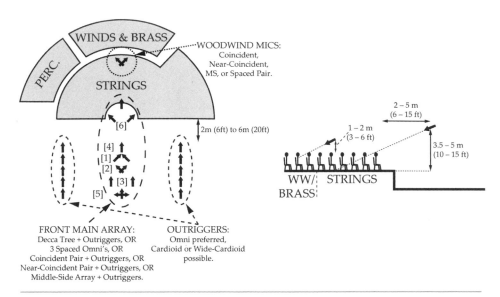

Figure 15.3 Top and side views of the orchestra or large ensemble microphone techniques discussed in the main text. The main front mics and outriggers need to be positioned at the same height, 3.5 to 5 m (10 to 15 ft) above the stage or studio floor, so that they pick up the front and rear of the orchestra more evenly, and do not focus on the front rows of performers. They should be no less than 2 m (6 ft) in front of the first row of musicians, so that they pick up a well blended sound, and do not make the strings too "scratchy." They can be up to about 5 m (15 ft) away, but the sound will be a lot more diffuse at that distance. They should be moved forwards or backwards in order to find the sweet-spot where the wet/dry balance, stereo image width, orchestral balance, perspective, and string timbre are appropriate and focused. Decca Trees are generally positioned much closer to the ensemble.

produce a very big, enveloping image. The center mic channel does not have to be used at the same level as the left and right mics – it should be used at a level that produces an evenly spread stereo image that does not have a hole in the middle or become too mono, narrow, and center dominated.

5. Middle-Side technique. As well as offering the utmost in image finesse and clarity, MS technique can be very useful in less than ideal monitoring situations because the non-matrixed M and S signals can be recorded raw, and then matrixed to stereo (and the image width precisely controlled) in a studio environment during post-production.

6. A Decca Tree produces a very immersive sound, but is a big awkward array to set up if space or visual aesthetics are a concern – which they might be in a live concert setting.

Increasing the separation between the mics in near-coincident and spaced pairs increases the width of the image – but only up to a point, after which the stereo image falls apart. The addition of a center mic to a spaced pair, to form three spaced omnis, can compensate for this.

Increasing the angle between coincident and near-coincident mics will increase the perceived image width – however centrally located sound sources are then more off-axis and subject to the mic's off-axis coloration. Hyper-cardioid mics are an alternative to cardioid mics, and exaggerate image width more than cardioid mics – but centrally located sound sources are potentially subject to more off-axis coloration because of the mic's increased directionality.

Moving the main array closer to the ensemble will increase the width of the stereo image – but positioning the mics too close will produce a scratchy, unblended, individualized string sound – particularly with "less than professional" ensembles…! Moving the main array closer to the ensemble also increases the direct dry sound, reducing the wet reverb or room acoustic picked up. Moving the mic array further from the ensemble produces a more unified, smoother, blended string sound, increases in the level of reverb and room acoustic (the "wet" in the wet/dry balance), but decreases the image width.

MAIN ARRAY POSITIONING – ART OR SCIENCE?

Main array placement is an art rather than a science – there are so many variables that all interact to change the perspective of the sounds recorded, the image width, and wet/dry balance, including:

- The type of array used.
- Mic choice.
- Angles of incidence between the mics in an array.
- The distances between the mics in an array.
- The distance and elevation of the mic array.
- The room acoustics.
- The sound of the ensemble, and how it interacts with the room.

It is impossible to accurately predict which techniques will be most suitable for each unique situation. Experimentation during rehearsals is essential!

15.3 OUTRIGGERS

If only a single stereo array is used, instruments located towards the edges of a large ensemble can sound distant and unfocused compared to those located directly in front of the array. A more even pick-up might be achieved by moving the mics further away from the ensemble – but the stereo image will be narrowed, and the sound will become more reverberant and distant, so it's not a perfect solution. A pair of *outriggers*, positioned in line with, and at the same height as the main stereo array, symmetrically spaced about two-thirds of the distance from the main pair to the edges of the ensemble will solidify the imaging of the sound sources towards the extremes of the stereo image. See **Figure 15.3**.

Omnidirectional mics are usually the preferred choice for outriggers because many sound sources are off-axis and benefit from their flatter off-axis response, and the image they create is easier to blend with the main array. Additionally, they offer better low frequency performance. However, recording in concert venues where audience or HVAC noise is present, cardioid or wide cardioid mics can be used to reduce pick-up of those sounds – although you might have to do an EQ boost of the extreme low frequencies to compensate for the low frequency roll-off of those directional mics.

The main array (usually panned hard left and hard right, but that is not always the case) should be used for the bulk of the pick-up, and to create a sense of the overall image width. The outriggers should be blended with this to solidify and extend the width of the image:

- If the outriggers are not turned up enough, the edges of the image will be weak and fuzzy, and the sound sources positioned towards the edges of the ensemble will not be as present or defined as they should.
- If the outriggers are turned up too much, the image will become extreme L and R heavy, and develop an unfocused center.

SETTING OUTRIGGER BALANCE

You should be able to clearly hear activity in the center *and* evenly spread throughout the entire stereo soundstage when the main array and outriggers are mixed together. To achieve this:

- With the main array faders at unity, turn the outriggers up until you start to hear them changing the stereo image. Make a note of that level.
- Continue to turn the outriggers up until the extremes of the stereo image become too loud, and the center seems weak. Make a note of this level.
- A good starting balance for the outriggers will be somewhere between these two levels.
- Mute and unmute the outriggers at different levels between the two positions previously noted. Increased presence and solidity of the extremes, and a little widening of the stereo image is what you're listening for. If there is a huge amplitude change, or the image gets drastically wider when the outriggers are unmuted, they are probably too loud.

15.4 WOODWIND MICS

The further away an instrument is from the front mics, the more distant its recorded perspective becomes, because the mics pick up more reflected sound, and less of that instrument's direct sound. Woodwind instruments are relatively quiet, and don't project as well as the brass or percussion – so they are prone to lack definition and to sound distant in the front mics.

A coincident or near-coincident array, or two or more (usually directional) spaced microphones can add definition to the woodwinds. They should be positioned several feet in front of the first row of woodwinds, and several feet above the player's heads, angled down into the center of the woodwind rows, as shown in **Figure 15.3**. Position them so the array's effective pick-up covers as much of the section as possible – both from a left/right and front/back perspective.

The woodwind mics may or may not need to be panned all the way left and right. Naturally, the woodwind section is not as wide as the whole orchestra, so it should take up less than the entire image width. However, if a less wide sounding woodwind mic array is used, it may be necessary to pan them partly, or all the way, left and right to obtain an appropriate image width.

To balance and blend the woodwind mics, repeatedly mute and unmute them, listening for amplitude and perspective changes. There should be a little woodwind amplitude increase, and the woodwinds should jump forwards slightly – sounding less distant, and less ambient and reverberant. They are too loud if they jump out or sound so dry that they don't blend with the rest of the orchestra. Use a balancing process similar to that described for the outriggers.

15.5 NATURAL REVERB AND ROOM ACOUSTICS

Large classical ensembles sound best in reverberant concert halls. Those same halls are the preferred environments for recording large classical ensembles – the acoustic experience can be captured naturally without using artificial effects. A large ensemble recording without reverb sounds strange, unnatural, and even unpleasant because the instruments lack the glue that bonds them together, and their sounds are too individualized.

The *critical distance* of a hall is the location at which the level of dry direct sound is equal to the level of reflected reverberant content. Reverb or room mics should be placed beyond that critical distance so that they pick up primarily reflections and not a time-delayed version of the sound picked up by the front mics. Do not assume that the critical distance is simply halfway back into the hall – it cannot be measured with a tape measure. It can be measured with acoustical measurement tools, or you can get a rough idea by walking from the front to the back of the hall (facing the back) listening for when the sound from the stage gets quite diffuse and unfocused.

Reverb mics should be high in the air, pointed towards the rear of the hall, and possibly upwards so they focus on where the best sounding reverb reflections are coming from. They should not be too far back or too close to any walls or surfaces because then they will focus on the reflections from only those surfaces and not the reverb characteristic as a whole. Reverb gives a hall, and therefore the recording, its character, so take the time to experiment and best position the reverb mics.

Any stereo mic array can be used for reverb mics, but those that produce wider images are recommended – because reverb promotes a sense of space, width, and envelopment.

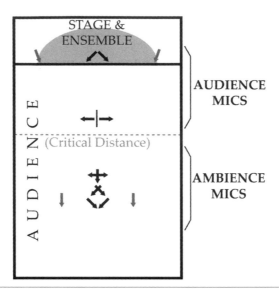

Figure 15.4 Ambience/reverb mics: Rear facing coincident, near-coincident, MS or spaced pair arrays positioned beyond the critical distance, aimed high into the reverberant space. Audience mics: A rear facing near-coincident pair, a spaced pair on the front of the stage, and a baffled A/B pair in the audience, in front of the critical distance. Any combination of audience mic options can be used.

FREE FIELD AND DIFFUSE FIELD MICROPHONES

Free field microphones are meant for use relatively close to a sound source where they pick up predominantly direct sound. Their frequency response is usually flat, or designed with presence peaks for character and projection. Most mics are designed for free field use.

Diffuse field mics are meant to be used at greater distances where the mic picks up predominantly reflected content – room and reverb mics, for example. Diffuse field mics have a slight high frequency boost to compensate for the natural attenuation of high frequencies over distance. This brightens up the sound so that the reverb is not dull or muddy. It also has the effect of bringing the sound forwards in the image, giving it a less "distant" perspective.

15.6 AUDIENCE MICS

Without an audience and the noise the audience generates, a concert hall or large church is ideal for large ensemble recording (if there is no HVAC, traffic, or other sources of noise audbile). With front, woodwind, and reverb mics you should be able to achieve good results. However if the recording is of a live concert, it is also necessary to capture the applause and audience responses so they sound good. The audience is behind the front arrays' and outriggers' mics, so directional front mics don't do a good job of it, and the rear room mics only pick up a small part of the audience – it is essential to set up dedicated audience mics.

GOOD AND BAD NOISE...

Audiences generate a lot of undesirable noise during performances, so only use the audience mics when there is applause, and between pieces – fade them into the mix quickly before applause starts, and then down subtly before the next piece starts.

Make sure the venue you're planning to record in is quiet. It's difficult to remove extraneous man-made sounds such as HVAC noise and vehicles driving past. Unfortunately, most churches are close to roads, so if possible pick a day and time when traffic can at least be minimized.

Rear facing microphones, in front of the critical distance, make good audience mics. Options (some shown in **Figure 15.4**) include:

- Directional mics (even shotgun mics) on the front of the stage, left and right, pointed into the center of the audience. Make sure they are high above the audience, angled down into the center of the audience so they don't focus on only the front rows.
- Coincident, near-coincident, or MS arrays positioned centrally, in front of (and above) the audience.
- A baffled AB array positioned *in* the front section of the audience will provide a less distant perspective.
- In larger halls, or if a closer audience perspective is desired, zone techniques can be employed – multiple audience mic arrays positioned throughout the hall, with outriggers to the sides in a wide hall. Unlike reverb mics, these audience mics should be pointed down into the audience.

15.7 SPOT MICS

Spot mics are close perspective microphones used in addition to the main front array, outriggers, and woodwind mics. Spot mics serve several different functions:

- They allow the balance of an instrument or voice to be increased so that important or subtle solos can be heard more clearly.
- They can change the perspective of an instrument or voice – bringing it closer and more up front in the stereo image.

- They can increase the clarity and definition of a sound source that is far from the main mic arrays. Blended in subtly at a low level, a spot mic can add definition and details without making the instrument or voice perceivably louder.

The most commonly used spot mics include:

- Soloists, vocal, or instrumental, in the ensemble, and in front of the ensemble. When deciding what soloists to spot mic, get the conductor's or director's input, and read the musical score while mixing and editing. If you can, fade them in and out subtly to avoid noticeable shifts in the stereo image, only use solo spot mics when necessary – that way the natural balance, perspective, and imaging of the ensemble are not permanently changed. If they do noticeably change the sound of the main arrays, it is best to leave them in all the time, but perhaps subtly fade them down by up to 6 dB when the soloist is not featured – this avoids such a drastic image shift.
- Double basses. Spot mics on one or more of the bass section add weight and low frequency definition to the more distant sound picked up by the main array. This is particularly effective when using directional front mics which can sound a little thin in the low end because of their inferior low frequency response compared to omnidirectional mics.
- Timpani. Most of the attack and definition of the timpani radiates upwards, and never makes it to the main mic arrays. A single mic, or a stereo pair, several feet above the timpani will restore these characteristics.
- French horns. With their rear facing bells, French horns can sometimes sound more distant than the rest of the brass section (which is often the goal). A spot mic or two behind the horn section will add projection and definition to their recorded sound.
- Harp and piano. If they are not soloists in front of the orchestra, harps and pianos can sound quite distant in the main mic arrays – they are relatively quiet instruments which do not project definition, attack, and details well. Even if a piano soloist is in front of the orchestra, the main mic array (which is focused on the orchestra) may not do a good job of picking up the piano sound – so spot mics can help.

Hyper-cardioid and cardioid mics tightly focus on the sound in front of them, isolating it from its surroundings. Sounds that are too isolated from their context are difficult to blend into the stereo image – they stand out as too different from their surroundings. Wide-cardioid and omnidirectional mics are preferred as spot mics, because they provide a less isolated sound that blends into the image more naturally.

But a single spot mic of any polar pattern is mono – compressing sound that comes from a wide physical space into a narrow point source panned somewhere in the stereo image created by the main mic arrays. Mono spot mics do not accurately represent the context of a sound source's location, nor do they make it possible to most accurately position the spot miked instrument, and the sounds around it, in the stereo image. On more important sound sources, or physically larger instruments, a stereo spot mic, with its own sense of width and space, can be panned and blended more naturally into the stereo image. This requires more setup time, equipment, and pre-amp or mixer channels, so is not always an option – but it is essential for large sound sources such as pianos and sections of instruments or voices. Stereo mics, which have two capsules (either a Left and Right, or Middle and Side) in the same body, are a great choice for faster setup and less visual distraction. They only require a single mic clip and stand, and no stereo bar. Many stereo mics feature adjustable capsules – the angle between the capsules, and the polar pattern of each capsule can be changed so that different stereo arrays can be used.

EQ SPOT MICS FOR THE MIX

EQ spot mics so they sound great *in the mix*. Do not spend too much time EQ-ing them so they sound great soloed out – you're not going to use them soloed out! It is often necessary to EQ spot mics quite severely, so that they provide only the sonic characters that the main array is missing. For example, on timpani spot mics the low and low-mid frequencies can usually be severely attenuated because there is plenty of that picked up by the main array. The spot mic is EQ'd so that it provides the missing upper-mid and high frequency attack and definition when mixed with the main mics.

In traditional classical recording, spot mics are not usually used to radically change balances. They are used to provide subtle lifts, give sounds a more forward perspective, add focus and definition, and to improve overall clarity. In modern contemporary productions, however, the balance changing possibilities of spot mics may be essentially exploited – there's just no way a singer can compete with a fully scored orchestra playing loudly, without being amplified via their own solo spot mic!

15.8 TO TIME ALIGN OR NOT TO TIME ALIGN?

There can be relatively large distances between spot mics and the front mics – 6 to 10 m (20 to 30 ft) or more. This means that the main mics pick up spot miked sounds 20 or 30 ms after the spot mics. When the mics are combined, this can cause phasing and comb filtering. Some engineers compensate for this by time aligning, or delaying the spot mics.

This is easy to do in a DAW, or on most modern digital mixers.

- Measure the distance (mic capsule to mic capsule) between the spot mic and main mic array.
- Calculate the time it takes sound to travel between them:

Sound travels 35 cm (1.13 ft) per ms at room temperature, meaning that it takes 2.9 ms to travel 1 m (or 0.88 ms to travel 1 ft). So if a spot mic is 10 m (30 ft) from the main array, the required delay on the spot mic is 26.5 milliseconds.

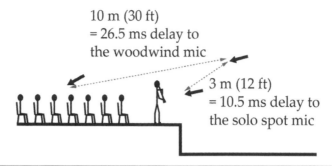

10 m (30 ft)
= 26.5 ms delay to
the woodwind mic

3 m (12 ft)
= 10.5 ms delay to
the solo spot mic

Figure 15.5   Delay times calculated for a solo spot mic in front of the orchestra, and the woodwind mics.

Required delay time (ms) = 2.9 × distance *in meters*

OR

Required delay time (ms) = 0.88 × distance *in feet*

Because of the relatively low levels of identical frequency content between front, woodwind, and spot mics placed throughout an orchestra, phasing and comb filtering artifacts are not usually a huge problem. In fact some engineers refuse to time align mics – instead allowing the law of first wavefront to bring closer miked sounds forwards in the mix. This means that less amplitude is needed to make the effect of the spot mics obvious and appropriate in the mix. Other engineers feel that time aligning the woodwind, section, and spot mics to the main front array gives the stereo image more clarity, clearing up some blurriness and smearing.

BALANCING ORCHESTRA MICS

- The bulk of the stereo image is provided by the main stereo array, which is panned and balanced to produce a smooth and even "center to mid-wide" portion of the stereo image. The array faders should be at around unity.
- Add the outriggers to the main array to increase the image width, and solidify the extremes of the image.
- Bring up the woodwind mics to focus the woodwinds, enhance their stereo imaging, and make them less distant.
- Add the reverb/room mics to make the sound more natural and glue the orchestra together.
- EQ the continuously used spot mics (double bass, timpani, French horn, harp, and piano) so they provide what's missing in the main arrays, and creep them up in the mix until they fill in what's missing.

- Finally, EQ and add the non-continuously used soloist mics to the mix, so they provide a slight amplitude boost where necessary, and focus the perspective of their sound sources.

15.9 ARTIFICIAL REVERB

If the natural reverb in a hall does not have the right sound or character (it may be too long, too short, too dull or too bright), artificial reverb can and should be used – possibly combined with the natural reverb. *Reverb for classical recording needs to be top quality though!* Cheaper reverb units or plug-ins usually have obvious and grainy characteristics which work well in pop music production but not for classical projects. Smooth natural sounding reverb that blends seamlessly with the acoustic sound and accurately recreates a real concert environment is necessary.

ARTIFICIAL REVERB TIPS

It is common to dial in more reverb on the closer and drier spot mics than on the main mics, to help them blend in.

Convolution reverb plug-ins model and simulate real spaces by applying processing based on the analysis of test tones and impulses recorded in real acoustical spaces. (These recordings are called *impulse responses*.) Convolution reverbs are ideal for classical music because they are so natural sounding – more "natural" than "noticeable."

Most classic outboard hardware and plug-ins are *algorithmic reverbs*. This type of reverb uses mathematical equations (algorithms) to generate the artificial reverb sound. The result is a less complex sound that is generally more "noticeable" than "natural," particularly at the cheaper, or stock plug-in, end of the market – although there are some very natural sounding algorithmic reverbs available these days. Algorithmic reverb is great for many commercial music styles, where it is used as a stylistic, deliberate, and obvious effect.

15.10 THE HOLLYWOOD SOUND

Orchestral film scores and "pops" recordings have a very different sound from traditional classical concert hall recordings – the orchestra as a whole has a closer perspective, and each instrument is more discrete. The following techniques can be used to achieve this sound:

- A Decca Tree, positioned above the conductor as the main array. It is closer to the orchestra than alternative main arrays that are usually located more in front of the orchestra/behind the conductor.

- Outriggers, to solidify the extremes of the orchestra image.
- Additional section/zone mics. These could be:
  - A couple of mics on each section of the orchestra (a few feet above, and slightly in front of the performers they're aimed at).
  - A mic on each desk of string players, plus individual mics on the woodwinds and brass, and multiple mics across the percussion section.
- Alternatively, each instrument can be individually miked, some even multi-miked.

In live sound reinforcement, miniature clip-on instrument mounted mics or pick-ups/transducers (on string instruments) can be combined with traditional free field mics, but clip-on mics and pick-ups are not commonly used in recording studios because they don't sound as good as traditional mics.

In order to increase isolation, and decrease the spill of louder instruments into the string and woodwind section mics, gobos or acoustic baffles are commonly positioned in front of the brass and percussion sections, and the physical arrangement of the ensemble is often changed so that the brass and percussion are located further away from the strings and woodwinds.

Scoring stages are large studio recording rooms used for orchestras. They are much smaller than concert halls and do not have the same reverb characteristics. They can be live, semi-dead, or anywhere in-between, but they are rooms and not cavernous concert halls – so artificial reverb is essential.

While six main mics plus a few spot mics can produce great traditional, natural sounding orchestral recordings, many more mics are necessary to get that intimate "Hollywood" or "pops" sound!

15.11 LARGE CHOIRS

A large choir has a significant physical width, but is only usually a few people deep. One approach to miking this type of choir is to use a main front stereo array, plus outriggers – similar to the front mics on an orchestra.

A good starting point for the main stereo array is 3.5 to 5 m high (11 to 15 ft), and 3 to 7 m (10 to 20 ft) in front of the choir, angled down towards the middle row of singers, if not just in front of that point to pick up more floor reflections and potentially increase presence and liveness.

- If the mics are too close they will pick up individual voices rather than a blended ensemble – but the sound will be drier and less reverberant, and the stereo image will be wider.
- If the mics are further away, the sound will be more organic and blended – but the stereo image will be narrower, and the mics will pick up more reverberant content.

The addition of outriggers will:

* Extend the width of the stereo image.
* Give the singers on the edges a more similar balance and distance perspective to those closer to the main array.
* Solidify the imaging of the singers on the extreme edges of the ensemble.

The outriggers should be positioned at the same height and distance as the main array. To balance the outriggers, follow similar steps to those discussed for orchestra recording earlier in this chapter. Reverb or room mics can also be added if the recording is taking place in a concert hall or large auditorium.

A greater number of less distant microphones can be used when a closer perspective is desired, or if a venue has inferior acoustics (necessitating the use of artificial reverb). Sections of singers can be miked – either groups corresponding to their voice part, or more arbitrary clusters of singers. Adhere to the 3:1 rule described in **Chapter 7** in order to minimize the effects of phasing and comb filtering between closer mics.

For large vocal ensemble recording, too many mics generally sound worse than too few mics:

* The more mics you use, the closer they have to go to adhere to the 3:1 rule.
* Too many mics, positioned too close, pick up voices too individually and not as a blended ensemble.
* Sound sources are picked up by multiple microphones, with different time arrivals at each – compounding phasing, comb filtering, and mono compatibility problems, negatively impacting clarity, timbre, and the stereo image.

Less *is* often more. **Figure 15.6** shows some different choir miking techniques.

Spot mics can be added for soloists within or in front of the choir. Even though the targeted solo sound source is a point source, miking it with a stereo mic will make it easier to blend into the image.

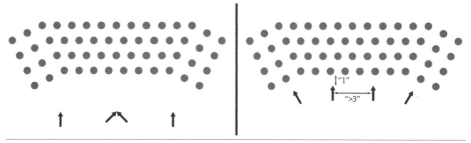

Figure 15.6   Left: Minimalist miking on a choir with just a front stereo array and outriggers. Any stereo array can be used. Right: A multi-miked "zone" approach, adhering to the 3:1 rule.

15.12 JAZZ BIG BANDS – CONCERT SEATING

In a live concert, big bands usually set up as shown in **Figure 15.7**, with the horn sections in rows behind each other (saxophones, trombones, and trumpets), and the rhythm section to the side (piano, guitar, bass, and drums).

DRUM SET

For a modern contemporary sound, rhythm section miking can be approached using the techniques described earlier in this book – but remember that a jazz drum set does not sound like a rock drum set. Jazz drums are smaller, and the kick often doesn't have a hole in the front – it produces a woofier, boomier sound that is an occasional accent, and has less attack and click than a rock kick drum. In rock and pop music the kick and snare provide time, and propel the rhythm forwards – in jazz, the hi-hat and ride cymbal are the timekeepers and driving forces, so make sure they can be clearly heard. Understand the jazz drum set and its sound before you try to capture and mix it faithfully.

- Five mics are a desirable minimum – kick, snare, hi-hat, and stereo overheads.
- A kick mic and two overhead mics would be an absolute minimum.
- Tom mics and a bottom snare mic can be also be added.

Over-processing the drums sounds is inappropriate because the jazz drum sound is more of a natural organic whole than a gated, compressed, heavily processed rock sound. Inevitable spill should be embraced to create blend rather than gating it out to create separation.

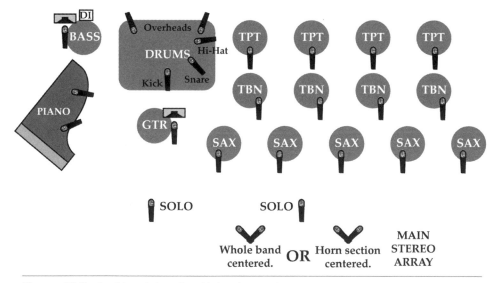

Figure 15.7 A miking strategy for a big band concert.

ACOUSTIC AND ELECTRIC BASS

- Acoustic bass: Blend a loudspeaker cabinet mic with a DI from the instrument's pick-up.
- Electric bass: Blend a loudspeaker cabinet mic with a DI of the instrument's output.

JAZZ GUITAR

Jazz guitar sounds are fat, warm, and clean. Unless soloing, they are often barely audible behind the band. While a dynamic mic is a respectable choice, a condenser mic will coax a little more bite and attack out of a sound that doesn't have much bite and attack – giving the guitar more clarity and exposure.

- Mic the loudspeaker cabinet – the amp and cone are essential parts of the sound.
- A DI can be blended with a loudspeaker cabinet mic, but *do not* use only a DI on the guitar – the sound will be flat and characterless.

PIANO

A jazz piano sound is somewhere in-between a punchy pop sound and a more distant classical sound:

- Close mics and corrective EQ are inevitable in a live concert or single room recording session. If the lid is open, the piano mics will pick up too much spill (particularly from the drums). Close, or half-stick the lid, and have somebody play scales up and down the piano, tweaking the mic positions until all the notes sound similar, none stick out or sound different, and phasing is minimized between the mics.
- Try leaving the piano on full stick, and drape a heavy comforter or duvet over the openings. This will allow the mics to be positioned about a foot above the strings for more even coverage, and a bigger, warmer sound that requires less corrective EQ.

Rhythm section mics can be panned to their actual positions towards the left of the image, or a more symmetrical image can forced by panning the bass and guitar centrally, and the drums and piano across the stereo image.

THE HORN SECTION

An accurate picture of a naturally well balanced horn section can be achieved using a single stereo array, 3 to 5 m (10 to 15 ft) above floor level, 2.5 to 4 m (8 to 12 ft) in front of the front row of saxophones. The distance, height, and angle of this array really affect the balance of the instruments picked up – particularly whether the saxes are too "close," too loud or too quiet, and whether the more distant trumpets are loud enough – so some testing and adjusting is necessary. Neither individual equalization nor compression of each instrument is possible using this technique, and it will also pick up a significant amount of rhythm section spill (particularly the drums). This section pick-up can be augmented with spot mics for soloists.

An alternate method is to individually mic each instrument. This is beneficial when:

- The horn section will require rebalancing during mixing.
- A closer perspective is desired.
- Individual EQ and dynamic processing of each instrument is desired.

Individual mics may also be blended with a main stereo array, and the individual mics can also be time aligned to the main array.

HORN SECTION MICS – CONDENSER OR DYNAMIC?

Condenser mics are recommended for close horn section miking, not only because of their superior sound, but because their increased reach means that the performers do not have to "get on" the mics as closely as they would with less sensitive dynamic mics. They do not have to adjust them so much when they change from seated ensemble playing to standing for solos.

A problem with this concert seating arrangement is that in the horn section only the trumpets have any real isolation in their mics – the trombone mics also pick up the trumpets, and the sax mics also pick up the trombone and trumpets! Imaging, clarity, timbre, balance, and processing options are compromised. One solution is to use a stereo array as the main horn section pick-up (as described above), and augment that with individual mics for solos and quiet passages – but you need to have a top notch, well balanced horn section to do this effectively.

15.13 JAZZ BIG BANDS – STUDIO ISOLATION SEATING

In a recording studio, the horns can be set up so that there is more isolation between their mics, allowing:

- More creative and clearer panning of each instrument.
- Individual equalization of each instrument.
- Compression to be applied to each instrument individually.

This can be achieved by setting the horns and director up in a square, as shown in **Figure 15.8**.

The piano and drums are best isolated – either each in their own room, or using gobos and sound barriers. At a minimum, try to isolate the drums in a different room – they are the loudest instrument and generate the most spill in other mics. If necessary, the piano, bass,

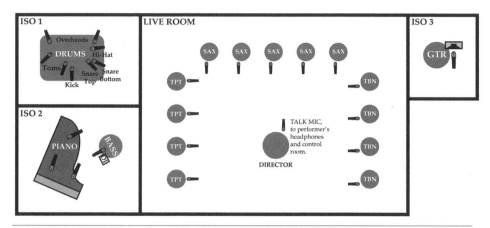

Figure 15.8 A miking strategy for a big band studio recording session.

and guitar can be housed in the same room, and barriers used to isolate them from each other within that room. Amplifier cabinets can even be completely "boxed" in a cage of sound barriers, with a lid or roof as well as sides.

Each instrument in the horn section should be individually miked. Cardioid condenser mics are obvious choices for the two sections that are to the left and right, opposite each other – this puts each section in the opposite mic's null points. For the section in the center, hyper-cardioid mics will minimize spill from the immediate sides – but with close positioning 30 to 45 cm (12 to 18 in) from each horn, spill should not be much of a problem.

The mix engineer can create different horn section images from recordings made in this way:

- The horn sections can be overlapped on top of each other, each across the entire width of the stereo soundstage – emulating a live setup with the players in rows behind each other.
- Or, each section can be panned similarly to how they are seated.

Solos can be tracked live, as the band performs, or overdubbed later. If a solo is recorded live, and the soloist isn't happy with it, the whole band needs to re-record that solo section due to the spill in the room. Overdubbing solos after recording the band backgrounds allows the solo to be worked on and perfected without holding up the whole band, but the rhythm section and soloists do not get to interact and play off each other as they would if they were playing together.

Jazz and jazz recording styles are about cohesive units. Spill should be embraced as a useful sound-shaping tool, and not treated as an enemy to be eliminated as it is in a lot of rock and pop production styles.

CHAPTER 16

Putting it All Together

IN THIS CHAPTER:

16.1 THE PRE-MIX

In addition to making sure there are no musical or technical problems with the tracks you are recording, you need to make sure all the sounds will work together in the final mix. The rough mix you build while tracking, the *pre-mix*, enables you to do this:

- Major EQ issues that have not been addressed through mic choice or placement during soundchecks or rehearsal run-throughs prior to recording should be fixed.
- Gentle compression should be added to tracks that have a wide dynamic range (vocals and bass would be prime candidates), but do not record this compression.
- Tracks that will obviously be panned away from center (drum overheads, stereo pairs, keyboards and synths, etc.) should be panned approximately.
- Each track's amplitude should be appropriately balanced on the return faders. While tracking, levels are optimized for the recording device. If all return or monitor level faders are left at unity the mix will probably be terrible and not at all musical – some sounds will obscure and mask others. Good musically appropriate pre-mix levels allow you to judge each sound in context, and have a good starting point for the performer's monitor mixes.
- Some generic, or stylistically suitable, reverb should be added to the vocals, solos, horns, and any other instruments that are obvious candidates. Any sounds that will rely on reverb or other effects as part of their character should have at least an approximate version of that effect applied from the outset so you can evaluate those sounds in context.

If the sound sources you are recording sound great, and are recorded with the right mics and mic techniques, a good pre-mix can be just a few minor EQ, monitor fader level, and processing adjustments away from the final mix – so creating a good pre-mix can be a good time-saver too.

16.2 THE MONITOR/HEADPHONE MIX

With most hardware and software recording systems, the easiest mix to send to the performer's headphones is the one that is being heard in the control room. But this is rarely the best plan:

- If you compromise the "on the fly" pre-mix in the control room, you may not hear technical or musical problems that need correcting while recording.
- Each performer will also probably want specific things in their personal mix, so a "one mix fits all" approach won't keep everybody happy.

A better approach is to create a separate mix for the performer, or separate mixes for each performer, and dial in only things they *need* to hear. This can be done by using aux sends on a hardware console (Aux 1 is left, Aux 2 is right), or a stereo bus routed to a dedicated pair of interface outputs connected to the headphone system when using a DAW.

Personal headphone monitor systems allow each musician to dial in their own mix on a control box they are given. Groups of sounds are sent to the system controller via auxiliaries,

Figure 16.1 Stereo sends used for multiple headphone monitor mixes in a DAW. Two sends (SENDS e and f, the top two small faders of each channel) are assigned across all tracks, with different mixes (amplitude and panning) dialed in for each. On the left of the mix window are the master faders for the main stereo mix, and the two headphone mixes.

busses, or other assignable outputs on the mixing console or DAW audio interface. These are then transmitted to each performer's personal mixer. These systems mean that you don't have to get everybody's mix right, or create a single "one mix fits all," and each performer is responsible for their own mix. But they can take longer to set up and might sometimes give inexperienced musicians too many choices, resulting in endless tweaking and little satisfaction! A good premix and setting each level control on the monitor mixers to a generic mid position will give the musicians a good starting mix they can tweak to their satisfaction.

Too much going on in a busy mix can be distracting to performers, so it's a good idea to strip down a thick mix to the essential elements needed to promote a great performance. For example, sixteen auxiliary percussion parts and six keyboard pads probably don't add any significant rhythmic or harmonic information that isn't provided by the drum set, rhythm guitars, and main keyboard part. Those extra layers may add textural interest to the final mix, but they will probably not benefit a headphone monitor mix.

STEREO OR MONO HEADPHONE MIXES?

There are mixed opinions on whether a mono or stereo headphone mix is better. The benefits of a mono mix are:

- It's quicker to create.

- The stereo image does not distract the performer – wide and active mixes can be off-putting to some performers.
- If the performer removes one headphone muff (or uses a single muff headphone), everything is still in the muff they are listening to.

The benefits of a stereo headphone mix are:

- Clarity is improved. It is easier for the performer to hear all elements of the mix because they each have their own physical space and are not all panned on top of each other.
- The performer will have more of a sense of being "in the song" and more intimately connected to it.
- The performer will have more of a sense of their place "in the mix," and with some stereo reverb added, the sound will be more natural and familiar.

A compromise is a mix with *some* panning (not extreme hard left and right) and keeping focal points and solo elements centered. As with any good mix, make sure the headphone mix is symmetrically balanced.

To perform well, performers need to hear rhythm, pitch, and form:

- Rhythm is provided by the drums. In rock and pop styles, the kick and snare are fundamentally important, followed by the micro-level groove information supplied by the hi-hat and cymbals. If the hi-hat and cymbals are too loud they become over-powering and kill natural groove because the performers don't relax *with* them, but instead try too hard to be on top of them. The opposite is true for jazz, where the hi-hat and ride cymbal are most important, and take the place of the kick and snare in rock music.
- Pitch information is provided by a combination of the bass and harmonic instruments (guitars and keyboards). The bass provides the musical fundamental of the chord – the note from which the singer calculates the melody's pitch. The harmonic instruments provide chord type and closer pitch-matching information.
- The form of the song should be obvious if the performers can hear the instruments providing rhythm and pitch, and the arrangement of the song is good!

Most importantly, the performers need to hear themselves! Some performers like lots of themselves in the headphone mix, while others will remove or partially remove a headphone muff so they hear lots of their natural sound in the room. For some, too much of themselves in the headphone mix is unfamiliar and will prevent them from giving their best performance.

The addition of some natural sounding reverb may mean that less of the performer is necessary in the headphone mix – the reverb tail provides an extra layer of acoustical feedback. This is the same effect reverb tails have in real rooms, and the reason people like singing in reflective bathrooms and lively halls.

Gently compress singers, wind, brass, and orchestral string soloists in the headphone mix, as you are doing the pre-mix – but do not record the compression. This allows the performers to "go for it" without suddenly hearing too much of themselves in the headphones.

Ultimately, the better the headphone mix is, the better the performance will be. A good headphone mix is especially critical for overdubs – final vocals, horn solos, string parts, etc. When the performer is drawn in by what they are hearing, their performance is always better.

OUT OF TUNE? TURN THEM UP. OR DOWN.

Turning some performers up in the headphone mix helps them stay in tune. But for others, turning them up makes things worse! If a performer doesn't notice they are out of tune, hearing themselves loudly in the headphone mix may suggest that they are "correct" because they are dominant in the mix. Turning the performer down can make the other instruments dominant and reinforce the actual correct pitch.

Single muff or double muff headphones? Many performers like to remove one muff from their ear so they can hear some of their natural sound in the room. Whatever they need to do to get a great performance is okay – with a few words of caution:

- An unsealed ear muff leaks sound which the microphone can pick up – so listen carefully for tinny headphone spill (and even feedback if the mic is cranked up in the headphone mix). Using single muff headphones will reduce this problem, and they are more comfortable than "half wearing" a muff.
- By removing an ear muff, the performer doesn't only lose 50 percent of their mix – they actually lose closer to 60 percent because of the way our hearing works. Approximately 40 percent of the auditory information is supplied by each ear, and the remaining 20 percent by the brain's processing of this information. Removing one muff probably means that the mix needs to be turned up more in the other ear – louder than it would need to be if both muffs were worn. This puts the performer at an increased risk of hearing damage in that ear.

A good approach to creating a good personal headphone mix for a performer is to:

- Put the performer themselves in their headphones so they are comfortable.
- Add the bass, then the harmonic instruments (guitars/keyboards) to their mix so they can match pitch but still hear themselves adequately.
- Finally, add the drums so they can hear time, rhythm, and groove.

Do listen to the headphone mix yourself as you create it – either in the room with the performer, or on identical headphones in the control room. This way you can hear problems, create solutions, and ensure the mix is at a safe listening level.

16.3 CLICK TRACKS

The drummer is usually the rhythmic timekeeper of the band – everybody else synchronizes to the drummer. Less than ideal drummers may push and pull the time quite significantly. Timing imperfections in the drum part will be revealed and magnified by the recording process and exist forever! Unfortunately for the drummer, the best solution to a sloppy drummer's time and rhythm problems is to get another drummer!

Or can a click track help?

Part of your pre-production discussions with the musicians should be regarding the use of click tracks and whether they are comfortable performing to them. Musicians who are not used to performing with click tracks usually have difficulty doing so. The recording studio is not the time to try it out for the first time. It may be only the drummer who needs to perform to a click – as long as they provide time for the rest of the band *throughout the entire song*. If the drummer is having difficulty playing to a click track you will probably get more musical results by turning it off – even though the tempo may fluctuate.

Click tracks can help maintain rhythmic accuracy in songs with tempo variations, or where the drums lay out for sections of the song – assuming that the musicians are familiar with playing to a click track. Many DAWs default to providing beeps as the click track. Some musicians prefer a more musical sound that blends better, while others prefer the artificial obviousness of the beeps. You need to be able to provide click track sounds that the drummer or other musicians are comfortable with.

One problem of using a click track is that the tempo becomes too static. Great songs often speed up slightly for the chorus, then slow back down for the next verse. This gives the chorus more excitement and energy. These subtle changes can be programmed into your click track!

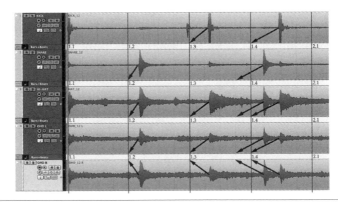

Figure 16.2   A recording made to an external click track (not shown) does not sync with the DAW tempo track, therefore the recorded drum tracks line up with themselves, but they do not line up with the "bars and beats" editing grid – making editing more difficult. The arrows show where the events should be to line up with the bars and beats grid.

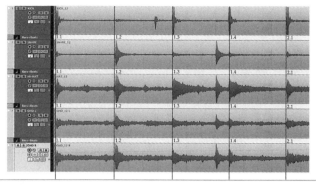

Figure 16.3 Drums recorded to the DAW's internal click (not shown) result in a performance that lines up with the DAW's grid – making editing much easier.

If you're using a DAW, it's best to have the DAW supply the click track, rather than an external metronome – the bars/beats grid of the DAW session line up musically with the bars and beats of the performance, making editing much easier, as shown in **Figures 16.2** and **16.3**.

16.4 KNOWING THE SONG

If the musicians cannot play their part of the song individually, and know their part upside down and inside out, they have no business being in the studio – although, billing by the hour, studio "practice" sessions could be very lucrative for the studio owner! If the musicians have not had much studio experience, discuss the recording process with all of the band members before the session – and make sure they know whether the process will be one instrument at a time, or the whole band at once.

Punching in and overdubbing can correct mistakes or build up a track section by section – but the more punches and edits there are, the greater the chances of volume, timbre, energy, and intensity inconsistencies between takes, making mixing more challenging.

ARE YOU THE ENGINEER OR A PRODUCER/ ENGINEER?

If you are the engineer your job is to record (and possibly mix), but not to express musical, performance, or other artistic opinions. That said, most engineers, on hearing something that they know is not in the best interests of the project will find a polite, tactful way to suggest a more suitable alternative – good methods include using subtle suggestions so the performers think they came to the conclusion or solution themselves, or taking a receptive band member aside for a discussion, and having them bring the issue up with the other band members.

In home, project, and many lower budget situations, there is no dedicated producer. Discuss your role with the band before the session to see if they will be receptive to your input as a producer/engineer, and then coach the performers, giving them the guidance and suggestions necessary to deliver that magical take!

If you are an assistant engineer, it is best to have no opinion, and keep your mouth shut! You should do what the engineer asks you to do, and proactively do *everything* to set up the session and ensure it goes smoothly. Assistants *should* answer client questions concerning the studio and how to best use it, but *avoid* saying anything that might be contrary to anything any other member of the production team has said or might say. "I'm sorry, I don't know. Why don't you ask the producer or engineer?" will politely move the question to a higher ranking member of the production team.

16.5 DON'T GIVE EVERYTHING AWAY AT ONCE

The arrangement, orchestration, and recording and mixing processes are uniquely intertwined – *together* they produce a successful record or a hit song. A band aiming for radio play or a hit record need a producer familiar with crafting arrangements that promote listener retention, and an engineer who knows how to deliver the sonic goods appropriate to the market and the band and song style.

If all the instruments thrash away throughout an entire song it will be boring, with little sense of form, progression, dynamics, or building excitement. A successful song leads the listener to its climax. The studio is an expensive place for a band to work out an arrangement, so ideally a "recording arrangement" of the song should be thoroughly worked out and practiced before coming into the studio.

If a professional producer is not part of the project, it's important that the band:

- Objectively evaluate their song forms, structures, arrangements, and orchestrations.
- Be receptive to outside advice from objective listeners and critics who are not obsessed fans.
- Be receptive to the input of the engineer – who hopefully has vast experience of making successful recordings, understands the musical genre and the target audience, and knows how to produce a product which will have maximum appeal.

You may be able to tactfully suggest that a guitar or keyboard drop out for a verse, then come back in for the chorus, for example. But if the recorded arrangement of a song is not perfect, you do have some important tools at your disposal to help create tension, release, and climax:

- The mute button.
- The copy/paste/delete capabilities of modern DAWs!

Experiment with muting textural sounds, additional riffs, and delaying the entry of percussion sounds until later in the song. Each chorus should have something new and extra added – making it bigger than the previous one. Before the final and biggest chorus, a breakdown can be effectively used – drop down to minimal instrumentation, then build back up to the biggest and final refrain.

A little bit of unpaid overtime is a fact of life for recording engineers. After the band have left you could create a quick alternate version with your mutes and re-orchestrations and see what the band think of it at their next session. If they like it, they'll value your input more and should hire you again. If they don't like it, hopefully there's no harm done and they'll be impressed you cared enough to go to that effort.

Percussion parts like congas, bongos, triangles, shakers, and claves, give extra lift and intensity to bridges, choruses, and hooks. Guitars can be multi-tracked using different sound and mic combinations, and provide additional textures that can thicken and intensify the guitar sound for bigger sections of the song.

A recording is a totally different aesthetic to a live gig. It is missing all the visual cues that allow us to perceive sounds more clearly. So, if a musical part is not really contributing anything useful to the song, try removing it, clearing up physical and frequency space, reveal other more important elements of the song.

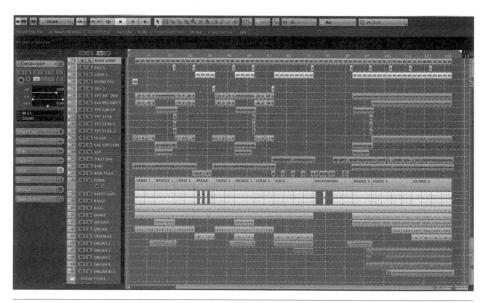

Figure 16.4   The edit window of a DAW shows an orchestration and arrangement map of a song. Note how the bridge (chorus) sections are more heavily orchestrated than the verses, the sparse breakdown, and the build to the end of the song.

16.6 LOUDSPEAKERS OR HEADPHONES? AGAIN…

As discussed in **Chapter 2**, headphones are not stereo, but binaural, producing a very different stereo image than loudspeakers. A mix created on loudspeakers translates to headphones much better than a mix created on headphones does to loudspeakers. It's always best to mix on loudspeakers – your product will sound best on the widest variety of systems, have a greater audience appeal, and longer lifespan.

That said, if you know headphone or earbud listeners are the project's target audience, do use headphones or ear buds to check the images of the stereo mic techniques you're using as you record the project, and the mix as you work on it – but do not use headphones or earbuds exclusively.

16.7 RECORDING FOR THE MIX

The purpose of this book is to give you the knowledge to record tracks that sound good, and sound the way you anticipate using them in the mix. Tracks "mix themselves" much more if you approach your recording this way – mixing becomes easier and quicker, and doesn't rely on after-the-fact processing and "forcing sounds into the mix" so much. For example:

- If you know you want a lead vocal to be front and center of the soundstage, record it so it sounds like that.
- If you know you want a sound to be further back in the mix and exploit the depth of the soundstage, mic it so it sounds like that and don't rely on EQ and effects processing to put it there.
- If you know you want a stereo sound source to be wide and expansive, or narrower and more focused, use stereo mic techniques that promote the desired image characteristic.

YOU DON'T HAVE TO USE EVERY TRACK YOU RECORD

Using analog tape, you have a limited number of tracks. With modern DAW systems, this is no longer an issue. It doesn't take very long to set up a couple of additional mics to record a couple of different perspectives of a sound source. A more distant perspective sometimes needs a little closer definition added to it for clarity and focus – so record that as well, and mix it in at a low level. (Checking for and correcting phase problems before you record of course!) Or you can decide you don't need the extra track, and don't use it. That's better than not recording the tracks and wishing you did have them!

With typical rock band instrumentation (vocals, guitar, bass, and drums) the only source that naturally has any width is the drums – via panned overheads and tom toms. That leaves many of the other sounds parked on top of each other in the center, fighting for clarity and frequency space. Mixing can be challenging, and the result boring to listen to. So record what you need to make an interesting mix:

- Double track rhythm guitars. The resulting symmetrical panning options relocate a lot of low-mid and high-mid frequency content to the sides of the image where it doesn't compete with other sounds. It will be much easier to keep the center panned bass, kick, snare, and vocals clear and intelligible.
- Record multiple vocal parts. You can then create different images and intensities depending on whether they are multiple unisons or harmonies, and whether they are all panned identically, slightly apart, or widely apart.
- Always record synthesizer and keyboard parts in stereo. They can be used to fill the stereo image. If there are multiple keyboard (or stereo guitar) parts, panning some to one side of the image, and some to the other may produce a clearer mix than panning them all hard left and right – depending upon the sound and musical role of each part. Do aim for symmetry – balancing an instrument or activity on one side of the image with one of a similar intensity of activity on the other side.

If you are stuck with limited instrumentation and minimal miking, use effects to widen the image:

- Delay effects, small room reverbs, chorus or pitch shift effects added to a single mono guitar track give you elements that can be panned widely to relocate the guitar from the center of the image to the wider extremes.

Do not simply set up mics in generic stock positions because somebody told you that was the only correct technique. And think beyond single mic, one take techniques.

Record *for* the mix!

16.8 CORRECT PROBLEMS EARLY (BUT KNOW WHEN TO LET THEM GO)

If you hear something is technically or musically not quite right – fix it. Immediately. Don't settle for second best. **"We'll fix it in the mix" is not a valid approach,** and technical problems are rarely fixable. A small glitch ignored until, or discovered during mixing is a big problem. The quality of the final product is compromised. The additional setup, studio, engineer, and performer time necessary to bringing everybody back to correct the problem is expensive. Correcting the problem immediately takes just a few minutes, and is time well spent.

Great musicality is what sells records to the majority of consumers. Only audiophiles are persuaded to buy something because it's a technically stunning recording. Getting a magical take can be more important than trying to fix a minor technical glitch in that take if the musicality is unrepeatable. Most listeners aren't going to notice a very minor technical issue – their focus is on being able to understand and sing along to the words, and not on the few milliseconds of slight distortion at the beginning of a syllable. You can do what you can to mitigate the problem – automate it to a lower level, make it less obvious through momentary use of EQ, cover it with reverb, re-draw the waveform in an editor or whatever – but know that you will always notice the problem, because unlike a consumer, you know it's there and you're listening for it.

> We should all want to create a perfect recording, and strive for that goal, but in the real and billable world, it's important to step back and realize that sometimes something that could be a little technically better is musically unique and wonderful – and worth keeping, because only we audio professionals find the problem distracting or annoying. *First takes often have freshness and magic to them, and even if you record three takes after that, you'll find most of what you use comes from the first one!*

16.9 "POLISHING A TURD"

Problems, either technical or musical, can only be fixed and polished so much. Even pitch and time correction software and plug-ins have their limitations and are time consuming to use properly, and there is no way to remove distortion or fix some stereo imaging problems. Most sound sources can be buffed over and made to sound a little better with some compression, EQ, and some reverb. But if the drums or guitar amp were just naturally horrible sounding, or the singer's performance was poor, no matter how much polish and buffing you try to give it, those problems will still exist – and it will be endlessly frustrating trying to make them less obvious! In the end it will probably still stink.... The only real fix is to re-record a better performance or better sounding instruments or vocals.

16.10 EXPLORATION AND EXPERIMENTATION

This book does not pretend to give you all the answers! That is impossible! There is no single way to achieve a great recording. But what this book should give you is the ability to:

- Think about the characteristics of a sound source and anticipate the recorded perspective the microphones will translate that sound into.
- Be able to use recording and mic techniques to capture accurate or stylized sound and timbres, different distance perspectives, and different stereo images.

You must have the mix in mind before you start setting up mics – otherwise how do you know what sound you need to capture? Thinking about the mix as you record, and recording for the mix will result in:

- Technically better sound that needs to be processed less during mixing.
- A more streamlined mix process.
- Knowing immediately during tracking whether a sound is going to work or not.

Artistic and technical skills you should be comfortable with before pressing the record button include:

- Listening critically to the source sound, and using appropriate techniques to capture it faithfully or appropriately for its role and place in the mix.
- Understanding the source sound, its musical role, and its place in the mix.
- Being able to choose an appropriate room, or adjust the room characteristics, to capture the best sound.
- Understanding mics, mic specifications, mic characteristics, and mic and recording techniques so you can choose suitable equipment and techniques for the job – guided by the mix you are recording for.

Combining the miking suggestions in the latter part of this book with the theoretical knowledge presented earlier on will enable you to capture the sound you're really after by adapting the techniques described, and importantly, being able to anticipate the effect of those changes. Just like a musician builds their musical vocabulary by emulating others, practicing, and eventually synthesizing many influences into their own unique style, you should explore and experiment to build up your library of recording techniques and solutions. Basic rules and techniques should be mastered in theory and sonically before completely "doing your own thing," because they'll help you recognize desirable sonic traits and avoid bad ones – but experimentation is key to developing your own style and being able to pair appropriate recording techniques with the aesthetic goals of different musical and production styles.

As important as these technical and artistic skills are though, they're nothing without good people skills and inter-personal skills. You need to be able to put clients at ease, quickly establish good working relationships, and be able to coax memorable performances from the musicians. Without clients and great performances, the best mics and techniques in the world are worthless!

You must aim for the highest audio quality possible. If we as professionals don't do so, we set precedents that lead to a decline in accepted audio quality, and don't provide the next generation of future audio professional with desirable material to analyze and learn from. True, the most common current consumer dissemination formats (lossy compressed audio files, played through bad sounding earbuds or tiny mobile phone speakers) do not reveal all the sonic details and definition we work hard to capture in a recording. But as internet speeds and storage device capacities increase, and listening habits change (as they always do), eventually better sounding dissemination formats and listening systems will be developed. And they *will* reveal any deficiencies in your work, giving your product a short lifespan and impairing your reputation as an audio professional.

Tips from the Professionals…

IN THIS CHAPTER:

17.1 TO CONCLUDE...

Specific models of mics have not been mentioned up to this point – to appear to "endorse" a small number of the many capable microphones available is inappropriate. It would be appropriate for some featured professionals to mention their favorite gear though! So let's close with some invaluable real world tips and tales from some practicing professionals in the recording industry. You'll notice common practices, as well as widely varying views and opinions as you read these interviews! One of the many great things about recording is that there's no single correct piece of equipment for a particular job, or a single correct way of doing something. As the interviews show, the essential skills any successful recording engineer should have are pretty universally acknowledged – and they are not all technical skills...

17.2 LENISE BENT

Independent Engineer, Producer, Post-Production, Los Angeles, CA, USA.

What type of recording work do you generally do?

"Mostly I record real musicians, typically bands, playing real instruments, and I track in a great sounding room. The room is very important to me – it's like another member of the band."

Where do you generally work?

"In various studios, mostly in Los Angeles these days. I have no typical day... ever! I do have a workflow, though. My goal for recording is to capture great performances – musicians playing together, some in iso-booths, but always having eye contact."

How long does a typical project last?

"There is no typical project, it depends on what is being recorded. I've worked on projects taking a few hours, or a few days, or several months."

Anything mic technique-related that unexpectedly pleasantly surprised you?

"On one tracking date I'd chosen two or three mics to shoot out and audition as the inside kick drum mic – an AKG D112, a Blue, and a Coles. A Shure SM7 was sitting about 3 ft away, on a tiny stand. In the control room, the faders for the D112 and SM7 just happened to be up on the console when I walked in and the sound was so rich and fat! I hadn't intended to use them both, and the SM7 hadn't been deliberately positioned, but the sound was so good I said, 'Let's do that!'

"Also, on another occasion, I'd just finished assisting on a session at the Village Studios in West Los Angeles, and had to tear that down and set up for a morning tracking date that included a Hammond B3 organ and a Leslie. I'd put some AKG 414's on the Leslie, side and bottom. While I was checking the mics in the control room, a colleague was noodling on the piano, which was 20 ft away in the opposite corner to the Leslie mics. The piano sound from these distant mics on the Leslie was so weird and freaky! I loved it! I've constantly looked for an opportunity to use this technique, but haven't had one yet...!"

How about any mic techniques that didn't work as well as you hoped?

"So many singers have heard about the Neumann U47 Tube mic and they want to use it. So I will do a blind test with the artist, using a U47 and some other mics I've determined might sound good on their voice. The favorite so far has never been the U47! It's usually the U67.

"I have used a U47 with Debbie Harry, for an old time, 20s sound. I'll often mix up vocal mics throughout an album – Neumann U67, U87, or even an AKG C414 for vocals on a brighter song."

What is the key to recording great sound?

"Capturing the performance the best way you possibly can, meaning using the right mic for that instrument or voice, put in the right place. And I prefer to work quickly while the energy is up."

What's the most important part of the recording signal chain?

"It's the source – without the source, nothing else matters. If you don't have a good singer or guitar player, or if you're recording a great piano player playing a lousy piano, you're not capturing anything good. Also, if it's not a good song, even great musicians and singers can't make it a good song."

What pre-production do you do before a session?

"I determine what songs, and how many we're going to record. We rehearse song structures, tempos, keys, and adjust lyrics to get the basic structure intact before we go into the studio. Once I know instrumentation I figure out what mics, what studio to record in, and where in the studio to set things up. What will the basic tracking be, and what will the overdubs be? I like to get the basics down so we don't have to think about that in the studio, and then the magic can happen."

What are your favorite mics and pre-amps for some different applications?

"I'm basically a Neve gal. 1073s are one of my favorite pre-amps because of the style of music I'm recording these days. If I have to pick just one, the Neumann U67 is my favorite mic. Each one sounds different, but it's a universal mic for vocals, mandolins, stand up bass, guitars, just about everything. That said, I've recently discovered the Audio-Technica 5040, love this mic and so does my current vocalist. It sounds great on everything we've tried it on.

"I also like Focusrite Red pre-amps.

"It also depends upon what the studio has, and the console. The studio is selected is based on the quality of the room, the gear, and the budget.

"I prefer not to use any EQ when I record, and I keep things as simple as possible so I can mix as I'm recording. I work very quickly and want to keep the session moving smoothly to keep creative energy and spirit intact. People forget that the technical equipment is there to serve the art, not the other way around. It's not about the gear – it's about the music, the performance, and capturing the emotion the best way possible."

What's your approach to recording in a less than ideal room?

"It's never completely impossible though it may be easier to record in a better room. It's important to really know your mics, and where to put them for the best sound. Use your ears! Use comforters or pillows to reduce standing waves and reflections in a bedroom, and turn off the AC."

What's your attitude to using less than top-of-the-line equipment?

"You just have to think "how good can we make it?" Determine what's less than ideal, and how you can upgrade the situation to be professional. I'm not going to pretend I can polish every situation, but it's got to be pretty bad for me not to be able to improve on it at all, because my style of recording is pretty simplistic, and there aren't a lot of elements involved.

"I have standards. Not only for me, but for the people who taught me, like Roger Nichols."

What do you want people to think when they hear your work?

"That it sounds great! The quality of the recording, mixing, and mastering are all equally important to me. I'm already thinking about the mastering when I'm cutting basic tracks."

17.3 DAVID V. R. BOWLES

Swineshead Productions, LLC, San Francisco, CA, USA.

What type of recording work do you generally do?

"Classical music recording, either live or in the studio."

Where do you prefer to work?

"The best recording rooms are meant for performances. Studios can sound too sterile, and are generally too small to allow for a diffuse reverb tail. A concert hall is better for the performers. They can all hear themselves and are comfortable with that acoustic, making for a better recording. These days a lot of orchestral recordings are compiled from different live performances, sometimes in different locations. That creates unique challenges!"

How long does a typical session last?

"A three-hour session is good for a large ensemble or orchestra. You'll get about fifteen minutes of 'finished product' from each session. For chamber music, two four-hour sessions, with breaks work well. In both cases you can get a complete project done in two days. Another possibility for live recordings is a post-performance patch session, usually lasting two hours. This allows coverage for inevitable audience noises and passages which weren't optimal during the concerts."

Anything related to mic techniques that unexpectedly pleasantly surprised you?

"Orchestras have a lot going on in the middle of the ensemble. I've found that spaced omni stereo pairs tend to have a hole, or wandering of the image, in the middle. Adding a center cardioid or figure-8 mic [to the main stereo array] helps to solidify the middle of the image, allowing me to space the left and right further apart, and get better separation between the left and right of the orchestra. That was a happy accident I've used ever since.

"I've always used some kind of coincident pair in orchestral recordings, to pick up winds or chorus. I've found this results in a very stable center of the image, as well as being a very accurate way to spot mic that central section."

Any mic techniques that didn't work as well as you hoped?

I've found the ORTF technique to be unsatisfactory. It works fine for listening on headphones, but on loudspeakers there's not enough width, and it tends to be too dry. If I moved the mics back, there could be too much ambience, especially in a bad sounding room. With a spaced pair of omni microphones, you get accurate low frequency response and, I think, a more natural high frequency sound. Omnis do pick up a lot of ambience so generally need to be placed closer, but not so close that one hears too many individuals. It goes back to needing good room acoustics to start with, and having enough of a blend coming through without having to move the mics back too far.

"I have found it difficult to get a pair of small diaphragm cardioids to have the same smoothness as a pair of omnis. Cardioids can work well as spot mics, but they can also bring out too much sibilance or 'fizz.' In general, avoid an omni or cardioid that has a high frequency bump around 2 to 3.5 KHz.

"The 'conductor's position' (i.e., as they would hear the ensemble) is not an optimal listening position. However, a mic placed about 1.5 metres above their head is a good recording position."

What's the key to recording great sound?

"Listening to the performers, and asking myself, 'how do I go about reproducing that?' It is dishonest to *want* a kind of sound without listening to the performers first, then striving to bring out the individuality of each performance and acoustic. Though I start with generic techniques for picking up vocal or piano sounds, these are starting points rather than fixed in stone. For this reason it's difficult to formulate what will work for different pieces, even performed by the same group in the same acoustic – this is why I change my technique slightly from recording to recording."

What's the most important part of the recording signal chain?

"The microphones, pre-amps, and A to D converters are all equally important. Look for good mics. There are fewer good mics than pre-amps, that is for certain. What colors do you want to get, and what do you want to avoid? Similarly, with A to D conversion, look for stable clocking, no jitter and very low self-noise specs. Test charts and measurements are important, but it's also important to try out equipment and ask colleagues what they think."

What pre-production do you do before a session?

"The questions I ask include what kind of music is being recorded, and what space is appropriate? I get copies of the printed music, and become familiar with it. If the ensemble has even a bad recording of a live performance, that will help me hear what they do with that particular music.

"Come into the studio with a mic list, setup and seating plan, and be prepared to change out mics if necessary.

"Performers need to be comfortable. I'll have a seating plan, but sometimes they'll react negatively to how I want them to sit – so I have to adjust accordingly.

"Discuss the recording schedule with the artists, be flexible with how much time is allotted to each piece, but keep in mind how much music needs to be covered in each session. Always ask discreetly which music poses the most difficulty, in order to allow enough time to cover that section adequately. For initial balance, choose a section which they are comfortable with, but has loud and soft sections."

What are your favorite mics and pre-amps for some different applications?

"Josephson C617SET for spaced omnis. For spot mics, the Sennheiser MKH series, or Neumann TLM 170. For percussion, the cardioid or hyper-cardioid models from the Schoeps MK series."

What's your approach to recording in a less than ideal room?

"I would probably mic a little closer than usual, and monitor with added [artificial] reverb so you get an idea of how you can transform that acoustic space into something more pleasing."

What's your attitude to using less than top-of-the-line equipment?

"I would make it clear to the client that if the equipment is less than optimal, the result will be less than optimal, and that more post-production work will be necessary to improve the sound."

What do you want people to think when they hear your work?

"The ideal listener reaction is to how good the performers are, how unique their interpretation is, and then how good the sound is. In that order.

"In one project I did, different sections of the same pieces were recorded in different locations, and then edited together. It was a challenge to match the sounds from each location. No reviewers picked up that this had been done, which to me is the ultimate compliment."

17.4 KERRY-ANNE KUBISA

Freelance Location Sound Recordist, UK.

What type of recording work do you generally do?

"Either live concerts, on location, usually in concert halls or churches, or location recordings with studio based production and without an audience. The genre of music can be varied, from opera to early music ensembles, from orchestras to string quartets, jazz to electro-acoustic and contemporary ensembles."

How long does a typical session or project last?

"Sessions can vary from four to five hours for a simple one-hour live concert, including setup, soundcheck, the concert itself and pack-up, to sessions which can last 12–15 hours, or even days."

Anything related to mic techniques that unexpectedly pleasantly surprised you?

"When I was a student, recording a band in a pub and wanting to capture the liveness and feel of the environment, I put up a pair of Sennheiser ME-80 shotgun mics. I positioned them to the left and right of the room, either side but behind the house PA, and aimed them at the audience. There wasn't anything more technical to it than wanting a mic that would pick up sounds further away. They are not the best sounding shotgun mics out there, but when I got the recording back in the studio, panned them hard left and hard right, and brought them up in the mix, wow, they gave me exactly what I was looking for. Obviously I hadn't invented that type of mic technique, it's quite common, but at the time, I felt like I'd found the holy grail of recording!

"I was working on an electro-acoustic/contemporary ensemble concert, which combined a front of house PA and some instruments that played acoustically without any amplification.

Doing a recording wasn't a requirement of the concert but I did feel this was an opportunity to do some mic technique-related experimentation! I wanted the production to be very natural, to be recorded from the perspective of the audience, and not to interfere with the stage setup in anyway. So I put a pair of miniature DPA 4060s, with their windshields on, in my ears and voilà, I had a dummy head! I sat very, very still in the sweet-spot of the hall for an hour – and the results were astonishing! There was no transference noise from them being placed in my ears, the stereo imaging was spot on, and the balance of the instruments was perfect."

How about any mic techniques that didn't work as well as you hoped?

"In the beginning of my classical recording career I was asked to record historically performed twentieth-century violin technique performances for an academic project to be submitted to the British Library. I proposed that we record from the perspective of the listener, with no close miking. I setup a Soundfield ST250 in B-format, a pair of DPA 4009 as a spaced pair, a pair of DPA 4011 in ORTF, and a binaural KU100 Neumann Dummy Head. Once we got back into the studio to listen to the initial recordings it became clear that there was just too much going on, and phasing between the pairs was a big problem. In the end we didn't use all the stereo pairs for each ensemble, just picked the best ones for each and that resolved the phasing. We also experimented with close up miking, and in the end went for a typically modern approach – a combination of stereo recording techniques *and* close up miking."

What's the key to recording great sound?

"Listening! You can have the best of everything but without the ability to listen to the music or sound of what you're recording you will never be able to get a good sound. You must also listen to what the artist wants. There's no point going all guns blazing with what you think is the best way of doing things if the artist goes away unhappy."

What's the most important aspect of the recording signal chain?

"Reliability! Well-maintained, solid equipment is key to a successful recording. Without faith that your gear will work time and time again, seeds of doubt and uncertainty set in. The last thing you want to be worrying about is, 'mmmm that input was a bit temperamental last time I used it, please don't die on me now!'"

What pre-production do you do before a session?

"Before I commit to any recording I sit down and discuss what the artists expectations are, to make sure that my skills and approach to recording that genre of music, and what the artist wants from the recording are the same. You don't want to find out down the line that you can't meet the artists' expectations.

"I ask for the score and listen to recordings of the pieces the artist wants to record, so I know the repertoire thoroughly before I start.

"A visit to the venue, if I haven't worked there before, is also essential. You need to look at access, power outlets, cable runs, health and safety issues, mic placement, etc."

What are your favorite mics and pre-amps for some different applications?

"My favourite pre-amp is the Earthworks 1024, and the mics I would usually reach for are Neumann and DPA, though AKG C414s are put on anything that's brass.

"I would typically use DPA 4009 or DPA 4006 for spaced pairs, DPA 4011 for ORTF, XY, etc.

"I love KM184s on strings and grand piano. They sound amazing and are my first choice for anything string related."

What's your approach to recording in a less than ideal room?

"I am often put in the position of recording drums *live* in a classical concert hall. The obvious way to avoid the drums becoming a muddy, noisy, over-reverberant mess is close miking. Maybe not so obvious is for the drummer to adapt what they play – instead of playing like 'Animal' from Sesame Street, they can use rim shots, brushes, tinkle the cymbals, or simplify the rhythms."

What's your attitude to using less than top-of-the-line equipment?

"Tricky. I think I would have to weigh up the negative and positive impact the project would have on my reputation, and either run away, or jump in feet first, depending on the odds. If you've got good ears, I think you could make the right sound, in the right room, sound great with a bag of SM58s and SM57s!"

What do you want people to think when they hear your work?

"I would like to say that I hope that they would hear the passion and commitment that went into the recording! Really though, what they should hear is the music. The listener should feel immersed in it, like they are sitting in the venue it was recorded in, surrounded by the audience and ambiance of the space, and forget about everything else!"

17.5 WES MAEBE

Engineer/Producer, Sonic Cuisine, London, UK

What type of recording work do you generally do?

"Anything from baroque to death metal, blues, jazz, pop, film scores, old hard rock, and stonking techno!"

Where do you generally work?

"A lot of my studio-based tracking happens at RAK Studios and British Grove, and then it's back to my Sonic Cuisine facility for overdubs and mixing. Classical sessions usually take place in concert halls and even stately homes. I've found there's always a road near churches, but stately homes are usually in the middle of nowhere so they're quieter!"

How long does your typical project last?

"The budget dictates the length. Most are a couple of days of tracking in a studio, and then back to Sonic Cuisine. The longest single job I worked on was about two months of recording and mixing at RAK."

Anything related to mic techniques that unexpectedly pleasantly surprised you?

"When I first used RAK's Studio 2… It has a very high ceiling, with the control room upstairs from the live room. The height was amazing for drums! I tried the Glyn Johns technique, with one overhead, one mic across from the floor tom, and a kick mic, plus some other spots. I put two Coles ribbon mics all the way up in the ceiling. I didn't need any artificial reverb. At the time, I hadn't done that before.

"Also on drums, I've put an SM57 or SM58 behind the drummer's elbow, in addition to a closer snare mic. I've had drummers comment 'Are you out of your mind? That's going to phase…' I've used that mic as the main snare mic, and got the best sounds out of it!

"I like to mic guitar cabs from the back, flipping the phase of the mic. It's been good on a Vox AC30 amp, but worked best on a Fender Concert."

How about any mic techniques that didn't work as well as you hoped?

"I started out as a classical balance engineer. Nothing was close miked in those sessions. My first time in the studio I close miked everything expecting full control of everything. But nothing breathed. There was no space. It was claustrophobic. The solution was to de-rig and start again. I went back to a classical approach.

"I once had a teacher tell me you need to walk the room and listen – that's really it. When I'm recording, I'm running around so much I lose weight! A lot of engineers sit and reach for EQ – I run out and move mics."

What's the key to recording great sound?

"Good players. The musician is more important than the mic. You can put a shit mic in front of a decent player and it will still sound cool. The best mics don't help bad musicians. The musicians must know how to deal with their instruments.... An amazing drummer with shit drums, or a good guitarist with a bad sound, it doesn't matter where you put the mic, it translates as bad sound.

"An engineer who knows how to use a mic is more important than the mic."

What's the most important part of the recording signal chain?

"That's a tough one, but I think the mic and pre-amp. I track virtually clean and don't use compression or EQ when recording. That's the same for analog and digital."

What pre-production do you do before a session?

"If it's a band, I go to rehearsals if I can. Hopefully we can tidy up some loose ends like song structures, and figure out a way to play songs so they pick up into the chorus. If the band has mediocre equipment, it gives me an idea of what we'll need in the studio, so I'll come up with a "hire list," or ask the studio if we can use their gear. I also put together a "wish list" of mics, pre-amps, compressors, DIs, and EQs, and funnily enough, mic stands! You'd be surprised how quickly you run out of little kick drum stands. For the Glyn Johns technique I use two heavy Brauner VM1s, so I also need enough heavy stands for heavy mics."

What are your favorite mics and pre-amps for some different applications?

"Brauner VM1s on drums. My favorite [stereo] technique for anything else is MS with the VM1s. I like the AKG 451 on hi-hat and acoustic guitar. I find the Neumann U47 valve mic very versatile on many vocalists. The Bees Knees Jade has never let me down on vocals. Royer R121 and Neve RNR1 on guitar cabs. Sennheiser MD421 on toms, Shure SM57 on snare. I also like a Neumann KM184 just above the rim of the snare, horizontally(!), blended with a 57. That's fun because it freaks drummers out..."

What's your approach to recording in a less than ideal room?

"It's possible. Here in my little Sonic Cuisine studio I record vocals using the SE reflection screen, which kind of works. I also use the pencil trick. [Rubber bands, or tape hold a pencil down the center of the mic, over the diaphragm, instead of a pop filter.] I hang up throws to get rid of reflections from windows.

"I had to record an eight piece jazz band in a very small room. I used only eight mics, because I only had eight inputs. It was a terrible room. I miked closer, and used polar patterns more, using figure-8 and hyper-cardioids more than I usually do, and moved the musicians around to exploit those polar patterns more."

What's your attitude to using less than top-of-the-line equipment?

"Fine! Let's do it! Blaming the equipment is the easy way out. You can make decent recordings with half decent equipment. If I know in advance, I'll take a few things with me, like my LunchBox [a powered chassis, originally developed by API, which can house a customized selection of boutique pre-amp, EQ and compressor modules], and a few mics."

What do you want people to think when they hear your work?

"They should hear open, organic sounds. I've been described as producing an edgy British sound, combined with smooth American production values. I like straddling those two markets."

17.6 MATT ROSS-SPANG

Producer/Engineer, Sun Studio, Memphis, USA.

What type of recording work do you generally do?

"I record bands of all genres, but mostly Americana, rock'n'roll and rockabilly! Nowadays genres are so blurred anyway. Mostly it's the whole band live, with minimal overdubs."

Where do you generally work?

"Ninety percent at Sun Studio. It's a very historic location, unchanged from the 50s. There's no isolation, so it's all about mic technique. I use the same type of gear they had: 1936 RCA

tube console with 5 mic inputs going live to a mono ampex tape machine or lathe. I also have a little Pro Tools set up, a 16 input Studer console, and a one-inch 8 track Studer A800, if the band wants that sound, or they're scared of live to mono. I rarely use more than eight mics at a time because of the nature of the room. The vocal mic is also the drum room mic – everything multipurposes!"

Anything related to mic techniques that unexpectedly pleasantly surprised you?

"Tambourine is one of the hardest things to record and fit in a mix, especially when you put the tambourine right on the mic. I left an RCA 77 ribbon mic up in the room as a vocal mic, and the guy was playing tambourine 20 feet back from that mic while I was patching in the control room. It sounded amazing! Now I always do tambourine that way – it mixes perfectly.

"The quieter you get someone to play drums, the farther away you can mic it and the bigger you can make it sound! That seems backwards, but if they play too loud, and you mic it too close, you get too much attack and not enough overtones. The distance gives you depth which you can't fake with a plug-in."

How about any mic techniques that didn't work as well as you hoped?

"When I was first engineering I thought in terms of name brands, monetary value, and industry staples. I would have bigger clients in and I'd try to use those mics because I thought I should – but I didn't like them, and they soon gathered dust in my closet. I love mics that have a unique character.

"Don't spend $5,000 and think you've got to use that mic on lots of things. A lot of times something cheaper will sound better. Do whatever you think sounds good."

What's the key to recording great sound?

"Because the room at Sun is so small, I have the whole band play together when soundchecking. I don't spend a lot of time EQ-ing or compressing. Instrument and mic positioning is a game of inches, and you have to treat the room as an instrument. Get it right upfront, and you know you're golden later on.

"I spend an hour, not a day, getting sounds dialed in, and I spend that time running around moving mics until I'm happy!"

What's the most important part of the recording signal chain?

"Whatever you're putting the mic on. And it's really the person playing. I have an old 60s blue drum set at Sun. It can sound amazing some nights, and others it can really bug me. It depends who's playing it – the tone is in the fingers of the player. And if you know your microphones, you know what to put up to accentuate the instrument's tone.

"A great microphone or pre-amp isn't going to save a bad acoustic guitar. But a great acoustic guitar played right will sound great miked with just about anything, if you mic it right."

What pre-production do you do before a session?

"Little to none. I think the art of pre-production is lost on most bands these days. Forty-five minutes after the band comes in we're usually cutting.

"Sometimes bands send me demos, but I don't necessarily listen to all of them. I like my first impressions to be in the studio since Sun is so different than most studios – that's why they come. You have to adjust to the room, and while I'm miking we're talking about arrangements."

What are your favorite mics and pre-amps for some different applications?

"I don't have many mics, but my go-to mics are:

Western Electric 639B (a ribbon and dynamic microphone from the 40's), Electro-Voice 666, RCA 77D, RCA 44, Altec M11, SM7, Ampex 1101, good ol' SM57, and my modded American R331 is the most beautiful acoustic guitar mic I've heard in my life.

"I love the RCA and Studer pre-amps on the consoles, but also have some tube Ampex 351s and funky old portable tube tape machines I use for certain sounds."

What's your approach to recording in a less than ideal room?

"A 'less than ideal room' has different meanings to different people. When I listen to major hits these days I don't hear character or the uniqueness of the room – it's all isolated tracks. Studios in the 1950s and 60s, like Sun and Royal Studios have a tone I really like – you can't fake that with digital plug-ins. You could tell where a record was cut by the echo chamber! I miss that!

"If the artist is inspired, then the room is now ideal, and there's a way to mic it and make it work.

"People are recording at home all the time, in less than ideal rooms, but they are getting great performances and often times those rooms have character. Sure you may have to work harder sound-wise, but that's a good thing!"

What's your attitude to using less than top-of-the-line equipment?

"The equipment should be invisible, and if you don't have the nicest microphone or whatever, that's not an issue. The goal is not to have nice toys to record with, the goal is to get a great performance. You just have to work really hard, and move the microphones until you get a good sound that the artist is happy with. Most artists don't get excited about the gear, they are excited about their songs."

What do you want people to think when they hear your work?

"Well first, I hope they think it sounds good! I'm such a fan of recordings by Sam Phillips, Rick Hall, Chips Moman, and Willie Mitchell, because five seconds into the track you know who engineered it and where it was cut, and then the rest of the song you think 'how the hell did they do that?' Not to mention they managed to do that while always serving the song! I hope my sounds inspire others the way those guys inspired me!"

17.7 MARK RUBEL

Instructor & Co-Director, The Blackbird Academy, Nashville, USA.

Owner, Pogo Studio.

Engineer, Producer, Audio Expert Witness.

What type of recording work do you generally do?

"I record all different styles, from death metal to Korean music to bluegrass, and everything in-between. I have also done a good deal of classical recording in concert halls – everything from soloists to symphony orchestras. I mostly do music recording, but also voice over work, video game soundtracks, and forensic audio – you name it!"

Where do you generally work?

"Mostly I record at my own Pogo Studio. I like to use it because I think of it as a musical instrument – I know its capabilities and I'm able to quickly get whatever sound I'm looking for."

How long does your typical session last?

"Infinitely variable! It might be an hour, or more lengthy, and like everyone else in this business I've also had a periodic thirty-two hour session."

Anything related to mic techniques that unexpectedly pleasantly surprised you?

"Hanging a small diaphragm condenser mic in a 5 gallon water jug, in front of a bass drum. I use that on almost every session. It gives you as much sub as you get from using a speaker in reverse, but it has more resonance so the low frequency tone lasts longer – it makes the bass drum sound something like a Roland 808!

"Occasionally for fun I will use a cell phone as a delay unit. I'll have a cell phone calling another cell phone, one sitting near the drum kit, the other isolated so I can mic its little speaker. You get a delay from the process of transmission, and because it goes through so many filters that are meant for voice you often get odd, syncopated, alien vocal sounds."

Photo: Della Perrone.

How about any mic techniques that didn't work as well as you hoped?

"I once did a workshop called 'Wacky Tracking' – the idea was to try and come up with as many silly, ridiculous, but potentially useful techniques as we could! It was actually difficult to come up with something new – I found just about everything I thought of had been done by Joe Meek in the 60s.

"In trying to come up with the most outlandish thing I could think of, I decided to put a microphone in a helium balloon, and it would be a pitch transposer. It turns out it doesn't work. I thought it was going to be fantastic, but it just sounded like a microphone in a balloon!"

What's the key to recording great sound?

"Listening. Listen to the instrument one's recording in order to know what the source sound is, even if you're going to change it. Listen to it from all directions and understand where the sound you like or don't like is. Listen to what the musicians have to say about their music.

"Listen to your internal voice – the process of recording is realization, trying to get the sound you have in your mind into the real world. Listen to your gut and move instinctively – is a sound pleasing you, or affecting you emotionally? If not, how can you get it there?"

What's the most important part of the recording signal chain?

"The instrument is the origin of the signal, and it's most important. If it sounds wonderful and you want to capture it 'as is,' that determines the rest of the signal chain. If the source isn't what you hear in your head, what can you do to the source or put in the signal chain to get it that way?"

What pre-production do you do before a session?

"Generally, get together with the client, listen to music and demos, and talk about the process. They might play me other music they like, so we're thinking in the same direction. We'll talk about arrangements; instrumentation; who plays what; when, where and how we're going to record; what will be overdubbed; and are we using their instruments or the studio's instruments?

"I prepare for the session by having everything set up, in place, tested and ready to go – so that they can walk in and make music as quickly as possible."

What are your favorite mics and pre-amps for some different applications?

"I like the concept of using a consistent set of pre-amps – it's more cohesive, and gives the record a tone. I love the sound of my vintage API.

"Electric Guitar: Beyer M88, fairly close, where the dome meets the cone.

"Vocals: It varies, but I'm never unhappy with a Neumann U67.

"Drum overheads: A small capsule stereo tube mic, like the Neumann SM2, or a pair of U67s, or a pair of ribbon mics, depending on the sound I'm looking for.

"An RCA 77-DX is a perfect match for saxophone."

What's your approach to recording in a less than ideal room?

"Generally, to move the mic closer to the instrument so we're not hearing the room as much. Don't set up in the middle of the room where most resonance problems are, and don't set up in a corner unless the problem is not enough bass.

"I would use more directional microphones, but also be careful to not mic too closely."

What's your attitude to using less than top-of-the-line equipment?

"I make it work. Something that is less than hi-fi can still be interesting. It depends upon the style of music and the sound we're going for. I would experiment with placement and settings to minimize what might not be great about it and maximize what's interesting about it."

What do you want people to think when they hear your work?

"I want them to think that the music speaks to them. That the recording is the frame around the picture, and the music is the picture. I would hope that the recording would serve the music to the point that it doesn't intrude."

Index